J.K.LASSER'S™

YOUR WINNING RETIREMENT PLAN

Look for these and other titles from J. K. Lasser—Practical Guides for All Your Financial Needs

J. K. Lasser's Pick Winning Stocks by Edward F. Mrkvicka, Jr.

J. K. Lasser's Invest Online by Laura Maery Gold and Dan Post

J. K. Lasser's Year-Round Tax Strategies by David S. De Jong and Ann Gray Jakabcin

J. K. Lasser's Taxes Made Easy for Your Home-Based Business by Gary W. Carter

J. K. Lasser's Finance and Tax for Your Family Business by Barbara Weltman

J. K. Lasser's Pick Winning Mutual Funds by Jerry Tweddell with Jack Pierce

J. K. Lasser's Your Winning Retirement Plan by Henry K. Hebeler

J.K. LASSER'S™

YOUR WINNING RETIREMENT PLAN

Henry K. Hebeler

John Wiley & Sons, Inc.
New York • Chichester • Weinheim • Brisbane • Singapore • Toronto

This book is printed on acid-free paper. ⊚

Copyright © 2001 by Henry K. Hebeler. All rights reserved.

Published by John Wiley & Sons, Inc.
Published simultaneously in Canada.

This publication is designed to provide accurate and authoritative information in regard to the subject matter covered. It is sold with the understanding that the publisher is not engaged in rendering professional services. If professional advice or other expert assistance is required, the services of a competent professional person should be sought.

Library of Congress Cataloging-in-Publication Data:
Hebeler, H. K. (Henry K.)
    J.K. Lasser's your winning retirement plan / Henry K. Hebeler.
      p.   cm. — (J.K. Lasser—practical guide series)
    Includes index.
    ISBN 0-471-41124-8 (pbk. : alk. paper)
    1. Retirement income—Planning.   2. Old age pensions.   3. Individual retirement accounts.   4. Social security.   5. Investments.   6. Income tax.   7. Finance, Personal.
    I. Title: Your winning retirement plan.   II. Title.   III. J.K. Lasser guide series.

HD7101 .H43 2001
332.024'01—dc21
                                      00-068605

Printed in the United States of America.

10 9 8 7 6 5 4 3 2 1

This book is dedicated to my family, past, present, and future. My mother and father encouraged me to seek knowledge, be innovative, and work hard. Mirriam, my wife, has supported me with this work and other endeavors beyond belief. Our children, now adults, have families of their own who we hope will prosper and have lives as interesting as ours. May the materials in this book be a guide to a better financial life for all of them, as well as those who seek the truth from what I have learned in this decade of research about retirement financial planning. With time, the financial world will change, tax laws will change, and people's objectives will change, but the fundamental principles of this book should persist well into the future.

Contents

Acknowledgments

There are a number of people who have gone far beyond my expectations by taking their time to review and help. Extra special thanks are due to Howard Stuverude, who tried out my written methods and became one of my biggest boosters; Bill Schultheis, author of *The Coffeehouse Investor*, who tested the programs I used with clients; Dr. John Broyles, professor of finance and economics, who challenged my theories; and Al Fischer, who fixed my computer whenever it went down.

Along the way, I received encouragement for my work and favorable published comments from Vanessa O'Connell, Tom Herman, and Jonathan Clements at *The Wall Street Journal*, Mary Beth Franklin at *Kiplinger's Personal Finance* magazine, Jersey Gilbert at *Smart Money*, Ellen Jovin at *Financial Planning* magazine, Robert Barker at *Business Week* magazine, and numerous others. And I am grateful to Global Financial Data at www.globalfindata.com, which came to my rescue as an economical source for historical return information.

When Bob Shuman, senior editor at John Wiley & Sons, Inc., called to ask if I wanted to write a retirement book, I was delighted. He knew exactly what he wanted, and that's exactly what I wanted to offer. This was a great opportunity to help the public understand the principles that can make their future retirement much, much better. To that purpose I have dedicated the last 10 years of my life without seeking any financial gain, wanting only the satisfaction of helping people live a more rewarding and comfortable life. Thanks to all of the people at John Wiley & Sons, Inc., who have made this book possible.

One of the hardest jobs is careful reading of technical text. I am indebted to some special people who labored many hours to reduce the mistakes that creep in as I enthusiastically brush by the words in a hurry to illustrate the points with graphs and tables, including Elaine Swenson, Barbara Benekas, Howard Stuverude, and Lee Mays. Mary Russell, a developmental editor, continued to push for further simplification; and Cheryl Brubaker did a marvelous job of copyediting. I appreciate all of their industry, enthusiastic support, and encouragement. The index was prepared by Stephanie Landis who went far beyond just listing the page numbers for some key words. Lisa Fickinger manipulated the figures and squeezed them into the right places.

Author's Note

For over 10 years, I have devoted the major part of every working day to evaluating retirement plans. A number of national publications published my results at various times. However, I have yet to find a good planning book for a do-it-yourself type person. There are many financial books that have a chapter on the subject, but, without fail, they are oversimplified, optimistic, and misleading. I am an avid computer user, so over the years I also have explored a large number of commercial software and Internet offerings. Unfortunately, with few exceptions, these programs are as bad as the books.

Although the majority of references employ defective math, they have a greater flaw. That is that they lack perspective. No one can predict the future, so we all rely on experiences from the past. There is nothing wrong with this, as long as you develop a plan that isn't based on average statistics that hide past problems. It also means that you need plans that have some tolerance for the inevitable difficulties that are sure to face you in the future.

For a half-dozen years I was the major planner and forecaster for The Boeing Company, known for developing advanced products in commercial aviation, space exploration, and sophisticated military endeavors. In that capacity, I benefited from broad exposure to economists, financial analysts, and government policymakers. But the real job was to present a credible forecast for the future and responsible budgets to the board of directors who were all top officers of some of the largest companies in the world. They demanded perspective.

With that background, I offer this book. Besides offering a more sanguine view of the numbers behind a plan, it introduces some new technology that is a rarity now because it is so simple to apply. I've included ample demonstrations using good, average, and bad times from the past to illustrate the power of the new methods. Although you could skip all this and go straight to Chapter 5 if you haven't retired or Chapter 6 if you have, I think that you'll find enough surprises that you'll go back to earlier chapters to develop your own winning retirement plan.

Introduction

It's likely that you and I have a lot in common. We started our working careers with little knowledge of the financial world. In fact, we probably could not have cared less. There were things that seemed much more important at the time—building our careers, enjoying our families, having fun. Our first exposures to any serious financial matter most likely included filling out our first tax return and applying for a loan, probably for a car or a house. Our money was in the bank, prudently tucked away in a savings account.

Then at some point both you and I came to the realization that we had to do something about retirement. Social Security wasn't going to be enough to live on, and we couldn't count on our pension alone to make up the difference. That's why I started reading about the subject, just as you are doing now. Sometimes this realization comes fortunately early. Sometimes it comes several years after retirement, often too late to reach the goals we imagined we'd achieve during the last part of our lives. Whether you are still working and trying to benefit from the incredible power of compounding, or whether you are past that stage and now trying to make your money stretch until you die, you recognize that you need help.

It is also likely that you, like me, are not a certified financial planner or public accountant; nor do we have a license to sell securities. Our exposure to the financial world most likely has come from an entirely different direction. In my case that evolved from a strong math background from my engineering degrees at the Massachusetts Institute of Technology (MIT). Like the cartoon character Dilbert, my analytical and often skeptical view of a sales pitch helped me evaluate and see what was really behind the mass of retirement planning materials

I was collecting from newspapers, magazines, books, radio, TV, software houses, and the Internet. Add to that my studies in finance and economics taught by Nobel Prize winners during a sabbatical to get my third degree from MIT as a Sloan Fellow. Mix in my exposure to broad policy issues as an economic consultant to the governor of Washington State and as a consultant to the U.S. Congress and Departments of Commerce, Interior, Energy, and Defense, as well as lessons learned doing business internationally, both as a merchant and as a member of international trade missions. And I learned a lot about compensation systems during five years heading one of Boeing's most financially successful divisions with 23,000 employees.

Finally, supplement that background with the gray hairs I have earned from many practical investment experiences in my personal life and two stints as The Boeing Company's chief planner and forecaster totaling almost six years. During those times I was responsible for presenting a credible plan for the future of Boeing to the board of directors and assemblies of financial analysts from Wall Street. Always there were people promoting new technical concepts with glorious prospects for the future. Again I used my Dilbert-like analysis and skepticism to tone down subordinate divisions' cries to get ever larger budgets for their projects: projects that had sales projections bloated far beyond their customers' budget capabilities.

But I found that all of the complex issues I encountered in these various settings were nothing compared to the barrage of baloney I was hearing from hawkers of financial material. They were misusing statistical information to promote securities. They were basing long-term forecasts on unrealistically optimistic circumstances. They were using math that did not model real past circumstances. They were omitting their own fees and costs to make their performance look better. Recommended securities were often already at their peaks. Taxes were regularly ignored. People were being encouraged to use retirement planning methods on the basis of the clarity and color of their graphs, not on the competency of their projection methods.

Higher-level Boeing executives received free investment and tax advice. By 1989 these advisors told me I had plenty of money to retire because I had saved and invested well. Still, I sorted through all of the retirement planning material I could find. When there was nothing that met my standards, like any good engineer, I put together my own spreadsheet with a year-by-year retirement forecast. This showed that not only could I retire comfortably, but also that I'd be able to provide substantial support to other members of my family, as well as to my favorite charities. My projections were much more conservative than those I found in the published material I reviewed. Now, after a decade of investigating retirement plans, I realize that except for the booming market my retirement plan would have been horribly optimistic, and certainly not the safe and conservative one I imagined. Spending at my original projected levels would have depleted my savings far too soon in a more typical stock market, and I would not have been able to do anything about it once the money was gone.

How could this happen? The main culprit was a principle I discovered several years after retiring. I call it *reverse dollar cost averaging.* Perhaps you have heard of dollar cost averaging. That's a phenomenon that benefits savers who make regular deposits in a fluctuating market because they effectively achieve a higher compound interest rate. I found that the opposite happens when retirees take money out on a regular basis. Retirees effectively get a lower interest rate in a fluctuating market. Hence my term *reverse* dollar cost averaging.

If you are deciding how much to save for retirement using conventional planning materials, more likely than not, their optimism and salesmanship will leave you far short of your goals. The thing you have to ponder is whether you'll be saved by a sustained and exuberant bull market as were those of us who retired in 1989. I wouldn't count on it. Of course, I'm hoping that this book will help you develop a plan that can withstand some severe economic shocks ahead, but I'm also hoping that financial researchers, with far more capability than I, will extend the principles I've initiated here and encourage their widespread use.

In my view, everyone in retirement needs to set and fulfill some goal. My initial goal was to enlighten the public about misleading retirement planning information. My subsequent discoveries in this area pushed me to a higher level when I recognized the similarity between controlling your finances in turbulent economic conditions and controlling an airplane in gusty wind conditions. Then I knew it was possible to apply new technology, economic principles, and my gray-haired experience to develop better systems for planning your future. I went back into my past aeronautical background and came up with something I call a retirement autopilot. That's what this book is about. It includes the information needed to add more realism to a plan, but the really new feature is the autopilot method. I don't promise you easy reading, but I can say positively that you will get a lot more out of your life as a result of the time you spend reading this book than you would from a comparable amount of time spent watching a couple of ball games on TV. And in the end, you won't be just an observer. You'll be a player armed with better equipment than those around you, and you'll have a better chance of winning.

Your plan will include a better choice of investments than you probably have now. If you are not yet retired, you will be armed with tools that will show you realistic annual savings to meet your goals for all your savings needs, not just retirement. If you are already retired, you will have a competent method that will show you how much you can budget so your investments will last until you reach your goal line. This book does not address detailed insurance and estate plans, which, at some point, require attention, but if you take the planning actions in this book, you'll be the winner with a winning retirement plan.

Caution Advised!

Virtually all financial organizations and software publishers include a disclaimer that says there is no warranty that their method is correct and the work is presented *AS IS,* just as a used car would be sold. Since these multi-billion-dollar firms have the sense to offer disclaimers in our current litigious environment, I want to caution you to read the disclaimer in this book that also says this material is presented *AS IS* and makes no warranties—implied or otherwise.

I do not sell any securities, insurance, trusts, or legal instruments. The information offered in this book is the result of many years of financial planning and investing in more securities than most financial analysts ever experienced in their own personal lives. If this book only helps you to ask better questions of professionals that assist you, the benefits may be very large, because even professionals make judgmental and analytical errors. If you need additional assistance, a good place to start is with a free call to the Financial Planning Association at 1-800-282-7526 for a recommendation of a certified financial planner in your area. So even if your decision is to engage a professional planner, before selecting anyone, review the material in this book. You'll get more for your money from the planner. A lot more!

CHAPTER 1

The Realities of Financial Planning

Confidence is the
feeling you have
before you really
understand the
problem.*

Very few people even know what a financial plan is, much less actually have such a thing. Before they retire, most people just try to save a reasonable amount of money, without any real understanding of whether it will be enough for retirement. After retirement, most people expect to live on Social Security, pension payments (if they get them), and the interest and dividends from their investments. Sadly, they may quickly discover that these funds are inadequate for their needs and all-too-easily demolished by a fluctuating market and unforeseen expenses. The problems are exacerbated for early retirees, who have more time to spend money but begin retirement with less of every financial resource: less Social Security, smaller pensions, and fewer savings. A long-delayed visit to a financial planner to get some help is inevitably followed by the question, "Why didn't I plan for this long ago?"

Everybody Needs a Plan

Most people need to do some planning if they expect their money to support their desired retirement lifestyle and last until they die. It's at least as important as an annual dental appointment or periodic physical examination. On reaching his 100th birthday, comedian George Burns said, "If I knew I was going to live so long, I would have taken better care of myself." He didn't have to add the word *financially* to that quote, but the vast majority of people would.

People who have not yet retired need a preretirement plan. That's a plan that

*Ogden Nash.

tells them where and how much to save to meet a retirement income goal. People who have already retired need a postretirement plan. That's a plan that tells them how to control their financial matters so that their investments will support them until they die. This book provides answers for both groups. Further, it shows how you can better grow your investments in either situation.

Although few people actually take the time to use them, there are an incredible number of planning methods available. They can be found in newspapers, magazines, books, and mutual fund publications, as software programs, and on the Internet. I hate to say it, but it's probably better to use even the worst of these than to have no plan at all. But what I've found is that even the best of them can lead you to a false sense of security about your future.

For several years I compared a large number of the most popular retirement planning programs using representative data for an imaginary preretiree. The results were awful. Some of the programs said that this person already had saved enough to retire comfortably, even though retirement was 20 years away. Others said he would have to save over a quarter of his income every year to meet his retirement goals. Different retirement planning programs produced the opposite results, even though they were using exactly the same data! My findings were incorporated into an article written by Vanessa O'Connell and published in *The Wall Street Journal,* December 27, 1996. You can check it out in the library and see how your favorite financial planning system measures up. I updated that work for another article published in *The Wall Street Journal,* November 30, 1998, which was written by Tom Herman. You can also find the details of these studies on my web site, www.analyzenow.com.

The sample cases I used to test the various financial planning programs were actually pretty simple compared to real-world conditions, since they tested only the math involved in the various programs and assumed that investment growth and inflation were the same values each year. More recently I have been doing work with real-world models, where the changes in security values and inflation come from actual historical profiles. My work led me to make some startling discoveries that were, for me, a real epiphany. One is a concept I call *reverse dollar cost averaging,* a technique that brings a vital element of reality to your financial planning. Another is a technique I call the *retirement autopilot method,* which works to smooth out the bumps in the financial planning world in the same way an autopilot works to counter turbulence on an airplane. Although we'll cover these items in detail later in the book, let's look briefly at the concepts now.

Perhaps you have heard of dollar cost averaging. That's a phenomenon that benefits savers who make regular savings deposits. Deposits made when the market is low generate more growth than an equal number of deposits made when the market is high. The net result is a larger overall growth rate than would be predicted using steady market conditions. Unfortunately, I found that the opposite happens when retirees take money out of their accounts on a regular basis, which is, of course, exactly what they need to do. Retirees effectively receive a lower interest rate in a fluctuating market. Hence the term *reverse dollar cost averaging*. This is *really* bad news when it comes to retirement planning projections. Unfortunately, all available long-term return data are based on the compound growth you would see in a preretirement situation and not the compound reduction you will experience in a postretirement situation. This means that you should really use a much lower rate of return in your postretirement calculations than traditional planning publications recommend. We'll look at this in detail in Chapter 4.

The second part of my retirement planning epiphany was the discovery that I could apply some airplane control technology to financial planning using a "retirement autopilot." Again, this is something that we'll review in more detail later, but consider this analogy. The autopilot in an airplane makes constant course corrections, automatically updating the plane's sense of direction and smoothing out the bumps during gusty conditions. Without the autopilot to compensate for various outside factors, the plane would behave more like a loose balloon on a windy day. Similarly, without the retirement autopilot, retirement plans soon go awry in fluctuating market conditions. When you finally get around to checking on your progress, you find that you must make changes so large your resulting recommended saving and spending levels bounce around just like the loose balloon. The retirement autopilot uses compensating equations to provide some stability and absorb some of the shocks that the outside world will inevitably deal you.

Real-World Planning Problems

In general, the biggest problems with most retirement planning methods are oversimplification and optimistic assumptions. The quickie plans you'll find on the Internet are often the worst, but those gleaned from many financial magazines run a close second. Let's take a look at the most common mistakes.

Mistake 1. Adding Apples and Oranges

For some reason beyond my ken, the authors of many retirement planning texts and computer programs believe that all pensions include cost of living adjustments (COLAs). Of course, that's just not true—only a few people are lucky enough to get a pension increase every time the cost of living goes up, and even then the increases are often capped at perhaps 2 or 3% per year. Still, many analysts persist in perpetuating this error in their calculations by claiming that you can determine the amount of income you'll need by doing a gap analysis. The gap to which this refers is the difference between the income you'll need during retirement and the sum of your Social Security and pension payments. The problem is sticky because in one sense the planners are right—it's not bad to do a gap analysis, but it needs to be done correctly. Theoretically, the gap would then be funded or closed by smart investing. But any explanation of a gap analysis must go farther because it can lead to dangerous misunderstandings about our money.

To explain means going back to grade school math. At that time you probably heard a teacher say, "You can't add apples and oranges." Likewise, Social Security and a fixed pension are two entirely different fruits. Social Security has a COLA. Fixed pensions do not. Therefore, they don't belong together in any kind of arithmetic, not to mention a calculation for retirement planning.

The real purchasing power of the lucky few who do have a COLA pension compared to those with fixed pensions is shown in Figure 1.1 for two arbitrary starting years: 1950 and 1960. The details will be different for any particular starting year, but the overall results will be the same. What needs to be understood is that a fixed pension is worth only a fraction of a COLA pension or Social Security after considering inflation. Therefore, you can add only a fraction of a fixed pension to your Social Security income in an accurate gap analysis.

Mistake 2. Assuming the Real World Is Smooth

To illustrate this mistake, let's consider an example that happens all too often. Mary is age 55. Her husband just died leaving her with savings and an insurance payment that we'll say totals a handsome $1 million. She goes to her accountant who is helping her settle the estate and asks for financial help. He asks her some questions and then recommends that she put 50% of her investments in a stock mutual fund and 50% in a long-term corporate bond fund.

Then Mary asks her accountant how much she can spend each year from her

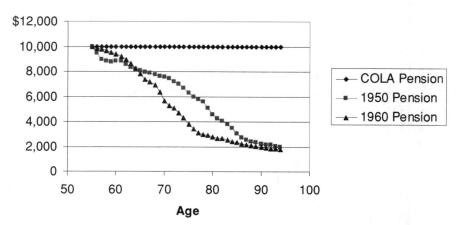

FIGURE 1.1 The actual value of a COLA pension compared to the real value of fixed pensions starting in two different years, after inflation has taken its toll.

investments. The accountant turns on his computer and brings up his latest version of a retirement planning program. He inputs Mary's age and the financial information. He asks Mary how long she thinks she will live, and together they decide to enter age 85 to represent her life expectancy. The program will let him enter his own assumptions about how the investments will perform, but suggests a certain return based on long-term averages of corporate long-term bonds and the most popular index for stocks, the S&P 500. (This is the Standard and Poor's index for the 500 largest companies in the United States, which included only 90 companies until 1957.) The accountant inputs the suggested composite return for this mix of bonds and stocks. The program also suggests a long-term inflation rate that the accountant also accepts.

The accountant hits the Enter key; the computer goes through the analysis in a fraction of a second, and shows two results on the screen. The first is how much Mary can spend this year as well as in the years that follow, assuming that Mary increases her spending each year by the amount of inflation. The second result is a plot showing what will happen to the total balance of Mary's investments each year. Then the program asks whether the accountant wants to see the results in terms of future dollars (which are worth less each year because of the inflation assumption) or with an inflation adjustment that shows results in the form of today's dollars. Knowing that Mary will get a better perspective of the future, he chooses the latter, and then prints the investment history on the screen. That's represented by the "Theory" line in Figure 1.2. At this point we're going to keep the example simple by not including Social Security and taxes.

The theoretical inflation-adjusted investment line from the retirement program is nice and smooth, just like the imaginary world represented by the com-

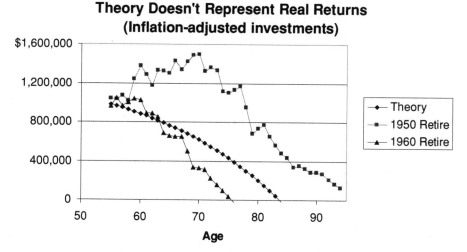

FIGURE 1.2 Inflation-adjusted investments are substantially different when comparing theory to real annual returns for retirement beginning in 1950 or 1960.

puter model where inflation and the return are the same year after year. The money runs out in 30 years, that is, on Mary's 85th birthday. Now the people who developed this computer program know that the returns represent an average of all the returns from 1926 to the present, and that about half the time the returns will be higher and half the time the returns will be lower. So the program includes some small print noting that these returns may not represent what may happen in the future.

In fact, there is a substantial difference in what would have happened in the real world if Mary retired in different periods of history. Figure 1.2 shows the performance of those same investments if Mary would have started her retirement in either 1950 or 1960. In the former case, she would have run out of money about 10 years earlier, far short of the time she wanted her money to last. In the latter case, she could probably leave some money to her children.

These real-world cases are based on my *The Real World* planning program (available from my web site at www.analyzenow.com), which uses copyrighted historical security data from Global Financial Data (find them at www.globalfindata.com). We'll use this program and the security data throughout the book to illustrate examples.

The smooth line data from the accountant's computer program are far different from those in *The Real World,* and they'll get even farther away after we consider some of the other problems that the real world presents. The problem illustrated here is that using average returns is just too misleading. It's like the man who drowned in a river that averaged only 1 foot deep. He still drowned, no matter how shallow most of the river was and how favorable a time it was to be in the water. At the same time, it makes a tremendous amount of difference to consider, as you estimate your retirement finances, the kind of economic environment you are wading through; there are deep spots in the river in any season, but there will be many more when the real storms come.

If Mary retired in 1950, she would have had three smashing years where investments increased by 52, 30, and 40%, even after adjusting for inflation and 1% investment costs. Less fortunate people who retired in the late 1960s were pummeled by market losses of 15, 23, 36, and 14% and another 14% after the same inflation and cost adjustments. Holders of small company stocks were hurt more. And bonds, supposedly the safe and solid investment, had loss years during the 1960s, nearly 50% of the time after considering inflation's toll.

It gets worse—especially if you are the owner of only a small number of stocks rather than the many stocks held in a mutual fund. If you have only one stock, be prepared for a wild ride. By spending just half an hour watching CNBC some morning, you'll see the sometimes painful gyrations of a free market swirling in volatile peaks and valleys—some deeper than is congruent with anyone's sense of well-being. Yet conventional planning methods, as shown in the Theory line of Figure 1.2, show the future as smooth as a baby's bottom.

There is one other point I want to make about Figure 1.2 before leaving it. At age 81, in the 1950 scenario, Mary's investment balance was almost $800,000 in inflation-adjusted dollars. If the dollars were not adjusted for inflation, Mary would have seen a chart showing about a $3 million balance. She could have been easily misled, but her accountant helped her avoid that trap. Nevertheless, investment firms, when showing investment performance, persist in showing the performance of their securities as if Mary's balance was really going to be worth $3 million.

That same kind of exaggeration applies to investment returns. Say you get a 6% return on your investment. Now let's say this year's inflation is 4%. You are really only netting 2%. In addition, all mutual funds, even no-load funds, have investment costs, which together with taxes and inflation can wipe out any real growth.

Mistake 3. Ignoring Investment Costs

Indexes used to measure stock and bond prices are based on a size-weighted average of the prices of the particular group of stocks or bonds represented by an index such as the Dow Jones Industrial Average of 30 very large companies, the S&P 500 for 500 large companies, or the Russell 2000 for 2,000 small companies. Since these are averages, you'd think that at least half of the mutual funds would be above the average and the other half would be below. In fact, because funds have large research departments that try to sort the bad investments from the good, you would think the average fund would do considerably better than the indexes' averages. Wrong! More than three-fourths of the stock funds fail to reach the average of the S&P 500, even though they can pick from over 5,000 stocks. Why? Because they must pay big wages to many people, do research, provide significant administrative support to their clients, pay for their impressive buildings, and so on. So the mutual funds either charge the costs directly in terms of a "load" when you purchase or when you sell, or take a little bit out all of the time, as do so-called no-load funds. We call those "costs" in this book. You cannot buy or sell an investment without paying someone to assist you, even if it's not in a mutual fund. And, on top of the cost of obtaining or disposing of the investment, you may pay an agent, advisor, or money manager a certain percent of your investment value each year. This adds to the cost.

Since very few funds were actually beating the averages, a number of mutual fund companies started marketing bundles of stocks or bonds that are contained in a particular index. That eliminated the research costs and the need for a highly paid guru to make the final buy and sell decisions. These index funds generally outperform the average funds but still don't quite reach the average, because there still are costs. Index funds' costs are most often under 1% of the fund's value. A small number are under 0.25%, but some mutual funds have costs in excess of 5%.

Yet people representing financial firms really try not to talk about the costs. Unfortunately, that's often true of planners and planning programs as well. I've attended numerous seminars given by planners, financial firms, and money managers who are seeking additional business. They will highlight examples showing how their client's money would grow under their auspices by using examples from stock and bond indexes. They make no mention of the costs in the mutual funds they recommend, nor their own costs. I've witnessed presentations by firms charging thousands of dollars just to recommend some investments who then invest the client's money in high-cost mutual funds with large commissions, and then charge an annual fee of 1 to 2% on top of that. The poor client will be lucky to get much more than from a bank.

So how does this affect Mary? She went to an accountant who charged a small one-time fee. He recommended she get a balanced fund with half stocks and half bonds. The fund she selected had a fee of 1.5%, which is a little high for someone who would shop around a bit, but typical of a large number of investors. It's also typical of money managers, who often charge an annual 1% fee and select funds with costs of 0.5%, which is decidedly below the average cost of mutual funds. Suppose that fund had exactly the same underlying investments as the one in Figure 1.2. Let's see what happens in Figure 1.3 as we include costs to add some more reality. Remember that the 1.5% cost really represents a 1.5% reduction in the investment's earnings each year.

Figure 1.3 has some valuable lessons. The accountant used the computer program's recommended return for the investment mix he selected. But that return was based on a long-term index for stocks and another for bonds. The accountant failed to reduce the return for his theoretical case by 1.5%. What happened to the real performance? It plummeted. If Mary had retired in 1960, the spending levels recommended by the computer would have exhausted her

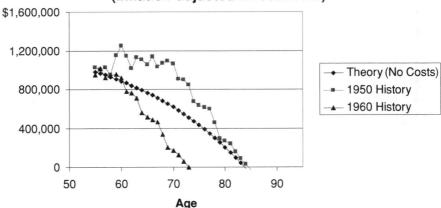

FIGURE 1.3 Inflation-adjusted investment balances, after accounting for investment costs, decline quickly.

funds at age 73! Mary's investments only would last her desired 30 years if she had been lucky enough to retire in a year like 1950.

Mistake 4. Not Defining Your Terms

It's important to know when to use before-tax returns and when to use after-tax returns. Returns are the annual growth of your investments, assuming all interest and dividends are reinvested. A fixed bond that pays interest generally has a return about equal to the interest rate. Stocks have a return about equal to their annual dividends plus any annual growth in the per-share price. A stock fund with reinvested dividends that began the year at $100 and ended the year at $110 would have a return of 10%. Before-tax returns represent the growth of investments without any tax considerations. You get before-tax returns from tax-exempt municipal bonds and the growth in a Roth individual retirement arrangement (IRA), assuming there are no state taxes. (Although most of us refer to IRAs as individual retirement *accounts,* the IRS uses the word *arrangement* in its definition.) You also receive before-tax returns from a deferred tax account such as a 401(k) or IRA, although you will later pay ordinary income tax on the withdrawals. Investments other than tax-exempt and deferred tax investments are taxed as soon as dividends, interest, and capital gains are realized. Such taxable investments grow at the slower after-tax rate, but the taxes may be at less than ordinary income rates when long-term capital gains are involved.

Most planning methods that try to separate IRAs and 401(k)s from taxable accounts make a mistake in preretirement planning because their definition of savings is incompatible with the conventional wisdom that deferred tax accounts grow at a before-tax rate and taxable accounts at an after-tax rate. They define savings as only that part of wages (including employer contributions) that go into your investments. They fail to ask if you are paying taxes on your investments from your wages. Except for unusual circumstances, most of us pay taxes from wages, not investments, because we don't want to make quarterly payments or face large year-end tax bills. Some people even overwithhold so that they get some money back at the end of the year. Since the taxes on the taxable investments are not deducted from investments but are paid from wages, even the taxable investments grow at a before-tax rate.

Therefore, preretirement planning programs that are mechanized to use after-tax returns for taxable accounts should define savings differently—and I've only seen one that does this correctly. In such a case, the correct definition of savings includes both the deposits from wages and that part of your income tax that was due on investment returns but was actually paid from wages, not investments. How many of us, for example, know how much of our income tax is actually due to the income from investments? You could do a separate tax calculation without including taxable interest, dividends, and capital gains and then subtract that income tax from the full taxes you owe. But how meaningful is that when the investment income changes your tax bracket? Albert Einstein was fond of saying that the most complex math in the world was on your tax return.

Very elaborate retirement planning programs, however, have been built around after-tax returns. I've written one of my own that got an extensive and favorable report by Ellen Jovin in the June 1999 issue of *Financial Planning,* a magazine for professional planners. The program is available from www.analyzenow.com. It's useful for people trying to make strategic decisions such as how to select IRA distributions or whether to get a reverse mortgage or buy long-term health care insurance. It requires very detailed tax and other information, including depreciation on investment real estate. Hundreds of professionals use the program, as do many laypeople, but the detail only helps to make better strategic decisions when comparing one alternative with another. With the possible exception of those with large real estate investments, it does not give a more accurate projection of how much you should save before retirement or how much you can spend after retirement than the very simple methods in this book. Nor does it offer the historical perspective we are introducing throughout this book.

There is also confusion in most retirement planning methods with regard to the analysis of debt payments and the associated definition of postretirement expenses. Most methods prefer to leave this as a fuzzy area and avoid bringing up the subject, but when mortgage or other loan payments are a significant part of your budget, you better use a method that competently addresses the subject. We are very specific in this book, so you won't have to puzzle over these issues.

For those few readers interested in delving into this subject, here's some more thought-provoking information: Most postretirement planning methods give you an annual budget that represents how much you will be able to spend each year in retirement. If the method asks you to subtract debt from investments, the budget does not include debt payments. If the method does not mention debt, the budget includes debt payments. In most preretirement planning methods any part of your debt payments that goes to paying off principal should be defined as savings, but I don't recall ever seeing that mentioned. In those preretirement programs in which you subtract debts from investments to determine a net investment value, at least part, if not all, of your interest payments should be considered savings. Net investment analysis assumes that debt is a negative investment. Therefore, debt interest reduces your returns. If you pay the interest to a creditor from your wages instead of from investments, the interest did not reduce your return.

Mistake 5. Using Calculations without Shock Absorption

The market goes up. The market goes down. Retirement planning gets whiplash. Lately, though, we've had so many successive good years that instead of whiplash we get complacency. People forget that a sudden drop in investment values plays havoc with their plans for the future. At some point it is inevitable that your plans will hit a brick wall, and then it's whiplash time again.

I don't know which is worse. Complacency leads to saving too little before retirement and spending too much after retirement. Preretirement whiplash abruptly changes both your future outlook and your projected savings needs before retirement. Whiplash after retirement does permanent damage to your future lifestyle.

I've been doing both before- and after-retirement planning for myself for many years now. One thing that always bothered me was the large change in my preretirement planning results from one year to the next when I compared how much I should save in the forthcoming year with the calculation made for last year. This is because when you near retirement, and your investments become significant, an increase in market value will obscure any need for additional savings. However, the reverse is also true. A significant market drop may make it impossible for you to reach your retirement goal with realistic annual saving.

I've found a comparable problem with postretirement planning, where the goal of the calculations is to find out how much you can afford to spend and still have enough investments to last until you die. Obviously there is no way to know what will happen to your investments in the future, but by looking back in history and plugging in what would have been my annual budget calculations during various periods, I found changes that would be very difficult to accommodate. One year my budget would be one amount, and the next it would be radically different.

It was then that I thought about the similarity of investment volatility to an airplane flying in gusty conditions. I used this idea to create the autopilot concept, and found that it worked very well in historical scenarios to provide a shock absorber and give some stability both to pre- and postretirement plans. Now I'm convinced that all financial plans need an autopilot, so it's built right into this book's methods.

You should not confuse the retirement autopilot with the work of statisticians in the financial industry who investigate the behavior of individual types of securities. This too involves a historical perspective, but its purpose is to characterize risk so that people can make better investment and allocation choices that suit their tolerance for market ups and downs. In contrast, the autopilot works with whatever mix of securities you choose and tries to give you the smoothest ride possible through the inevitable turbulence.

Mistake 6. Ignoring the Effect of Reverse Dollar Cost Averaging

Most people have heard of dollar cost averaging. If you methodically put the same amount of money into a volatile market on a regular basis, your investments will grow faster than the same deposits in a steady market that has the same long-term return. Reverse dollar cost averaging is just the opposite. When you take money out of an account on a regular basis instead of making deposits, more often than not you will achieve a lower effective return. We will demonstrate this in Figure 1.4, where $10 is withdrawn each year.

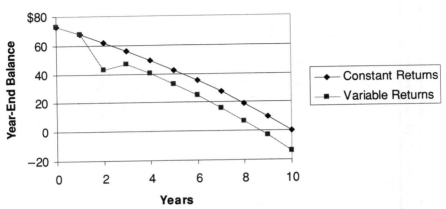

Reverse Dollar Cost Averaging Is Damaging

FIGURE 1.4 Reverse dollar cost averaging in action. When investments go down in a volatile market and you are withdrawing principal, you seldom bounce back.

Figure 1.4 has two lines. The upper one is labeled Constant Returns because the returns are the same every year. The bottom line is labeled Variable Returns because in two of the years the returns are different values. The average return in both cases is 7% over the 10-year period. However, in the case of the variable returns, the 23% loss we encountered in the second year is not fully compensated by the 37% gain in the third year, even though the average of −23% and +37% is still 7%. The net result is that the money runs out sooner with variable returns than it does when we assume constant returns. Since almost all planning methods assume constant returns, they optimistically predict that any investments will last longer than they will in the real world of varying market prices.

As a historical average, retirees effectively receive a return on their investments that is about 0.5% lower than that for preretirement savers. However small this 0.5% difference in return may seem on the average, this is another illustration of the man who drowned in a river that averaged only 1 foot in depth—because he happened to step in a big hole in the river bottom. Only in this case the "holes" are those many historical circumstances where there was a sudden drop in security values. It's one more instance where conventional retirement planning methods show a lack of concern for conservative, realistic planning. Neglecting the ups and downs in the market is just too cavalier for an analysis this important.

The Hazards of Postretirement Projections

It's not possible to do preretirement planning without first knowing how much money you will need after you have retired—it's the figure from which all the calculations start. So we're going to review the major postretirement planning methods before we look at the preretirement ones. There are a variety of methods you can use to make your postretirement projections. We'll start with the worst of them, and end with the best.

Spend-All

The spend-all approach basically assumes that after retirement you will be able to live comfortably on your after-tax income, as long as you don't spend your principal. It is the oldest approach to postretirement planning; in fact, it was featured in the majority of the references I encountered when I first started doing my research in the 1980s. It was probably most applicable during the years after the depression, when inflation was very low and you could count on the stability of such things as preferred and utility stocks. In more recent times, the spend-all method is nonsensical if you have investments with a fixed rate of return, such as fixed pensions, bonds, or certificates of deposit (CDs) because they effectively go down in value every year due to inflation. It is also nonsensical when considering stocks or stock funds because dividends are a lot smaller than they were in the past, and funds distribute capital gains that, although income, vary appreciably from year to year and invade the basic principal.

As old as the spend-all method is, it did wisely advise shifting to more conservative investments such as bonds instead of stocks as you grow older. When life expectancies are short and savings are relatively small, a shift to bonds or CDs makes sense.

Inflation-Adjusted Spending

During the 1990s, planning methods based on financial planning equations, long used by professional planners, started showing up more widely in magazines, books, and, of course, computer programs. The equations account for returns, inflation, life expectancy, and the present value of your investments. The computer programs had the virtue of simplifying the math needed to make various calculations and eliminated the need to use multiple tables to manipulate data. Unfortunately, the initial software was pretty bad—most, for example, did not account for the difference between fixed pensions and COLA pensions. With time, the computer programs advanced, while the written literature seemed to stand still. Quicken, Vanguard, Fidelity, and others upgraded earlier flawed programs with so many versions that it was hard to keep track of them. Then came the enhancements that made provisions for irregular expenses or one-time receipts, such as cash from the sale of real estate. A few programs started to include provisions for a choice of allowable methods to meet the Internal Revenue Service (IRS)-mandated required minimum distributions (RMDs) from an IRA after age 70½. The Financial Engines web site examined the security investment situation statistically to show what your past (or purported future) chance of success would be by using some dramatic scenarios representing your own combination of mutual funds.

None of these wonderful programs can predict the future accurately, and the level of detail in a method does not necessarily ensure a more precise outcome. No one is able to predict what inflation or the stock market will be in 10 or 20 years, for example. The detail offers the ability to compare what might happen if you make one set of choices with the results for another set of choices where both cases otherwise have the same assumptions. Such data may help you decide whether you should buy a long-term-care insurance policy or when it's better to sell some real estate or whether to get a reverse mortgage. You must make a number of assumptions in such detailed investigations, and those assumptions are unlikely to be exactly right. Nevertheless, you'll get some quantitative idea about your retirement prospects in different situations. One of the most popular features of the current retirement programs is their ability to use financial payment equations to determine how much someone can spend this year and still leave sufficient savings to provide for the future. These equations are also built into the financial calculators sold in office supply stores and most spreadsheet programs, such as Microsoft's Excel. You input your estimate of future returns less inflation, life expectancy, and the current balance of your retirement savings. The output is the amount of money you can withdraw from savings this year. Of course, in the computer solution, the money eventually runs out precisely at the end of your life expectancy, because the math is designed to work that way. This is the ideal world of the planner. In the real world, the money will probably run out much sooner because your real returns will not remain constant from year to year. Unless your real returns turn out to be substantially higher than you assumed in your initial calculations, you are in for a nasty surprise down the line. This is reverse dollar cost averaging at work.

An even more important flaw in the inflation-adjusted spending method becomes evident when people do such an analysis only one time and then actually increase their annual spending by the amount of inflation in each year, which is, of course, the basis of the theory. I've seen texts written by professional planners that make this recommendation and even some computer programs. This is always a disastrous thing to do, especially if the calculation happens to be made just before investments take a nosedive. But even when a drop in the market is not imminent, without annual adjustments to your data to allow for changing conditions, your savings are highly unlikely to last the rest of your life.

Fixed-Percent Withdrawals

Another popular postretirement planning method recommended by some planners is to withdraw annually some percentage, most often 6%, of the previous year-end investment balance to pay for the forthcoming year's expenses and taxes. For example, if your retirement savings totaled $100,000 at the end of the year, you would be able to spend $6,000 of your savings this year. The exact percentage is often argued by these planners and is also dependent on how your investments are allocated. Even if your portfolio has more stocks than bonds, conservative planners say you should withdraw only 4% to allow for some significant ups and downs in security values. Other planners, whom I consider to be optimists, say 8%. We'll use the more common 6% figure in our examples to illustrate the principle. Keep in mind that the size of this withdrawal should not be confused with the mandatory required minimum distributions after age 70½ for an IRA or 401(k). When the RMD exceeds 6% (or whatever percentage is being used for your budgeting purposes), the excess should be reinvested in some other account. We'll take a look at how this method compares to the others later in the chapter. You'll see that it can quickly lead to disaster unless you have a portfolio made up predominantly of stocks and a bull market most of your retired life.

Successive Annual Calculations

The financial planning method known as successive annual calculations requires you to establish an annual budget based on a new analysis each year using long-term market returns, long-term inflation, and a new life expectancy each year. The potential problem with this method is in the data you are putting in—remember, garbage in, garbage out. Sometimes the equations get fouled by overly optimistic returns and inflation assumptions when compared to historical records. I've seen cases where the returns came from one period and inflation from another to make the numbers look better.

The better applications of successive annual calculations account for the fact that the longer a person lives, the more likely it is that he or she will die at a still older age. In spite of added sophistication, computer programs using this method seldom account for the actual mutual fund costs, management fees, or broker charges of owning securities. Instead they use the market indexes directly, which, as we've seen, are seldom actually matched in real life because they do not include the costs that investors pay, either directly or indirectly.

Retirement Autopilot Method

This is the method used in this book, and there are several aspects that make this retirement planning method the one I believe to be the best available at this time. First, it uses new technology incorporating methods long used by engineers in dynamic systems. (We'll explain this in a moment.) Second, unlike most methods, it factors in that returns in retirement most often lose the battle to reverse dollar cost averaging and investment costs, and finally, it accounts for the fact that your savings must be used for things other than retirement. To the best of my knowledge, there are no other methods that use the autopilot, only a small number of very complex computer programs account for real-world returns in historical retirement scenarios, and only the more sophisticated computer programs account for the purchase of high-value items before or during retirement.

Let's take a look at how it works. In an airplane, an autopilot is an electronic device that can either control the airplane without the pilot's assistance or provide better performance even with the pilot in control. In a missile or space vehicle, it provides control at all times without any human intervention. An autopilot is mechanized so that it provides the smoothest ride possible as it guides the vehicle to its intended destination. Our retirement autopilot has the same goal, controlling your finances so that you save and spend at levels that are intended to get you through retirement smoothly and successfully.

An airplane is continually buffeted by wind gusts. Its autopilot cannot foresee the turbulence ahead, so it must continually compensate by adjusting the airplane's flaps, ailerons, elevator, rudder, and throttle. In the same way, your retirement autopilot cannot foresee future security prices and inflation, but it can make continuous small adjustments based on the ever changing economic climate. It can then adjust your saving and spending accordingly to provide as smooth a ride as possible, and to ensure that you don't run out of fuel (money) before you die.

If an engineer for your home heating system would have developed this type of retirement planning system, the engineer might have called this same system a retirement thermostat, because a thermostat does something similar, though much simpler. The thermostat controls the furnace to adjust for temperature changes outside the building. It doesn't know what the future outside temperature will be, but it still provides a comfortable and a relatively steady temperature inside the building. Besides facing an uncertain external environment, airplane electronics, building thermostats, and the retirement autopilot method all have something else in common: They rely on a concept called *feedback* by an engineer. The concept in all cases is to measure something that is happening and use that measurement to adjust the controls. So we "feed back" the information to the system. In the case of a thermostat, we feed back the internal temperature and compare it to the control temperature. If the internal temperature is too low, the system turns on the furnace until reaching the desired temperature. For an airplane we feed back the current heading (direction), pitch (nose up or down), or yaw (nose right or left) and compare it with the desired position. The system then adjusts the flight controls to bring the vehicle back into the correct position. With the retirement autopilot, we feed back the year-end balances of your investment account and last year's inflation and compare the new projection with an inflation-adjusted projection from last year. Like an airplane autopilot or thermostat, the retirement autopilot acts as a shock absorber to reduce the disturbances to your planned savings and/or spending levels that would otherwise result from turbulent external conditions.

Comparing the Different Methods

Now let's consider how the various postretirement plans work in the real world. To do that, we'll look at how a hypothetical retiree might have done using the different methods if he or she retired during two different historical periods, beginning in 1955 and 1965. For simplicity's sake, we will assume the funds are in deferred tax accounts such as IRAs or 401(k)s. The amounts withdrawn are taxable, so the withdrawals always cover both living expenses and taxes. (Things in the real world get a little more complex, of course, and when it comes time to do your own plan we will also account for taxable investments, debts, and unusual expenses that do not repeat year after year, such as the purchase of new automobiles, a vacation house, and so on.)

Our imaginary retiree is retiring at 60 years of age with $1 million in investments for retirement. (We could have started with some other number, but a million is a nice round figure, and not a bad objective for many people. You could use a number with more or less zeros, but the results will be proportionately the same.)

Fifty percent of the investments are in a S&P 500 index fund. Each year the portfolio is rebalanced so that the amount of stock is 1% less than it was the year before, so 49% would be in stock the second year, 48% the third year, and so on. Ten percent of the investments are always in short-term Treasury bills or money markets (which have a similar interest rate). The remainder of the investments are in long-term corporate bonds. Each part of the portfolio has its own return. We will also subtract 1% from the market indexes for the costs of funds, brokers, agents, advisors, services, and bad timing. A few index funds and those using discount brokers sometimes fare better than 1%, but there are people who have costs in excess of 5%. (The planning chapters will let you pick your own security allocations and costs.) Let's examine what would happen under real-world conditions over a 30-year period as we let the different postretirement scenarios play out.

First, look at Figure 1.5. Each point on each line represents the amount of money the retirement plan calculations say can be withdrawn. In this deferred tax case, that is equivalent to a budget for living expenses and the taxes due on the withdrawals.

You can see that life would have been difficult for those who retired in 1955 and used the fixed-percent withdrawal method to take out 6% of their remaining investment assets each year. Shortly after committing to a budget of about $60,000, the budget starts a steep decline that finally levels off to roughly $13,000 in 1980. Thus, the one-time millionaire who initially spent $60,000 for living expenses and taxes will ultimately struggle at what would have looked like poverty level back when he or she started making those fixed-percent withdrawals.

The inflation-adjusted budget, on the other hand, nicely supports the retiree's original lifestyle for much of his or her life, albeit at a somewhat reduced budget compared with the fixed-percent withdrawal's initial $60,000. Even so, by 1980 the budget is down to zero! At that point, support would have to come from welfare or, with luck, some affluent and generous adult children.

Only Autopilot Helps Expenses Late in Life

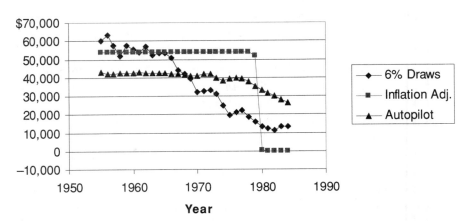

FIGURE 1.5 Annual withdrawals (adjusted for inflation) for three different retirement methods starting in 1955.

The autopilot budget starts a little lower but provides funds throughout what would reasonably be considered a practical life span—in this case, the person who left work at age 60 in 1955 would be 90 years old in 1985 and still would have a little money in the bank. In spite of security fluctuations, the autopilot calculations are relatively stable, making it possible to maintain a good lifestyle for many years without continual worry about what will happen in the market.

Retirees who used the inflation-adjusted spending method to calculate a budget would be able to maintain a very stable lifestyle—until 1980 when they flat ran out of money! That's age 85 for a person who was age 60 in 1955. We'll see next that a retiree who was 60 in 1965 would have run out of money at only age 75. That wouldn't be very comforting to all of the people over 80 years old we have in our community.

So, what would have happened to you if your retirement had started in 1965? As you can see in Figure 1.6, there would have been a rough time ahead no matter what method you used. Especially hard hit were those who tried to maintain their initial lifestyle by using the inflation-adjusted method, and went belly up at age 75. My father, who lived to be 96, started retirement quite comfortably, readjusted his budget numerous times in his life to severely reduce costs, and ultimately, no matter his frugality, had to depend on his children for support.

The autopilot budget was about $10,000 lower initially, but, compared to the person using the 6% withdrawal method, ultimately provided $5000 to $10,000 more each year for the person who retired in 1965—especially during the important middle years of retirement. The fixed-percent withdrawal method's budget left our millionaire at poverty level early in retirement. The inflation-

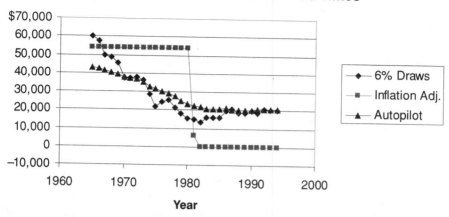

FIGURE 1.6 Annual withdrawals (adjusted for inflation) for three different retirement methods starting in 1965.

adjusted method would leave the millionaire in poverty for almost half of his or her retired life.

Unfortunately, one of the lessons we can draw from these examples is that there is no perfect way to overcome really bad economic times. The particular controls used by the autopilot system, however, were chosen so that, in most scenarios from past history, they would have provided the best possible results. If the future is anything like the past, the autopilot method will do so in the future as well. You can see that it's important to use a good planning method and, just in case, preserve some reserves for the unforeseen. Those who do this will be the eventual winners.

The Hazards of Preretirement Planning

Preretirement planning is not as demanding as postretirement planning, though it's important to do an analysis periodically. There is more tolerance for errors when you still have some time left before retirement, and people who are still putting money into their accounts benefit from dollar cost averaging as opposed to the retiree's reverse dollar cost averaging. In addition, you might have the option of retiring a little later if your savings aren't yet what they should be. Working longer offers a number of benefits. Existing investments have more time to grow, and there can be additional savings contributions. Social Security benefits will increase. If the employer has a pension plan, its value can grow immensely in the last few years. That's because the pension formulas are based on the number of years of service multiplied by the wage rate near retirement. In fact, a few pension plans allow "spiking" in the last year of work, which means some people will greatly increase the income from which their pension will be calculated by doing such things as working unnecessary overtime and taking pay in lieu of vacation and sick leave.

The person who is still working also has the ability to take more risk, especially at quite young ages. A younger person can invest in a portfolio composed largely of stocks or stock mutual funds. As an example, over a 20-year span, a person with a portfolio heavily weighted with stocks could well retire with twice as much as a person with a portfolio weighted heavily with bonds. Over a 30-year span, instead of doubling, your retirement savings could triple. (We'll see this in action in Chapter 3, when we look at asset allocation.)

No one needs to be told that the difficult part of preretirement planning is saving enough money early enough to do you the most good. However large the benefits from the incredible power of compounding may be, there are many impediments that prevent young people from saving. There is the down payment on a new house, furnishings to purchase, cars to finance, and the next thing you know it's time to start saving for their children's college expenses. The autopilot method that we'll describe in Chapter 5 will show you how to account for these things, but here we are going to look at some simplified examples so that we can look at the difference in the various planning methods you will encounter. Keep in mind, though, that if the planning method you use does not look at your overall savings to achieve the unique requirements of your preretirement years, be wary. You cannot have one plan to save for things like college that is independent of a plan to save for retirement. You must save for both at the same time, or one or the other will suffer accordingly. What this means for practical purposes is that, most likely, your greatest retirement savings will come as you near retirement.

It really helps to develop the mind-set that you are going to save a certain percentage of your income no matter what. Essentially, you live on an income that's a little smaller than you actually could afford. Perhaps you can start by saving all of your next few raises. As you get nearer retirement, you may have to really save quickly if your annual savings were low or the markets were unkind to your investments.

What are the current planning methods for preretirement? We'll look at the major ones in a minute. Then we will test them in a real-world scenario, just like we did for the postretirement plans. And let me just say up front that the results aren't pretty. Why? Because the real world isn't smooth. The simulations we will look at illustrate the problem I confronted when I tried to forecast my own retirement needs in the 1980s. If you do a new calculation each year to check on how you are doing, you will find that the closer you get to retirement, the more variation you will see in your needed annual savings. The reason is that your calculation is largely dependent on the value of your investments at the time, and these values go up and down, particularly investments in stocks or stock mutual funds. The autopilot can help smooth things out some, but don't forget that you have to come up with the money to begin retirement, whether that means saving more sooner or working a few years longer.

Open-Loop Shortcut

The first preretirement method we'll look at is the open-loop shortcut. This is the method used by people who have taken one step above the worst method, which is to do nothing. We call it open-loop planning because there are no annual corrections. The term *open loop* is engineering jargon. In an engineer's mind, if you took your hands off the steering wheel of your automobile, it would be in an open-loop mode. On the other hand, when you continually steer the car, you are "closing the loop." Open loop implies it's out of control. At the same time, this method is a shortcut because you bypass more competent methods that take more time. You can find various versions of the open-loop shortcut for free on the Internet, in magazines, or in brochures from banks, brokers, mutual fund salespeople, or insurance agents. They all like it because it shows optimistic results for their products. The reason is that returns are artificially high, either because they are averages (as opposed to compounded) or they come from a favorable historic period. To make things worse, they almost universally ignore investment costs. Better versions of open-loop planning calculate the percent of wages you should save each year, and this in itself should boost your annual savings as your wages grow. The worst of these shortcuts calculates an annual savings value without any recommended increase in the future. It's disastrous to keep your annual deposits at the same dollar amount because inflation reduces the value each year. Yet that's what the government does with IRAs when it limits maximum savings without an annual adjustment.

The good thing about the shortcut is that it is simple and better than no plan at all. In terms of numbers, a plan of this kind generally will lead you to input figures of 3% inflation, 8% return on investment before retirement, and 7% return on investment after retirement. These translate to a 5% real return before retirement and a 4% real return after retirement. To illustrate, let's use numbers that are all inflation adjusted. For example, consider a 50-year-old person wanting to retire at age 60 with a $40,000 annual before-tax budget that would last 30 years. This means she'll need about $692,000 in investments (based on 4% real return) at retirement. Let's say she is starting with current investments of $350,000. To reach her goal from there, she has to save about $9,700 per year, and that figure has to be increased each year by the amount of inflation.

We'll further assume that this is a moderate investor who, at age 50, has 55% large company stocks, 35% long-term corporate bonds, and 10% in a short-term Treasury bill money market fund. The overall investment costs are 1% (which is lower than average). Each year, this person reduces the stocks by 1% and replaces those with bonds. That means that at age 60, there will be 45% stocks, 45% bonds, and 10% in a money market.

Now let's take a look at what happens when we plug these data into the open-loop shortcut using three different periods in history. Figure 1.7 details what would have happened if we started saving in 1950, 1955, and 1960 and retired 10 years later. Each case assumes 10 years of inflation-adjusted savings of $9,700 before retirement followed by retirement spending of $40,000 each year after retirement at age 60. (Note that the charts begin their calculations with data from the *end* of the first year, which accounts for the varying starting points in the graph.) You'll see, as in the postretirement examples, that it makes a huge difference which piece of history you use as a point of referral.

In our examples, the person who started using the open-loop shortcut method in 1950 went broke at age 82. The person who started using this method in 1955 went broke at age 75, and the person who started in 1960 went broke at age 71, just 11 years after retiring. How can this happen? Well, the real world got in the way. The open-loop shortcut method didn't take into account investment costs and reverse dollar cost averaging. It also used a return that was an average kind of value that made no provision for those years when the returns will be less than average.

You'd think it couldn't get much worse, but many people using the open-loop shortcut retirement assumptions can fall prey to even more dramatic overspending. Consider a case in which someone uses the open-loop shortcut method just before retirement to make a new estimate of how much he or she can spend using his or her current investment balances. In the 1950 scenario, the investments during the 10 years of savings did better than expected, exceeding $800,000, so the method would now say that the retiree could spend $54,600 per year instead of $40,000. Figure 1.8 shows the results.

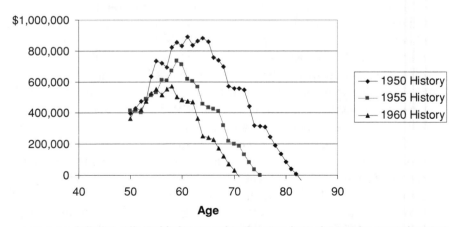

Open-Loop Shortcut Runs Out Fast!

FIGURE 1.7 Inflation-adjusted balances using the open-loop shortcut for scenarios starting in 1950, 1955, and 1960.

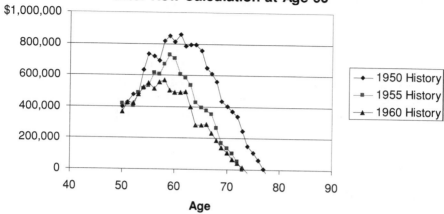

Open-Loop Shortcut Results May Get Worse after New Calculation at Age 60

Legend:
- ◆ 1950 History
- ■ 1955 History
- ▲ 1960 History

X-axis: Age (40, 50, 60, 70, 80, 90)
Y-axis: $1,000,000; 800,000; 600,000; 400,000; 200,000; 0

FIGURE 1.8 Making a new estimate with the open-loop shortcut just before retirement does not always improve results, as in the 1950 scenario.

Spending at this new higher level in the 1950 case turns into trouble. While the investments will last till age 82 with spending at $40,000 a year, as we saw in Figure 1.7, spending at $54,600 per year depletes the investments at age 77. The 1955 scenario has the same kind of effect, though not as dramatic, and investments actually last a little longer in the 1960 scenario because the age 60 calculation recommended spending only $32,200 per year instead of $40,000.

If there is a lesson here, it's to be very cautious with the retirement planning advice you receive. You also need to get a firm handle on the kind of return you can expect from your investments—something we'll talk more about as we go on.

Quick and Dirty

Quick and dirty planning offers a touch of realism compared to the open-loop shortcut. I developed it for people who were willing to take only a few minutes to look at their future finances as contrasted with a more comprehensive method that I recommend. (Both methods are discussed in Chapter 5.) Quick and dirty lets you calculate your results for three different kinds of investment allocations: one for the conservative person investing mostly in bonds, another for the moderate person with about half his or her investments in stocks, and a third for someone who invests aggressively in stocks with only a few bonds. Costs are assumed to be 1%, which is a little lower than average because we hope you will learn something from Chapter 3 on investments. The quick and dirty tables in Chapter 5 provide some conservatism relative to returns, especially in retirement, and it's easy to do a new analysis periodically. We don't encourage the use of this method for a number of reasons, including that it is not very detailed and doesn't allow for people's need to save for things other than retirement while they are saving for retirement. Still, if you don't have much time, the results are more likely to be practical than the shortcut methods you find in magazines or on the Internet.

Figure 1.9 shows how someone would fare with quick and dirty. Here the savings last much longer than they did with the shortcut method in Figure 1.8. That's because, to reach the goal of a $40,000 annual retirement income, the annual savings in this method would have to be substantially higher, as a consequence of using more realistic returns. As you'll see in Chapter 5, quick and dirty does have the advantage of making it easy to strike a balance between saving before retirement and spending in retirement.

Recalculation Methods

Most professional planners recommend that their clients reassess their retirement plans about once a year by recalculating their results. (This should not be confused with the *recalculation method* used to determine required minimum distributions from an IRA.) I've found that this really is as important as an annual dental or physical exam, and a lot more important timewise than an hour or so in front of a TV. The principal benefit of recalculation is that you will get an annual reminder of the importance of making sacrifices now in order to achieve the income benefits you expect in retirement. If you haven't gone through this process at least several times before retirement, you are very likely to be in for the shock of your life. People are generally astonished at the low

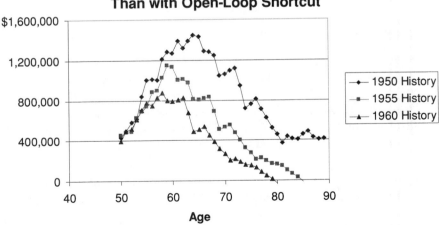

FIGURE 1.9 The quick and dirty method shown here uses more conservative returns than the open-loop shortcut in Figure 1.8 and so demands more saving before retirement and lower spending after retirement.

level of income they will get from investments during retirement because they had no idea of the quantitative relation between their savings before retirement and their spending after retirement.

Recalculation uses the same kinds of methods we looked at earlier. The quick and dirty methods will show better results than open-loop shortcuts. Using some of the best computer programs will, of course, give even better results. Recalculation with the retirement autopilot is a step better yet. We've already seen the benefits of recalculation using the retirement autopilot method in the retirement part of the scenario in Figures 1.5 and 1.6.

I do want to alert you to a potential problem as you approach retirement and the stock market goes through one of its typical up-and-down cycles. As you do your annual recalculation you may well run into the same effect that confounded me: One year you are told you can save a lot less and the next you are told you must save a lot more. By using the autopilot method, it's unlikely you will have to relive my own levels of frustration with these calculations.

As an illustration, Figure 1.10 shows how investments would increase during preretirement if you recalculate each year using three separate methods. The goal of each method was to achieve $1 million before retirement. The first method is the open-loop shortcut we investigated before, but it is now used in annual recalculations. The second method uses a computer program that could be any high-quality commercial program where we inserted realistic returns less investment costs. The third method is the preretirement autopilot that you can find in Chapter 5.

These simulations assume that 70% of the investments are in large company

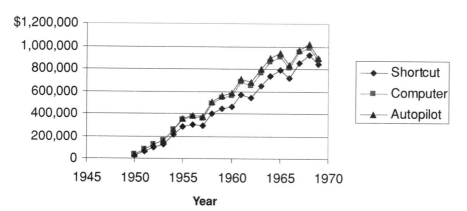

Stock Market Shocks Shortly Before Retirement Hurt Investment Growth

FIGURE 1.10 No planning method gives happy results when the stock market takes a plunge after a sustained bull market, but the autopilot method produces the least trauma.

stocks, 20% in long-term corporate bonds, and 10% in short-term Treasury bills. Investment costs are 2%. When people are close to retirement, a drop in the market may dramatically increase the calculated demand for new savings, as we will see in these scenarios, so much so that it may be impossible to ever meet their retirement goal. As a practical matter, people then compromise their expectations. In the cases here, we'll reflect that reality by arbitrarily limiting the actual maximum savings amount to twice their recent annual savings even though the demand is greater, because that is about as far as most people can go. This is equivalent to saying that if our normal savings were 15% of wages per year, we would never be able to save more than 30% per year, even if our goal demanded more (as it does several times in Figure 1.11).

As you can see in Figure 1.10, both the autopilot and the computer program did better than the shortcut. The principal reason is that the shortcut, being optimistic, always thought that the future was going to be brighter than what actually materialized. However, that's not the point I want to make. The point is that this particular bit of history had some serious stock market problems that cropped up just before retirement. Which recalculation method did the best job of coping with the market dips?

This question is answered in Figure 1.11. All of the methods get lulled into a false sense of security by 1965 because of the previously great market conditions. The demand for annual savings diminishes. (Incidentally, the same situation unfolded in the year 2000. National savings rates were almost zero, at least in part because investment values went up so much.) But then the investment values fall abruptly in 1966, which signals all of the planning methods to tell you to increase your annual savings. But the market rebounds, so the plans call for

Shortcut Goes Berserk,
but Autopilot Returns to Normal

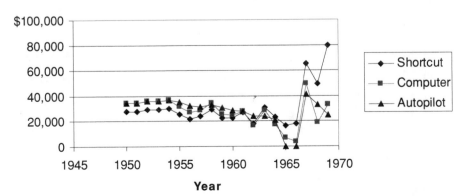

FIGURE 1.11 All of the planning methods try to cope with adverse market conditions near retirement. The shortcut calls for unreasonable savings in the last year.

more moderate savings. Then the market hits another hole, and both the shortcut and the computer programs call for another savings increase. The autopilot just returns to a more normal level. The shortcut method goes berserk.

If you review the details of Figure 1.11, you'll see that the autopilot provided the most reasonable response through the years. But there is no question which turned out to be the worst. That's the shortcut. It's highly unlikely that anyone who was used to saving $20,000 to $30,000 a year would be able to come up with $80,000 to meet his or her goal. If you want the shortcut to give more reasonable results using recalculation, you must use a more conservative return on investment than the long-term average return for the types of securities in your portfolio.

Now that we've reviewed some of the most important planning methods, we can see that doing a recalculation each year is one of the most important things you can do to ensure a comfortable retirement. And the autopilot method, which requires recalculation, provides much more practical savings conditions before retirement and spending conditions after retirement than the other methods we discussed. Even with the autopilot, however, it may be impossible to reach your retirement investment goal when the market plummets just prior to retirement. At that point, you'll either have to compromise by taking a lower retirement income or work longer.

One of the keys to successful retirement planning is to avoid optimistic theoretical assumptions about future investment performance that are likely to lead to disappointing real-life retirement benefits no matter what method you select. It is also essential to have realistic data that reflects all of the outside forces that will come into play during your retirement. In the next chapter we're going to look at some of the fundamental forces the real world will add to the mix: death, inflation, and taxes.

CHAPTER 2

Some Fundamental Planning Facts

Nothing in this world
is certain but death
and taxes.*

Spend Now and (Really) Pay Later

Most people don't really know what spending costs them. When they near retirement, though, they get much smarter about what things really cost. Cost is not just the price paid for an item, or even any associated interest costs. The cost is really in lost savings that could have compounded into very significant numbers to help out in retirement—and remember that retirement can easily be one-third of your total life. Spending too much too early after retiring is devastating. There is no way to recover other than with budgets that get smaller every year.

Let's look at some specific numbers to illustrate this point. We'll use $1,000 as our base amount. Perhaps it represents some additional options we just had to have on our new car, or it could be an upgrade to our computer, or a high-speed integrated system of cell phones and Internet service, or any one of the hundreds of things we can come up with all too easily to spend $1,000 on—and watch those things become valueless in just a few years.

The real cost of those unnecessary items is dependent on a number of factors. The first of these is how many years you could have compounded the savings until you reach that point in retirement when you would withdraw the money. The next is whether you are purchasing for cash or credit. If you buy on credit, you can really run up your cost with interest payments. If your interest rate is 15% and you spread the payments over four years, you really pay $1,749 for your $1,000 item. Many people who buy with credit cards end up with 18%

*Benjamin Franklin, in a letter to M. Leroy of the French Academy of Sciences, 1789.

interest and let the balance run for up to 10 years. That would increase the amount you pay to $5,235.

But this isn't the full extent of the real cost to you. The real cost is the amount it reduced your retirement savings. This in turn depends on whether you could have saved the money in a tax-deferred account such as a 401(k) or an IRA. If you have to reduce your contributions to a tax-deferred account to pay for your $1,000 purchase, then you lose the initial tax deduction as well as the benefits of tax-deferred growth.

But even without the tax reduction, that $1,000 item can cost you dearly. Let's assume you pay cash, use no credit, can take the $1,000 out of your current checking account, and have already made the maximum contributions to tax-deferred savings accounts, so you aren't actually losing any deductions. Consider what happens if you have 30 years until you retire and your mutual fund returns a steady 10%. In this scenario, the least that $1,000 could cost you at retirement would be a reduction in your savings of $17,400. Now you can begin to see why most wealthy people are penny-pinchers and great savers.

Let's take that example a step further. The costs get significantly higher if you buy the article on credit and the money you have spent prevents you from putting it into an employer's savings plan. (We don't have to tell you that you should *always* save enough to get the maximum from your employer's matching contributions, do we? That's like throwing away a gift.) For example, if you are 30 years away from retirement, that $1,000 plus the credit card interest, ignoring any employer's matching contributions, would reduce the amount you put in savings by $5,235. Then there is the tax deduction you get from sheltering the $1,000 in a deferred tax plan. At a 15% tax rate, that's another $785, because you could have used that $150 tax saving to reduce your credit card debt. Now, compound the sum of $5,235 and $785 for 30 years at 10% and you get a loss of $105,000 in retirement savings. If you had foregone the opportunity to contribute to an employer's savings plan with 100% matching contributions, that would have cost $210,000!

Face it. In retrospect, wasn't most of that stuff just junk? Look in your basement. Look in your attic. Think about the beating you took when you tried to sell your old computer; think about how fast the newness and pleasure of most of your toys wore off. We've all blown money on dumb purchases. But those who can recognize a dumb purchase before actually turning over the money are the ones who will still have something to spend during that last one-third of their life.

The Preretirement Blowout

It's very common to see a couple in early retirement do two things: (1) buy a new car that will be comfortable and supposedly last most of their remaining life, and (2) go on an expensive once-in-a-lifetime vacation. Others add a third item: buy a vacation home or time-share.

What really happened is that they have just reduced the time their retirement funds will last by about one year for each of the first two items, and, who knows how many years for the vacation home. And the truth is that the more expensive car won't really last any longer than a less expensive one, and it certainly doesn't cost less to operate. The expensive vacation ended with some nice additions to the scrapbook for memories, but a less expensive one could probably have produced the same result. And the vacation home or time-share will ultimately be sold at a fraction of what the equivalent investment in stocks or bonds would have yielded. Let's assume that the new car or the vacation cost our newly retired couple an extra $10,000. Let's also assume that the couple has a return of 7% from their retirement investments. Let's say they expect to live another 20 years or so. That $10,000 could have grown to almost $39,000 over those 20 years, which, together with their Social Security, might have supported them for another year.

I have a neighbor who has really taken this to heart. Every time his wife makes an expensive purchase he tells her, "Honey, this is okay by me, but I hope you realize that you'll have to take another year off your life to compensate." There's no doubt about it—spending now really costs later!

What If You Outlive Your Current Life Expectancy?

You have a 50% chance of outliving your current life expectancy. Sound strange? Well, it's true. To see why, we have to look at how life expectancy is defined. Insurance companies generally cite an age. Government publications more often define life expectancy as the additional number of years you have left to live. So a life insurance company might say that a person would be expected to live to, say, age 80. On the other hand, the Internal Revenue Service (IRS) would say that you have 20 more years to live. We're going to use the latter definition as well as the IRS data in this book, because it provides a slightly more conservative planning result than insurance mortality tables and isn't dependent on variables like your sex, race, physical condition, and so on, so it is simpler for us to use. But by either definition, life expectancy is an average, which implies that 50% of the population will die at a younger age than the data shows, and 50% will die at an older age.

Should it somehow transpire that you are among the 50% of people your age who will die later, the good news is that you'll see a ripe old age. The bad news is that you'll have to finance it. That's where our autopilot method can help you to feel good, as well as covered, on both accounts.

Your Life Expectancy Depends on Your Age

Here's another surprising fact. Statistically, each year that you live, the age at which you can expect to die increases. A 65-year-old single person has a life expectancy of 20 years according to the IRS (see Figure 2.1). This means he or

Find Out How Long the IRS Thinks You Will Live

Age of Single or Older Person	Single Life Expectancy	JOINT LIFE AND LAST SURVIVOR LIFE EXPECTANCY (YEARS) Other Spouse Is Younger By										
		Equal Ages	1 Year	2 Years	3 Years	4 Years	5 Years	6 Years	7 Years	8 Years	9 Years	10 Years
55	**28.6**	**34.4**	**34.9**	**35.4**	**35.9**	**36.5**	**37.1**	**37.7**	**38.4**	**39.0**	**39.7**	**40.4**
56	27.7	33.4	33.9	34.4	35.0	35.6	36.1	36.8	37.4	38.1	38.7	39.5
57	26.8	32.5	33.0	33.5	34.0	34.6	35.2	35.8	36.4	37.1	37.8	38.5
58	25.9	31.5	32.0	32.5	33.1	33.6	34.2	34.8	35.5	36.1	36.8	37.5
59	25.0	30.6	31.1	31.6	32.1	32.7	33.3	33.9	34.5	35.2	35.9	36.6
60	**24.2**	**29.7**	**30.1**	**30.6**	**31.2**	**31.7**	**32.3**	**32.9**	**33.6**	**34.2**	**34.9**	**35.6**
61	23.3	28.7	29.2	29.7	30.2	30.8	31.4	32.0	32.6	33.3	33.9	34.6
62	22.5	27.8	28.3	28.8	29.3	29.9	30.4	31.0	31.7	32.3	33.0	33.7
63	21.6	26.9	27.3	27.8	28.4	28.9	29.5	30.1	30.7	31.4	32.0	32.7
64	20.8	25.9	26.4	26.9	27.4	28.0	28.6	29.2	29.8	30.4	31.1	31.8
65	**20.0**	**25.0**	**25.5**	**26.0**	**26.5**	**27.1**	**27.6**	**28.2**	**28.9**	**29.5**	**30.2**	**30.9**
66	19.2	24.1	24.6	25.1	25.6	26.1	26.7	27.3	27.9	28.6	29.2	29.9
67	18.4	23.2	23.7	24.2	24.7	25.2	25.8	26.4	27.0	27.6	28.3	29.0
68	17.6	22.3	22.8	23.3	23.8	24.3	24.9	25.5	26.1	26.7	27.4	28.1
69	16.8	21.5	21.9	22.4	22.9	23.4	24.0	24.6	25.2	25.8	26.5	27.1
70	**16.0**	**20.6**	**21.1**	**21.5**	**22.0**	**22.5**	**23.1**	**23.7**	**24.3**	**24.9**	**25.6**	**26.2**
71	15.3	19.8	20.2	20.7	21.2	21.7	22.2	22.8	23.4	24.0	24.7	25.3
72	14.6	18.8	19.4	19.8	20.3	20.8	21.3	21.9	22.5	23.1	23.8	24.4
73	13.9	18.1	18.5	19.0	19.4	20.0	20.5	21.0	21.6	22.2	22.9	23.5
74	13.2	17.3	17.7	18.2	18.6	19.1	19.6	20.2	20.8	21.4	22.0	22.7
75	**12.5**	**16.5**	**16.9**	**17.3**	**17.8**	**18.3**	**18.8**	**19.3**	**19.9**	**20.5**	**21.1**	**21.8**

Age												
76	20.9	20.3	19.7	19.1	18.5	18.0	17.5	17.0	16.5	16.1	15.7	11.9
77	20.1	19.4	18.8	18.3	17.7	17.2	16.7	16.2	15.8	15.4	15.0	11.2
78	19.2	18.6	18.0	17.5	16.9	16.4	15.9	15.4	15.0	14.6	14.2	10.6
79	18.4	17.8	17.2	16.7	16.1	15.6	15.1	14.7	14.3	13.9	13.5	10.0
80	**17.6**	**17.0**	**16.4**	**15.9**	**15.4**	14.9	14.4	14.0	13.5	13.2	12.8	**9.5**
81	16.8	16.2	15.7	15.1	14.6	14.1	13.7	13.2	12.8	12.5	12.1	8.9
82	16.0	15.5	14.9	14.4	13.9	13.4	13.0	12.5	12.2	11.8	11.5	8.4
83	15.3	14.7	14.2	13.7	13.2	12.7	12.3	11.9	11.5	11.1	10.8	7.9
84	14.5	14.0	13.5	13.0	12.5	12.0	11.6	11.2	10.9	10.5	10.2	7.4
85	**13.8**	**13.3**	**12.8**	**12.3**	**11.8**	11.4	11.0	10.6	10.2	9.9	9.6	**6.9**
86	13.1	12.6	12.1	11.6	11.2	10.8	10.4	10.0	9.7	9.3	9.1	6.5
87	12.4	11.9	11.4	11.0	10.6	10.1	9.8	9.4	9.1	8.8	8.5	6.1
88	11.8	11.3	10.8	10.4	10.0	9.6	9.2	8.9	8.6	8.3	8.0	5.7
89	11.1	10.7	10.2	9.8	9.4	9.0	8.7	8.3	8.1	7.8	7.5	5.3
90	**10.5**	**10.1**	**9.6**	**9.2**	**8.8**	8.5	8.2	7.9	7.6	7.3	7.1	**5.0**
91	9.9	9.5	9.1	8.7	8.3	8.0	7.7	7.4	7.1	6.9	6.7	4.7
92	9.4	8.9	8.5	8.2	7.8	7.5	7.2	6.9	6.7	6.5	6.3	4.4
93	8.8	8.4	8.0	7.7	7.4	7.1	6.8	6.5	6.3	6.1	5.9	4.1
94	8.3	7.9	7.6	7.2	6.9	6.6	6.4	6.2	5.9	5.8	5.6	3.9
95	**7.8**	**7.5**	**7.1**	**6.8**	**6.5**	6.3	6.0	5.8	5.6	5.4		**3.7**
96	7.3	7.0	6.7	6.4	6.1	5.9	5.7	5.5	5.3			3.4
97	6.9	6.6	6.3	6.0	5.8	5.5	5.3	5.1				3.2
98	6.5	6.2	5.9	5.6	5.4	5.2	5.0					3.0
99	6.1	5.8	5.5	5.3	5.1	4.9						2.8
100	**5.7**	**5.4**	**5.2**	**5.0**	**4.8**							**2.7**

FIGURE 2.1 Life expectancies depend on your age. (Based on data from IRS Publication 590.)

she could expect to live to age 85. Once having lived to age 85, however, the new life expectancy is about 7 years, which brings us up to a likely life span of 92 years. And so on.

Take for example the true story of my friend's father who finally retired at age 96. At that point he had a life expectancy of 3.2 years per the IRS table, so he would theoretically live to age 99. Now he's 102 years old, and his current life expectancy is about 104. If you update your life expectancy each year, you simply can never outlive it. It's a sort of statistical immortality. We use this same principle to make sure that you will always have some funds for your retirement even on the day you die. Ideally, we'd like you to spend your last nickel on your last day. Our method doesn't quite do that (if I could predict your last day, I'd be in another line of work altogether), but it does offer a way to adjust your spending to your current life expectancy so that you can be assured of having funds until you do die, because each year we make a new plan using a new life expectancy. Since you can never outlive your life expectancy, you can never outlive your remaining investments.

Working with Life Expectancy Data

The life expectancies in Figure 2.1 are based on the current IRS Publication 590. Although the IRS may abandon some detail on life expectancies when it simplifies IRA calculations, Figure 2.1 is useful to demonstrate representative life spans of both single people and the surviving spouse of a couple. To illustrate, if one spouse is 60 and the other 58, you would look in the row for age 60 and the column for 2 years' age difference to find 30.6. This means that one spouse has about a 50% chance of living another 30.6 years while the other would have died earlier. It does not distinguish between male and female, and the numbers may be conservative when contrasted with actuarial tables—especially for males who tend to have shorter life spans than females.

After you are age 70½, the last column of Figure 2.1 is important to you if you have a deferred tax investment like an IRA or 401(k) because that part of the table is used to determine your RMDs. You can withdraw more than the RMD, but if you withdraw less, you will receive a horrible tax penalty. In essence, you divide the balance in your IRA (or other similar account) on December 31 of the previous year by the number of years (in the last column of Figure 2.1) corresponding to the IRA owner's age. If that number is more than our calculations indicate that you can afford to spend, reinvest the difference in a taxable account. Keep in mind that although these numbers have not changed for many years, you should make RMD calculations using information from the latest IRS publications. Also, there are special rules that come into effect when spouses are more than 10 years different in age or for a beneficiary after the original IRA owner dies. Before selecting beneficiaries, check the implications with a knowledgeable professional.

Making Your Money Last a Lifetime

We are going to use the life expectancy table shown in Figure 2.2 to determine how much retired people can afford to spend every year and still have enough to last for the rest of their lives. It is really just a copy of the column in Figure 2.1 for a couple of equal ages. However, we're going to use it with a little twist. Instead of entering the table using the age of the older spouse or a single person as you do in Figure 2.1, we enter Figure 2.2 using the age of the younger spouse or a single person. This provides us with a simple way to calculate a slightly longer life expectancy. That, in turn, makes the analysis using the retirement autopilot method slightly more conservative, because our money must be stretched over several more years.

For a single person who is 65, Figure 2.2 would forecast a life expectancy of 25 years, which is 5 years more conservative compared with the 20 years from Figure 2.1. If the 65-year-old had a spouse who was 10 years younger, you would enter Figure 2.2 using age 55 and get 34.4 years for a life expectancy. We use this number to represent the life expectancy of the surviving spouse, which could be either the younger or older one. The full IRS table in Figure 2.1 would give 30.9 years, so Figure 2.2 is more conservative by 3.5 years in that case.

Autopilot Life Expectancies

Single or Younger Spouse Age	Life Expectancy	Single or Younger Spouse Age	Life Expectancy
55	**34.4**	75	16.5
56	33.4	76	15.7
57	32.5	**77**	**15.0**
58	31.5	78	14.2
59	30.6	79	13.5
60	**29.7**	80	12.8
61	28.7	81	12.1
62	27.8	**82**	**11.5**
63	26.9	83	10.8
64	25.9	84	10.2
65	**25.0**	85	9.6
66	24.1	86	9.1
67	23.2	**87**	**8.5**
68	22.3	88	8.0
69	21.5	89	7.5
70	**20.6**	90	7.1
71	19.8	91	6.7
72	18.8	**92**	**6.3**
73	18.1	93	5.9
74	17.3	94+	5.6

FIGURE 2.2 The autopilot method uses this life expectancy chart to calculate affordable expenses in retirement.

Of course your actual life expectancy depends on many factors, including the fact that longevity seems to run in some families. Married people tend to live longer than single people. Statistics show that a nonsmoker might live two to three more years than a smoker. An overweight person might not live as long as the average person, nor may people who live in high crime neighborhoods or don't wear seat belts. However, with that said, you can't afford to run out of money just because you happen to live longer than the average person. My wife and I visit elderly people every month to offer some conversation, comfort, and occasional help. Most of these people are already beyond the life expectancies that would have been projected using IRS or life insurance tables when they and their spouse first retired. They demonstrate a difficult if obvious concept: Sometimes you think you know what will happen, and the results turn out quite differently. My father was 12 years older than my mother. Logic would say that even if they were both the same age, my father would die first because women generally outlive men. Reinforce that logic with the reality that, all other things being equal, the older person will die first. Neither of these generalities were true in this case. My father outlived my mother and exceeded the IRS statistics by 11 years beyond what was projected for him at age 65.

That's why using the retirement autopilot method is so critical. You will never outlive your life expectancy with it because the calculations readjust to your new life expectancy each year as you get older—and, although your budget will go down (as it would in any realistic plan as you live longer), it will allow you to make gradual and relatively painless adjustments along the way rather than suddenly discovering that you have run out of money.

Inflation Really Hurts

Many current retirees remember when they could buy a new house for under $6,000. A loaf of bread cost only 7¢. People who retired in 1965 saw prices increase by almost five times in the period between 1965 and 1995. They watched inflation eat away at the returns from their fixed income investments until they were practically worthless. If you are more than 20 years from retirement today, you'll have to allow for inflation for the years until you retire as well as the years in retirement. This could well be 40 to 60 years, and the cumulative effects of inflation are likely to be terrifying. Inflation is something that compounds, just as interest on an investment compounds. Its growth accelerates because the base is bigger each year, even if the rate of inflation remains constant. Four percent of what costs $100 today is only $4. But after 20 years of 4%, the item now costs $219. After 60 years the item costs $1,052.

In Figure 2.3, we show a lifetime of increasing prices. It begins with something that cost $1.00 in 1925. During the Great Depression, you'll see that prices actually fell for a number of years. But, whether fortunately or unfortunately, that's something we haven't seen since. From the 1930s on, prices increased slowly until about 1970. That period of very moderate inflation influenced the writers of the retirement books of the time. Because there seemed to be little inflation, essentially, they ignored it in their calculations. There just wasn't much difference between a cost-of-living-adjusted pension and a fixed pension for a person who was only going to live 10 to 15 years maximum in retirement anyway, using the shorter life expectancies of the time. Then inflation raised its ugly head. It quickly started to erode the value of fixed pensions and investments that paid a fixed interest rate, both of which returned less valuable dollars each year. And life expectancies started to grow appreciably.

My parents retired around 1970, and they were forced to do what most people do when their savings are eaten away by inflation. They moved into a less expensive home. They were forced to sell their homes two more times as inflation tore apart their plans. Then they moved into an apartment. The rent soared as the years went on, and the need for some assisted care added to my father's woes.

As a more recent case, I retired in 1989 at age 55. At 65, the purchasing power of my fixed pension was only about two-thirds of its value when I was 55—and by historical standards inflation over most of those 10 years had been about one-half as high as much of modern history's inflation rate. I'm fortunate because I had other retirement savings and had planned on even more inflation than we had in the last few years, and I've been blessed by a real bull market. But you can't count on luck to finance your retirement.

When I was born in 1933, you could buy a new automobile for under $600. As I write this, most new cars sell for about $20,000. Before I die, average sales prices could well exceed $60,000 for a very modest automobile. We've seen inflation destroy the value of fixed pensions, investment returns, and savings. As an

A Lifetime of Increasing Prices

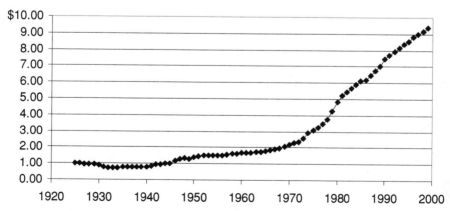

FIGURE 2.3 In the last three decades, prices have risen markedly compared with times past.

extreme example, I have a friend in Russia who had saved 10,000 rubles, which was enough to purchase a small car. Horrible inflation set in, and in just a few years, that 10,000 rubles was worth only a couple of dollars—just enough to buy a small meal.

The Truth about Compounding

It is popular to show how a little savings can compound to very large values over many years. But I want to tell you how misleading those investment growth tables can be. Those compounded future investment values won't have anywhere near the same purchasing power that the same number of dollars will have today. The real message the popular press should be conveying is that it takes great sacrifices to save enough to provide for 20 to 30 years of retirement life—and you're going to have to share your retirement earnings with the government through taxes as well.

Figure 2.4 shows how much purchasing power it's possible to lose during retirement or, for that matter, during the time before your retirement. It's the inverse of the previous chart, which showed the increase in prices over the years. This graph shows how much less you can buy for a dollar compared to what you could in 1925. Lots of security sales people ignore this part of reality when they describe the large appreciation of the investments they are hoping to sell. An investment that grew at about 10% per year from $1,000 to $7,000 over 20 years in a period of 4% inflation is really worth only $3,200—or less than half the advertised growth.

There's another lesson in Figure 2.4 as well. Books on retirement planning usually cite the long-term inflation rate as 3.1%, measured from the end of 1925

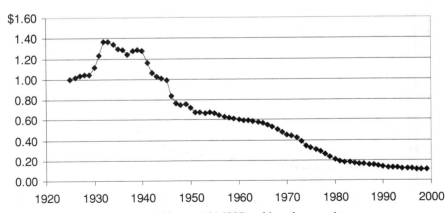

A Dollar Buys Much Less Today!

FIGURE 2.4 What a dollar would buy you in 1925 and in subsequent years.

to the end of 1999. If, however, we begin with a period that might be more representative, starting just after the Great Depression at the end of 1939, the long-term inflation rate increases significantly, to 4.3%.

It gets worse. Inflation in the 20-year period from 1960 to 1980 compounded at a 5.3% rate, but the 20-year period from 1970 to 1990 compounded at a 6.2% rate. Pessimists will say that we're trending to higher inflation rates. Optimists will point to very long term histories to show inflation compounding at about 3% and say that modern government controls will keep us under that, as perhaps it has in the last few years.

Inflation in Retirement

Then there is the argument about whether today's retirees have lower or higher than average inflation rates than the rest of the population. I tend to believe the latter, as does the American Association of Retired Persons (AARP) as well as the Seniors Coalition. How can one sector of the population have higher inflation rates than another? They spend more of their money where prices are going up faster. This hits retirees hard because of their great dependence on the service part of the economy. If you look at what has happened to your costs for health insurance and prescription drugs, you'll be able to confirm what has been happening. Costs for such things as medical, dental, and support services tend to increase faster than many of the other items in the "market basket" used to calibrate inflation. Additionally, the need for these things increases with age. This compounds the problem for retirees because none of the inflation indexes are adjusted to account for what happens to an individual over time.

I hear some retirees say that their inflation rate is lower than the average American. They argue that their mortgage payments are a large part of their expenses and those payments don't increase with inflation. That's true until they make their last mortgage payment. Then their view changes pretty quickly. They still have to make property tax and insurance payments, which often increase much faster than inflation. (Incidentally, although it doesn't have anything to do with the method in this book, if you are using a computer program that inserts loan payments into a spreadsheet to calculate your budget, you should use an inflation rate that doesn't include your mortgage payments, and that means a higher inflation rate than normal. That might add another 1% to your personal inflation rate if your mortgage payments are about one-third of your expenses.)

Inflation tends to be higher in other areas too, such as the recreation industry. Retirees would actually like to spend more for recreation than working people, and of course they have more time for it, but sadly many can't afford it. The July 28, 1994, *The Wall Street Journal* ran a relevant headline: "Some Take a Second Honeymoon at First Honeymoon Hotel Rates." The article went on to say, "Manhattan's Plaza Hotel . . . is charging 55 former newlyweds the same price they paid way back when. One couple, married in 1944, will pay $6.11 for a room that now costs about $225 a night." This corresponds to 7.5% inflation (significantly above the Consumer Price Index [CPI] growth of the period). Or consider the report in the April 16, 1997, *Park Record* from the skiing town of Park City, Utah, which says that for a limited time they are letting people get tickets on the gondola at the same $3.50 price they were charging when it opened in 1963. That represents an inflation rate of over 8% when compared to today's prices. Unfortunately, you can't count on nostalgic promotions like these to finance your retirement fun.

The government doesn't know how to cope with a different inflation rate for seniors than the population at large, so it doesn't acknowledge that there is a difference. To increase Social Security payments at a rate faster than average inflation would be unaffordable as far as the government is concerned. There are already enough problems trying to figure out how to support our existing Social Security system. To support even higher payments would be unthinkable.

What will inflation be in the future? No one knows what will happen, of course—and each economist has his or her own prediction. George Bernard Shaw once said that if you laid all of the economists end to end they would never reach a conclusion. That pretty much sums it up.

Calculating Your Personal Inflation Rate

For a different kind of perspective about inflation and its effects, you might want to calculate the rate of inflation you have personally experienced in the past and then see what would happen to your costs if you had that same rate in the future. To some extent, everyone's inflation rate is different. If you live in a reasonably large city, you can go to the library and find an inflation rate not only for the nation as a whole but for the place in which you live. These local indexes are often used to determine wage increases in labor contracts. But your own inflation rate is likely to be different than either of these, especially if you are retired.

Bill Dickenson, author of *The Retirement Letter,* often said retirees have twice the inflation rate of working people. To test that, I asked three retirees if they could make a five-year estimate of their personal inflation rate. Two found that their personal inflation was, indeed, much higher than that of the country as a whole. The third said his inflation was lower, but he was the only one in the group that had a mortgage.

Figure 2.5 shows how costs compound at various inflation rates. Over 20 years with 5% inflation, for example, costs will increase by 2.65 times, or, over 40 years, by 7.04 times. This same figure is a useful guide to determine the inflation rate of your own personal expenses. All you have to do is look back to some previous year and find out what you were paying for something then, for example, your property taxes, utility bills, or even the total of all of your expenses. Let's say your annual utility bills totaled $1,000 fifteen years ago. Divide your current total, $2,000 perhaps, by what you were paying previously, in this case, 15 years ago. Look in the table for the corresponding number of years, and read across the row to find the number closest to your calculation: $2,000 \div 1,000 = 2.0$. In the example, 2.08 (in the 15-year row) is the nearest number to 2.0. Your inflation rate is at the top of that column. In this example, your utility inflation for the 15-year period was about 5%. It's not hard, and it can be quite illuminating.

If you want to know how much a fixed income will buy in future years, see Figure 2.6. You may find that your dollars won't be worth very much. Here's an example: You get a $10,000 annual fixed income from a pension or interest from bonds, and you estimate that future inflation will be 5%. If you live 20 more years, how much could you buy with your $10,000? In the 5% column and 20-year row of the table, you find 0.377. Multiply that by the your $10,000 for a total of $3,770. In 20 years' time, you'll only be able to buy the equivalent of what $3,770 will purchase today.

THE RULE OF 72

There's a standard formula for determining the effects of inflation that you can also use, called the Rule of 72. If you want to make a rough estimate of inflation's effects, and you don't have our tables handy, divide 72 by your estimate of what the future rate of inflation will be. That will tell you the number of years it will take for something to cost you twice as much money, or, conversely, when a dollar will be worth half of its current value. For example, if you wondered what 6% inflation would do, $72 / 6 = 12$. That means that it would take 12 years for the price to double or the value of the dollar to be worth only 50¢. For example, in 12 years the cost of college tuition would be twice as much. (Incidentally, tuition has been increasing much faster than inflation for as long as I can remember.)

TODAY'S VALUE AND FUTURE VALUE

You already know that the value of $1 will be vastly different in the future than it is today. In the retirement autopilot method we use in this book, we will describe those future values in terms of today's dollars (in financial equations, the standard term for today's dollars is *present value*). Let's see how this works. Suppose that in the next 10 years your investments grow to the point where your fund would report a $100,000 value. You know that $100,000 in 10 years is not going to be worth $100,000 of today's dollars because the price of everything is likely to be much higher. Using the autopilot method, therefore, we would show a lower value because we always want you to see results in today's dollars. If you expect the future inflation rate to be 4%, you can use Figure 2.6 to give you the value of that investment in today's dollars. Under the 4% column, in the row for the 10th year, you find the number 0.676. Our method automatically does the

Future Value of One Dollar

Year	With Inflation Of							
	2%	3%	4%	5%	6%	7%	8%	10%
1	1.02	1.03	1.04	1.05	1.06	1.07	1.08	1.10
2	1.04	1.06	1.08	1.10	1.12	1.14	1.17	1.21
3	1.06	1.09	1.12	1.16	1.19	1.23	1.26	1.33
4	1.08	1.13	1.17	1.22	1.26	1.31	1.36	1.46
5	1.10	1.16	1.22	1.28	1.34	1.40	1.47	1.61
6	1.13	1.19	1.27	1.34	1.42	1.50	1.59	1.77
7	1.15	1.23	1.32	1.41	1.50	1.61	1.71	1.95
8	1.17	1.27	1.37	1.48	1.59	1.72	1.85	2.14
9	1.20	1.30	1.42	1.55	1.69	1.84	2.00	2.36
10	1.22	1.34	1.48	1.63	1.79	1.97	2.16	2.59
11	1.24	1.38	1.54	1.71	1.90	2.10	2.33	2.85
12	1.27	1.43	1.60	1.80	2.01	2.25	2.52	3.14
13	1.29	1.47	1.67	1.89	2.13	2.41	2.72	3.45
14	1.32	1.51	1.73	1.98	2.26	2.58	2.94	3.80
15	1.35	1.56	1.80	2.08	2.40	2.76	3.17	4.18
16	1.37	1.60	1.87	2.18	2.54	2.95	3.43	4.59
17	1.40	1.65	1.95	2.29	2.69	3.16	3.70	5.05
18	1.43	1.70	2.03	2.41	2.85	3.38	4.00	5.56
19	1.46	1.75	2.11	2.53	3.03	3.62	4.32	6.12
20	1.49	1.81	2.19	2.65	3.21	3.87	4.66	6.73
21	1.52	1.86	2.28	2.79	3.40	4.14	5.03	7.40
22	1.55	1.92	2.37	2.93	3.60	4.43	5.44	8.14
23	1.58	1.97	2.46	3.07	3.82	4.74	5.87	8.95
24	1.61	2.03	2.56	3.23	4.05	5.07	6.34	9.85
25	1.64	2.09	2.67	3.39	4.29	5.43	6.85	10.83
26	1.67	2.16	2.77	3.56	4.55	5.81	7.40	11.92
27	1.71	2.22	2.88	3.73	4.82	6.21	7.99	13.11
28	1.74	2.29	3.00	3.92	5.11	6.65	8.63	14.42
29	1.78	2.36	3.12	4.12	5.42	7.11	9.32	15.86
30	1.81	2.43	3.24	4.32	5.74	7.61	10.06	17.45
31	1.85	2.50	3.37	4.54	6.09	8.15	10.87	19.19
32	1.88	2.58	3.51	4.76	6.45	8.72	11.74	21.11
33	1.92	2.65	3.65	5.00	6.84	9.33	12.68	23.23
34	1.96	2.73	3.79	5.25	7.25	9.98	13.69	25.55
35	2.00	2.81	3.95	5.52	7.69	10.68	14.79	28.10
36	2.04	2.90	4.10	5.79	8.15	11.42	15.97	30.91
37	2.08	2.99	4.27	6.08	8.64	12.22	17.25	34.00
38	2.12	3.07	4.44	6.39	9.15	13.08	18.63	37.40
39	2.16	3.17	4.62	6.70	9.70	13.99	20.12	41.14
40	2.21	3.26	4.80	7.04	10.29	14.97	21.72	45.26

FIGURE 2.5 Your future requires more money.

Future Dollars Are Not Worth As Much

Year	With Inflation Of							
	2%	3%	4%	5%	6%	7%	8%	10%
1	0.980	0.971	0.962	0.952	0.943	0.935	0.926	0.909
2	0.961	0.943	0.925	0.907	0.890	0.873	0.857	0.826
3	0.942	0.915	0.889	0.864	0.840	0.816	0.794	0.751
4	0.924	0.888	0.855	0.823	0.792	0.763	0.735	0.683
5	0.906	0.863	0.822	0.784	0.747	0.713	0.681	0.621
6	0.888	0.837	0.790	0.746	0.705	0.666	0.630	0.564
7	0.871	0.813	0.760	0.711	0.665	0.623	0.583	0.513
8	0.853	0.789	0.731	0.677	0.627	0.582	0.540	0.467
9	0.837	0.766	0.703	0.645	0.592	0.544	0.500	0.424
10	0.820	0.744	0.676	0.614	0.558	0.508	0.463	0.386
11	0.804	0.722	0.650	0.585	0.527	0.475	0.429	0.350
12	0.788	0.701	0.625	0.557	0.497	0.444	0.397	0.319
13	0.773	0.681	0.601	0.530	0.469	0.415	0.368	0.290
14	0.758	0.661	0.577	0.505	0.442	0.388	0.340	0.263
15	0.743	0.642	0.555	0.481	0.417	0.362	0.315	0.239
16	0.728	0.623	0.534	0.458	0.394	0.339	0.292	0.218
17	0.714	0.605	0.513	0.436	0.371	0.317	0.270	0.198
18	0.700	0.587	0.494	0.416	0.350	0.296	0.250	0.180
19	0.686	0.570	0.475	0.396	0.331	0.277	0.232	0.164
20	0.673	0.554	0.456	0.377	0.312	0.258	0.215	0.149
21	0.660	0.538	0.439	0.359	0.294	0.242	0.199	0.135
22	0.647	0.522	0.422	0.342	0.278	0.226	0.184	0.123
23	0.634	0.507	0.406	0.326	0.262	0.211	0.170	0.112
24	0.622	0.492	0.390	0.310	0.247	0.197	0.158	0.102
25	0.610	0.478	0.375	0.295	0.233	0.184	0.146	0.092
26	0.598	0.464	0.361	0.281	0.220	0.172	0.135	0.084
27	0.586	0.450	0.347	0.268	0.207	0.161	0.125	0.076
28	0.574	0.437	0.333	0.255	0.196	0.150	0.116	0.069
29	0.563	0.424	0.321	0.243	0.185	0.141	0.107	0.063
30	0.552	0.412	0.308	0.231	0.174	0.131	0.099	0.057
31	0.541	0.400	0.296	0.220	0.164	0.123	0.092	0.052
32	0.531	0.388	0.285	0.210	0.155	0.115	0.085	0.047
33	0.520	0.377	0.274	0.200	0.146	0.107	0.079	0.043
34	0.510	0.366	0.264	0.190	0.138	0.100	0.073	0.039
35	0.500	0.355	0.253	0.181	0.130	0.094	0.068	0.036
36	0.490	0.345	0.244	0.173	0.123	0.088	0.063	0.032
37	0.481	0.335	0.234	0.164	0.116	0.082	0.058	0.029
38	0.471	0.325	0.225	0.157	0.109	0.076	0.054	0.027
39	0.462	0.316	0.217	0.149	0.103	0.071	0.050	0.024
40	0.453	0.307	0.208	0.142	0.097	0.067	0.046	0.022

FIGURE 2.6 One dollar will buy less in the future.

multiplication for you and will show the value of that investment in today's dollars as $100,000 \times 0.676 = \$67,600$.

Defining Wages, Income, Savings, and Expenses

In order to create a solid retirement plan, there are a few more terms you need to understand. It is fundamental that you know how we define wages, income, savings, expenses, and taxes. If you get these wrong in your retirement planning, you've put garbage into your program, and you'll get garbage out. You won't have to remember all of these definitions because we'll explain them again briefly when we need your input, but we want you to start getting familiar with our use of some financial terms.

- *Wages:* This is the simplest of all definitions. Wages are the annual amounts that you get from your employer. These are gross wages, that is, wages before any tax or other deductions from your paycheck. When we want you to include matching contributions your employer makes to a savings plan, we'll tell you. Our planning method assumes that your wages will increase with inflation.

- *Income:* In this book we use the word *income* in two different ways: For preretirement planning, we use *income* to imply the equivalent postretirement wage you would need to cover retirement expenses, including debt payments and any related income tax. This does not refer to the kind of income you would report on your tax return. So in this case, when we ask what *income* you would like to have in retirement, we're asking for the amount of money you would like to receive in retirement that would be analogous to your wages today. Specifically, in quick and dirty, that is the amount that you will need in retirement to pay your normal living expenses, related income taxes, and debt payments.

  In postretirement planning, we use the word *income* as you would on a tax return. Income then includes Social Security, pension payments, annuity payments, wages from part-time work, and, of course, the returns from investments that you would enter on a tax return. It also includes any tax-exempt income from investments, even though, for tax calculations, tax-exempt income is deducted from gross income on your return. The kind of income we are talking about here has no direct relation to expenses or budgets. It's used only for planning purposes, to calculate what we call a net tax rate that we'll explain later.

- *Savings:* We try not to use the word *savings* as a synonym for investments except when very common usage makes it seem natural. When it comes to inserting a number into a calculation, we will be specific and use the word *investments* where it means the total of all of your mutual funds, stocks, bonds, CDs, money markets, real estate equity, or similar financial resources.

Whenever we ask for an annual savings input, it means an annual amount that you take from your wages and deposit in a bank or investment account. We assume you will increase the amount you save each year to account for inflation. Such savings also include any employer annual contribution such as matching funds for a 401(k). This is not the total value of your investments, it's only the annual contribution that you and/or your employer makes. By our definition, you can have only annual savings before retirement. After retirement, the only thing we would call *savings* might come from new income you save from part-time work. Therefore, if you have surplus income, that is, more than you have budgeted for your needs in retirement, that is automatically reinvested. Otherwise, you would be withdrawing additional money from your investments and then adding it back in as savings. In retirement, you only withdraw as much as you need from your investments. If you reinvest any dividends or interest from investments, those are not considered part of savings at any time, either before or after retirement. If you are spending any part of your dividends or interest before retirement, however, these should be deducted from your annual savings, because our calculations are made on the assumption that dividends and interest will always be reinvested. If you need part or all of your interest and dividends to support retirement, by our definition those are withdrawals from investments. You could look at it as if dividends and interest were first deposited to a money market investment or checking account before you "withdrew" part or all of them to pay for expenses.

The planning methods in this book are completely consistent with the preceding definitions. This is not true of many of the planning methods that you will find elsewhere. The majority of methods fail to define what they mean by savings, and often the particular mathematics used would require that you add debt payments to savings and even the taxes due on investment returns that you pay from your wages instead of from investment income. Did you follow that? This can be a very confusing and thought-provoking subject. If you are using a method from a publication or a service on the Web, only an expert would be able tell you what to include in your annual savings number. Unfortunately, the instructions seldom will.

• *Expenses:* In this book, expenses include both unusual and infrequent expenses, as well as all normal living costs that would be paid out in the course of one year. Thus, normal living expenses always include food, utilities, clothes, and so forth. We will ask specifically for a separate total of the kind of expenses that are unusual and would not generally occur each year. In the process of preretirement planning, this would include your estimate of both large expenses before retirement, such as college costs, as well as a separate entry for major purchases after retirement, such as automobiles or a retirement condominium. In postretirement planning we will ask you to set aside a reserve for large items that are not part of your normal annual living expenses. Such items might include a retirement condominium, new automobiles, an exceptional vacation trip, and so on.

In preretirement planning (in contrast to postretirement planning), expenses that would occur in retirement also include income tax and debt payments. In postretirement planning they do not. The reason for the difference is that in preretirement planning the most important thing is to build investments, so we use a preretirement planning method with that focus. On the other hand, in postretirement planning, the focus is more on the detail of how much we can spend without depleting our investments, so, in effect, we provide separate budgets for normal living expenses, unusual expenses, income taxes, and debt payments.

We assume that both normal living expenses and unusual expenses will always grow with inflation. Figure 2.7 shows how cost compounds at various inflation rates for an item that originally cost $1,000. All of these rates existed at various times in our economic history. Each of the lines for inflation rates of 3, 5, and 7% starts at $1,000. Of course, actual rates aren't likely to remain constant over a 60-year period; this chart is simply designed to give you an idea of what inflation can do to your costs over the years. Inflation makes costs grow at compound rates, just like investments. In our planning, however, we will always show the results in *today's* dollars ($1,000 in this example) instead of future dollar values. If we showed you answers in future dollar values, you would throw up your hands in shock.

Future Costs Are Hard to Comprehend

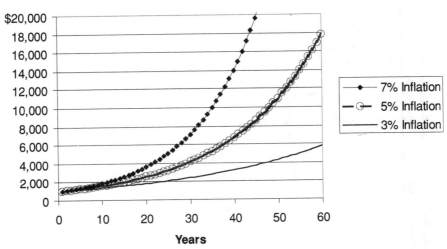

FIGURE 2.7 What a $1,000 item will cost you in the future at three different inflation rates.

For example, with sustained 5% growth, something that cost $1,000 originally would cost over $6,000 forty years later and almost $18,000 after sixty years. You may think it's odd to look at something as far off as 60 years, but there are going to be some 30-year-old people reading this book who will live that long.

Consider my own example: I was 27 years old in 1960 and was spending about $1,000 a month on food, utilities, insurance, and the like. At that time, I couldn't relate to spending over $6,000 a month for the same kind of purchases, even in what seemed then like the far distant future. Well, here I am 40 years later at age 67, and the same kind of items are costing me far more than $6,000. Part of that is my own greater affluence, which I would not have projected, but the larger part of it is just plain inflation. After another 20 years of inflation I will be age 87, and 5% inflation could take the same expenses to $18,000 a month. I'm likely to live that long or longer, and I'm fairly confident that if I don't, my wife will, because she's younger (she'll be pleased I noted that) and comes from a long-lived family. We're not going to ask you to guess how much your expenses will be in future dollars, not only because you won't be able to relate to them, but also because none of us knows what future inflation will be. This does not mean that we are going to ignore inflation. Quite the contrary. It just means that we are going to use inflation-adjusted investment performance and let the appropriate mathematics work in the background out of our sight while the math translates the answers into today's values. As far as you are concerned, you will still see the real cost of the item as $1,000 whether after 40 years it would cost $7,000 future dollars or after 60 it would cost $18,000 future dollars, or whatever the number may be. It will show on our charts as $1,000.

You do not need to understand the mechanics of this translation from future dollars to today's dollars, but if you are inquisitive, the main trick is to use inflation-adjusted returns instead of actual returns. The latter requires the final projection to be reduced to today's values with present value theory based on what I believe is often an inappropriate measure for inflation.

• *Affordable expenses:* It's one thing to talk about expenses in general, but in real life, your expenses have to fit within a budget that you can afford. That often means that expenses have to be constrained so that you don't draw down your investments too quickly in retirement. You cannot afford to run out of money before you die. We call the level of expenditures that will get you through retirement *affordable expenses.*

When you reach retirement we ask that you make a calculation to determine a new annual budget for affordable expenses each year. As you'll see clearly later on, the annual changes in inflation and in your investments due to the stock market alone would be reason enough to make a new budget calculation. But even in the absence of those economic effects, your affordable budget will change each year, as we'll now explain.

In Figure 2.8 we see two lines. The upper line represents a retiree's afford-able expenses each year in future dollar values. This is one of the few times we will show values in terms of future dollars, but we have a reason. When you do your annual calculation, you will be doing it in the dollar terms of that year. You won't go back and say, "How much could I spend now in terms of what dollars were worth when I was age 65?" With the highly idealized constant inflation and investment performance postulated in Figure 2.8, you can see that this retired person would calculate a slightly larger budget each year to compensate for inflation. However, by the time the retiree has reached about age 85, the budget starts to decline. This is because the analysis is starting to recognize that this retiree is not going to die as soon as was predicted back at age 65. In fact, age 90 is about the time he should have died according to that analysis. What is hap-pening is that the calculation is trying to stretch the investments to last longer as the likely age to die increases.

To illustrate this point with the example, the calculation at age 65 is based on a life expectancy of 25.0 years, which brings us to a final age of 90. The calcula-tion made at age 66 uses a 24.1 year life expectancy, or an age at death of 90.1 years, which is not much different than 90.0. But when the calculation is made at age 85 the projected age at death is 94.6, and the calculation at age 86 gives us until 95.1. Not only is the age at death increasing, but the difference between the calculations each year is getting greater.

You can get a better perspective of what is really happening if you look at the lower line in Figure 2.8, which is what we will normally do in future charts in this book. It represents constant dollar values, or today's dollars. You can see that the retirement planning method we use does quite a good job of providing the retiree with almost constant purchasing power each year until you note

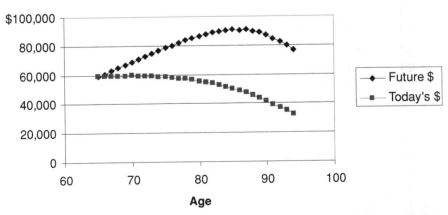

Your Budget May Go Up, but Its Real Value Won't

FIGURE 2.8 Idealized affordable expense history shown both in future dollars and today's dollars.

some drop as age 80 approaches. But by age 95, the budget will be about half of what it was at age 65 in real terms. If this was a plan for a married couple, this drop might be tolerable because somewhere along the way, the sad truth is that one of the two is likely to die. Or if the initial budget represented a degree of affluence not needed late in life, that too could be acceptable. (Also keep in mind that Figure 2.8 shows only the budget contribution from investments. Including Social Security and any COLA pension would make the curves flatter so that the reduction at older ages would not be as severe.)

But what if you wanted to be able to preserve the same budget in today's dollars all the way to age 95, or even 105? How would you do it? The answer is that you must spend *less* than the budget that we calculate. Often a budget reduction of only 5 to 10% will fulfill this objective. Conversely, overrunning the budget continuously by 5 to 10% a year can bring financial disaster quickly.

Your own history will be different and will also depend on whatever economic conditions persist throughout your life, including inflation and the results of your investment performance. But the fundamentals will always be there. Inflation will continue to degrade the value of your money, and your expenses will consume your investments. In the real world, investment performance and inflation will not be smooth, and there will be many unforeseen economic changes. If you want to be a winner, you can't determine a retirement budget by grabbing a number out of thin air. And you certainly don't want to use a method that is likely to encourage you to spend too much too early. That's a loser's plan.

Oh Shoot! I Forgot!

One term I found common to both the construction business and the aerospace business was commonly known as OSIF, or Oh shoot! I forgot! (Except that we had another word for *shoot*.) This refers to the items that were unintentionally left out of the estimate for a bid price. We always knew that there would be some, but we never knew how large they would be. Once the price was submitted, you had to eat any of the OSIFs that came up, because the customer would never reimburse you for them.

Retirement planning is the same way. Once you have made that commitment to retire, you'll find the OSIFs. Here are some that I and my retired friends and neighbors have found:

- Dental costs increase and are uninsured.
- Medical costs increase both with inflation and age.
- The need for drugs increases with age, and they are more expensive and most often uninsured.
- Medicare drops services such as blood testing, home care assistance, and so on.

- There will be major repair costs on your home: roofing, furnace replacement, remodeling, painting, and the like.
- You get major assessments from your condo or other association.
- That old automobile won't last until you die. Nor will your dishwasher, washing machine, hot water heater, computer, and so forth.
- You don't recover from severe market drops and can't risk buying after the drop.
- Rolling money from matured bonds into new bonds does not maintain the same income.
- That once profitable real estate partnership is now a dog.
- The pension will be lower than listed in the benefit report because you take an option to pay your surviving spouse on your death.
- A few years of high inflation wipe out the value of a pension, annuity, CDs, bonds, and so on.
- The prospects of high inflation cause a plunge in the stock market.
- Social Security increases lag behind actual inflation, so there is irrecoverable damage.
- A child gets in major financial trouble and has nowhere else to turn for help.
- An elderly parent desperately needs financial help.
- Relatives die, requiring unplanned travel expenses.
- Grandchildren are born, requiring unplanned travel expenses.
- Assisted care for you, spouse, or a parent was not in the budget.
- Infirmity forces you to hire help for maintenance jobs you once did yourself.

Unfortunately, professional retirement planners are, by definition, not retired, so they can hardly speak with any authority about this unless they have been supporting retired parents or watching them struggle. They often feel they have done their duty when they wave clients off telling them they should do fine on 60% of their working budget. Or even worse, they ask them to fill in a retirement budget sheet with an estimate of how much less they'll need for each item in retirement. (This is a major source of OSIFs!) Instead, they should suggest a significant retirement reserve and often recommend that the clients work a little longer before retiring instead of facilitating their early retirement.

It's true that many retirees live on Social Security with a small fixed income supplement. It's also true that their incomes are a fraction of their income during working years. This is not by choice. The fact that a large part of the retired population is in this condition should have no bearing on the goals of a person planning for retirement, except to act as a wake-up call. Until the planners have actually seen the stress from living on such incomes and the need for supplemental help from younger family members, they should be cautious about using gross statistics to imply that preretirement and postretirement lifestyles will be comparable when retirement budgets are much less than preretirement budgets.

This is not to say that low retirement incomes equate to unhappiness. It does, however, mean that before entering retirement, people need a realistic look at their retirement financial future to make sure that the new lower-cost lifestyle will fit the image they have of what may be the last third of their life. And a good dose of realistic planning is your best means of avoiding the really ruinous alternative, overspending in the initial retirement years. This is the most disastrous of all, because it reduces the savings that most certainly will be needed for all of those unforeseen OSIFs.

Uncle Sam Will Share Retirement with You

There are so many tax laws that vary from one year to the next that it is impossible to determine the best actions to save taxes on a long-term basis and equally impossible to predict tax rates with any precision. Probably the best advice I can give is to be conservative; that is, estimate that your tax rate is more likely to increase in the future than to decrease.

There may be years where politicians make it look like they are lowering tax rates. Beware! The government has many more ways of taking money away from you than is shown in federal or state income tax rates. Often the federal government will change allowable deductions, or impose special excise taxes, or shift tax burdens to your state, which then must obtain funds from property, sales, or use taxes, or taxes from businesses or individual incomes. You pay many taxes that are hidden because they are paid by the industries that make and supply your goods.

In periods of sustained economic growth, low inflation, and low interest rates, it is easy to promise reduced income taxes. But what the one hand gives, the other takes away, if not immediately, then ultimately. In this book we look only at income tax, but to those of you who are 20 or more years away from retirement, it's immaterial whether your retirement purchasing power is reduced by income tax, property tax, sales tax, or whatever future tax states and the federal government will invent or whatever deductions they will eliminate.

To make things worse, the future demographics appear devastating! We are just beginning to enter a phase where we have some massive changes taking place. The baby boomer generation is flooding the schools with children at an unprecedented rate. You would think that would bode well for retirees. However, in the near term, state taxes will increase to support the new schools, and, in the long term, demographers tell us that within the next generation, there are likely to be only two-thirds as many people working to support each retired person. This would require that Social Security and Medicare taxes increase by almost 50% to maintain the same level of support (unless each individual's Social Security and Medicare tax contributions are saved and invested instead of being used to pay current government expenses, as often happens now).

Of course, it probably won't happen just that way. Government benefits may be reduced or taxed more, and, in the long run, increased income taxes likely will share some of the burden. The 1996 Department of Commerce's population projections cite the following statistics, which must be discouraging to the few remaining taxable wage earners: In 1900, 7.3% of the U.S. population was over 65. In 1995, that number increased to 20.9%. By the year 2020, it will be almost 28%, and by the year 2040, it will be almost 37%!

It's hard to stop government spending. Government spending really took off after 1913 when it became legal to levy an income tax after the passage of the Sixteenth Amendment of the Constitution. Ever since then, Congress has had unlimited power to use or otherwise redistribute our income to other people. In good economic times with high employment, enough extra taxes come in that the individual tax rates may temporarily be reduced until a period of bad economic times when tax receipts are down. We are rapidly approaching the point where we will be spending 40% of our income on taxes of one kind or the other. This is not too surprising considering that almost one-third of our population either works for the government or is supported by the government. The trend is ominous.

For a final bit of perspective about your future income taxes, consider this bit of history. Prior to World War I, the maximum tax rate was 7%. During World War I, it peaked at 77%. After the war, the maximum rate was cut by about two-thirds, but when World War II came, the rate peaked at 94%. Of course, practically no one paid the highest rates because deductions were so large. The average American's effective tax rate (taxes divided by taxable income) after World War II was lower than it is today. High rates persisted after World War II until 1988, when the maximum rate dropped to its lowest postwar value of 28%. In 1991, the maximum rate increased to 31%, and in 1993, to 39.6%.

These tax rates do not include state or local taxes, Social Security and Medicare taxes levied on workers (and some retired people with severance pay), nor any possible excise taxes. Considering these and the current trend toward phasing out deductions, current maximum tax rates on income are really significantly higher than 39.6%.

It's not impossible that tax rates can go down a little on a temporary basis after a string of good economic years. But don't think that the combination of federal and state governments isn't capable of taking even substantially more than now, in the long run. Besides the depressing ratio of nonworkers to workers out ahead of us, whenever there is a national emergency, tax rates can soar and deductions can be eliminated. Who knows what will be determined to be a national emergency in the future? It could be a war with another country. It could be any number of building internal pressures: government workers striking for higher wages, the need to improve the country's infrastructure of schools, roads, airports, and so on. Or it could be retired and welfare groups' growing dependency on public support because savings rates are now so low. I don't think that you want to be complacent about taxes 10 or more years from now.

Computing Your Net Tax Rate

In the planning sections of this book, we are going to ask you to use your *net tax rate* to determine how much you will be able to spend in retirement after you have paid your taxes. This is a special calculation we will ask you to make for the autopilot method. There are numerous definitions of tax rates besides net tax rate, such as average tax rate (income taxes divided by taxable income) and marginal tax rates (the highest tax rate used in computing your income tax). We have a special definition because we want to make sure that it is compatible with our budget analysis. Net tax rate is defined here as

$$\frac{\text{State income tax} + \text{Federal income tax}}{\text{Gross income}}$$

Income tax is the annual amount that you calculate on a tax return. It is *not* the tax that is deducted for Social Security or Medicare, nor any of the other taxes you may pay, such as a tax on your real estate, automobile, or personal property.

Our definition of gross income is broader than you'll find in the section of your tax return where you compute your adjusted gross income. For the majority of people, as a practical matter, there won't be much difference, but there will be for those people with Roth IRAs, municipal bonds, and investment real estate. We do this to greatly simplify the planning process by combining a number of different kinds of investments that you would otherwise have to analyze individually. This gives us a very close approximation of the results you would get if you had used a very detailed analysis—and the amount of effort to do the calculations is much, much less. Gross income for our purposes is defined as the annual total of wages, alimony, Social Security, pension, and/or annuity payments, and all income from investments, including dividends, both taxable and tax-exempt interest, capital gains, income from businesses, both Roth and regular IRA distributions, and before-tax cash flows from investment real estate.

Although we really would like to know what your future retirement net tax rate would be, this will always have to remain an estimate because of the continuous changes in the tax laws and the fact that you may change to different types of investments later in life. The best approach we can offer is to calculate your current net tax rate and then perhaps adjust the number up or down a bit depending on what you think may happen in your particular situation. Certainly the past long-term trend has been to increase the amount of taxes that the average individual pays, but if you expect that your taxable income in retirement will be significantly lower than it is now, you may want to use a lower net tax rate than your current value. I personally think that it is prudent to add a percent or so to your current tax rate when making an estimate for the future. For example, if your current net tax rate calculates to 0.12, that is, 12%, then I'd use 13% for the future. It's a judgment call for you to make.

Although inflation will probably increase the number of dollars you might receive later in retirement, generally the IRS adjusts income taxes so that inflation by itself does not increase your tax rate. However, there could be some additional upward tax-rate creep if the government trims the consumer price index for political reasons or needs additional taxes to meet ever growing social pressures.

Use caution when you are doing your retirement tax calculations: Selecting your net tax rate is like establishing the budget that you will pay for taxes. Fortunately, the net tax rate for retirees changes very little from one year to another unless there is an unusual change in income. If your tax rate looks like it will be changing, try to select a net tax rate that will be on the high side of your new estimate.

Now let's determine you net tax rate. First add last year's state, federal, and local income tax together to get your total income taxes. See Figure 2.9.

Then determine your gross income. You can either use your adjusted gross income from your 1040 return and add in your untaxed Social Security, Roth IRA withdrawals, municipal bond interest, and depreciation on rental properties, *or* add up last year's income sources, using Figure 2.10. (There may be a small difference between the two methods if you make both computations. If so, use the smaller of the two numbers.)

To get last year's net tax rate, simply divide your total income taxes by your gross income. For example, if your total income taxes were $23,000 and your gross income was $100,000, then 23,000 divided by 100,000 is 0.23 or 23%. Remember, if you expect a significant change in your future taxes (perhaps from losing a child's

Last Year's Income Taxes

Federal income taxes	$
State and local income taxes	$
Total income taxes	$

FIGURE 2.9 Calculate your total income taxes.

Last Year's Gross Income

Wages if working	$
Pension and annuity payments if received	$
Alimony if received	$
Business before-tax net cash flow	$
Real estate before-tax net cash flow	$
Interest, dividends, & capital gains	$
Nontaxable investment income	$
Roth distributions if received	$
IRA distributions if received	$
Social Security if received	$
Other income	$
Total equals gross income	$

FIGURE 2.10 Add up your gross income.

deductions and tax credit), you should try to estimate your future net tax rate instead.

Other Stuff You Really Should Know about Taxes

I find that most people don't know that income taxes can be significantly different for one kind of investment than they are for another. Over a period of years, this can make a huge difference in the amount of wealth you accumulate.

For example, those people who buy a growth stock mutual fund in a Roth IRA get a fantastic break. Normally, the managers of growth funds do a lot of stock trading. Each time they do this, the government steps in and wants its share of the gain and any dividends from the underlying stocks. With a Roth IRA, none of this is taxed.

High-income people often buy municipal bonds, which are exempt from tax by the federal government and, most often, the state. However, they pay lower interest rates than corporate or federal government bonds, so you usually have to be in a tax bracket of 28% or higher to benefit under current tax rate schedules. (Your tax bracket is the highest rate used in calculating your income tax, which for most people is 15%, but for the highest taxed people it's currently 39.6%.) If your tax bracket is 28%, a CD, corporate bond, or government bond paying 6% interest would have an income tax of 28% times 6%, or 1.68%. Therefore, after taxes, it would net 6.00% minus 1.68%, or 4.32%. It's likely that you could find a municipal bond that would pay a rate greater than 4.32% with the same maturity. Maturity is the amount of time before you will automatically get back your principal; for example, a CD that matures in five years. In the preceding illustration, the interest rate of 4.32% after paying income taxes is called an after-tax return, while the original 6.00% interest rate is your before-tax return. After-tax returns are used only to determine the ultimate growth of investments for investments that are not tax deferred. The reason is that deferred tax investments grow at a before-tax rate. The taxes aren't taken out until the money is withdrawn.

Almost anyone benefits from deferring tax payments until many years later. That's the great thing about deferred tax investments like IRAs or 401(k)s. You don't have to pay tax on these until you start taking out cash, and then you only pay tax on the particular part you take out, thereby leaving the remainder to continue to grow tax deferred. What you are doing is earning interest on what the government would otherwise get in early taxes. So if you defer $1,000 of taxes for 20 years, and you have stock investments growing at 10%, the $1,000 that is still in your accounts instead of the federal government's will grow to $6,727 less $1,009 tax on withdrawal at a 15% tax rate, for a total of $5,718. So you are richer by $5,718 than the person who wasn't able to defer taxes.

If you have investments that aren't in a deferred tax account like a 401(k) or IRA, then you may be able to benefit from capital gains tax rates, which are lower than ordinary income tax rates. When you sell something for more than you paid, you have a capital gain. For example, if you paid $1,000 for a stock that had grown in value to $3,000 when you sold it, your capital gain would be $2,000. If you sold the stock in less than one year, it would be a *short-term gain,* while if you sold it more than a year after the purchase, it would be a *long-term gain.* Short-term capital gains tax rates are the same as your ordinary income tax rates, but long-term capital gains tax rates are much lower, almost half as much for the top income brackets. Thus a high-income person might do even better with capital gains than with a deferred tax investment by holding on to the same stock for a very long period.

People who have deferred tax investments often are forced to take their payments after a certain age, most often age 70½, but perhaps as late as age 85 for some insurance products. At that time, the amount that is withdrawn each year is taxed at ordinary income tax rates. The year 2001 changes for RMDs from an IRA did two things: First, it simplified the calculations, and second, it reduced the size of the RMDs. (See Chapter 6.) Actually, few people will be able to delay withdrawals until age 70½ and even fewer will be able to withdraw only the minimum. Nevertheless, lower minimums offer additional tax-deferred growth possibilities for those with substantial resources outside an IRA but increase the tax problem for heirs. This becomes a complex subject for estate planning, especially for those widows or widowers who inherited their spouse's deferred tax investments. It gets even worse for the subsequent beneficiaries when the second spouse dies. Many of the benefits from deferring taxes may then be lost without good tax planning. If you think you will leave an estate in the millions to your heirs, you should get help from professional estate planners.

Coping with Uncertainty

There are many things in your future over which you have no control. You can't predict exactly what will happen. You have no control over the economy, government policies, or the medical problems that will strike your family. Practically every piece of data we will use in our analysis is uncertain. For example:

- We do not know how long we are going to live.
- No one can predict what future inflation rates will be.
- Return on investment will vary every year.
- Your pension fund or insurance company can go belly-up.
- The government can change the income tax rate.
- The government may reduce your Social Security benefits.
- There will be many unforeseen financial requirements, some very large.

Some weakhearted people use this uncertainty as an excuse for not planning for the future. That kind of ostrich mentality is almost surely going to lead to disastrous results.

Fortunately, modern mathematics gives us a method to help cope with uncertainty. The method involves the use of feedback. With feedback, we continually make corrections to keep us on course. At one time, some of the principles of feedback were considered so important that they were classified by the government because they were used in defense work. Sophisticated methods were developed to achieve the most accuracy for weapon systems in the face of uncertain readings of instruments, mapping errors, and environmental changes and effects.

Norbert Wiener, one of the world's greatest mathematicians, tried to explain feedback in his book *Cybernetics* in the early 1950s. My first exposure to the subject came in a seminar given by Dr. Wiener at MIT in that same time period. Today feedback is used in many commercial applications for mechanisms as simple as the modern thermostat in a home to complex systems that keep an airplane on course. All of these systems are trying to steer toward some objective with a lot of uncertain events happening outside the system. The thermostat has to accommodate uncertain temperatures outside the house, and the airplane is continually buffeted by unpredictable winds coming from all directions.

We are going to use the principle of feedback to keep us on a course that will lead to the best retirement plan we can create. Our timescale will be considerably different than the electronic systems in a thermostat or airplane, which frequently update their information in fractions of a second. Our timescale is going to be one year. Doing an update more frequently will not improve the answer significantly unless there has been some major change in your data caused by economic tragedy or (we can always hope) incredible luck such as buying a Picasso at a garage sale. Doing the update less frequently can leave us exposed to compounding errors.

In addition to feedback, the autopilot method includes a means to cope with what might otherwise be intolerably large changes in your data when the market experiences large changes. In the preretirement analysis, this includes a limiting equation when the market suddenly increases. In the postretirement analysis, this includes a different type of limiting equation for large market surges. *Limiting equation* is simply a statement that if something goes beyond a certain limit the equation doesn't apply anymore. It's like a girl who is interested only in boys who are taller than 5 feet 6 inches. She limits her search to boys above that height. She doesn't have to know what a psychologist would say was going on in her brain that causes her to reject shorter boys, and you don't have to understand what is going on in the math behind the limiting equations in your retirement plans. If you really want to know, however, it's there for you to see in the retirement planning sections.

We wouldn't need any of these things in a nice, smooth, theoretical world, where there are no ups and downs. This theoretical world is envisioned by virtually all financial planners, but we're not falling into that trap. Our methods work in the real world, and they are practical and easy to apply. You perform only a few simple steps each year.

So stick with us. We'll show you how to create a good and usable preretirement plan or postretirement budget on a few sheets of paper. You'll provide the feedback by doing an annual analysis using your current data: investment balances, estimates of investment returns, Social Security inputs, the new value of your life expectancy, and so on. We provide the autopilot method that helps control any potential variability in your personal finances. Together, we will produce an excellent retirement plan that is custom-made for your situation.

CHAPTER 3

Investments

The path you're on
looks different when
you turn around.*

In the previous chapter we looked at things that are largely beyond your control: life expectancy, inflation, unforeseen expenses, and taxes. In this chapter we're going to show you something you can control, namely, the selection of your investments. First, by allocating classes of investments, we'll strike a balance between getting maximum performance and the risk you may be willing to accept. Then we'll look at various tax shelter vehicles and consider which ones might be best in your situation. Finally, we'll offer some help in selecting the particular investments that will fit your requirements.

Owners and Lenders

It's interesting how the futures of two people, each with the same basic wages and annual savings, can end up so different financially. I'm not talking about one being lucky and winning a jackpot while the other one doesn't. I'm talking about the gains that come from having some knowledge about investments. Over a 30-year span, the person with the knowledge often has more than three times as much financial capability as the one who doesn't. I know a retired school teacher who, now in her 70s, has all of her money in a bank savings account, just as she has had all her working life. She won't even consider putting her money into a mutual fund's money market, which would ensure almost the same safety, have check-writing privileges, and yet pay twice the

*Cynthia Copeland Lewis, *Really Important Stuff My Kids Have Taught Me,* Workman Publishing Company, 1994.

interest. With some investing that still would be conservative, she could probably have financial resources of perhaps five times the funds now at her disposal.

A little financial education early in her life would have made the difference. Someone should have told her that you make much more money being an owner than loaning money to an owner. Let me explain. A person who buys a piece of property, perhaps a house to be rented out, is an owner. The owner takes some risk because the value of the house may go down or there may be months without someone paying rent. To buy the house, the owner borrows some money, usually in the form of a mortgage. The lender of the money wants to minimize risk and so only lends enough money so that if the owner defaults on payments the lender can take possession of the house and sell it. Since the lender is in a much lower risk position, the interest rate on the mortgage is less than the owner expects to get as a return on the equity invested in the house.

In this example, the owner gets better interest (in the form of rent and appreciation) than the lender. As time goes by, the owner's position gets even better because the value of the property increases and the rental rates go up. Not only can't the lender increase the interest, but the value of the mortgage goes down, not just because of principal payments, but because inflation has made the principal value worth less and less each year. In periods of very high inflation, the lender really has poor results.

A person who puts money into a bank account is a lender. That person is lending money to a bank that will invest it in securities that will give higher returns. If that weren't possible, we wouldn't have banks. The greater the difference between the rate paid to the lender and the rate earned as an owner, the better off the bank. That's why the bank can afford marble floors and highly paid executives. And that's why my school teacher friend does not do very well financially.

Stocks and Bonds

People who invest in stocks are owners. They actually own a small fraction of a company. Those who own a large enough fraction can have a lot to say about how the company will be managed. Owners thrive when the company thrives because others would like to enjoy some of that success. People offer ever increasing prices to entice the current owners to give up their shares. The reverse happens in bad times. Stocks are very liquid, so unlike real estate, you can sell them on a moment's notice. For every sale there must be a buyer, even in a down market. So what looks like a losing situation to one person has to look like a winning situation to another.

Firms that buy and sell stocks bring the buyers and sellers together. For this assistance they generally receive handsome fees, often disguised as percentages that make them look like a small amount, perhaps *only* 1 or 2% of the transaction. Many shareholders don't realize that this small percentage adds up to a large bite out of the amount that they will earn on the stock, especially when the stocks are sold and bought in the form of mutual funds that charge annual fees, sometimes very well hidden even in so-called no-load mutual funds. (We discuss mutual funds in more detail in the next section.)

In the good old days, the size of the dividend paid by firms to their shareholders was very important. That's not as true today. Many of the best stocks pay no dividends at all because they reinvest all their earnings to improve their growth, and that growth increases the perceived value of the company. So the stock price increases, which is the main goal anyway.

People who invest in bonds are lenders, just like my school teacher friend. They are lending money to a corporation to help fund its growth or to a government for some kind of a public project. Interest rates on bonds are lower than the growth of the owner's stocks because lenders take less risk, especially when lending money to the government. Therefore, interest rates on government bonds are lower than corporate bonds in most cases. Municipal bonds, usually sold by cities or counties, have lower interest rates yet, but they are not taxable by the federal government, nor by many of the states. Bond holders suffer badly in times of high inflation, just as my friend does with her savings account.

In investment language, bonds pay interest, not dividends, but mutual funds that own only bonds pay out the interest in the form of dividends, just as they do with stocks. Bond prices go up when interest rates go down, and vice versa. Therefore, mutual funds that hold only bonds will sometimes have capital gains dividends as well as ordinary dividends.

Fixed Income Investments

Bonds, certificates of deposit (CDs), and other investments that pay a fixed interest rate are called fixed income investments. Probably the most secure fixed income investments are Treasury bills (T-bills) that are sold by the U.S. Treasury. They mature in months rather than years, as do bonds. Although individuals can buy them, they are most often bought by financial firms like mutual funds. Mutual funds that are based on fixed income investments alone, such as T-bills or bonds, are also classified as fixed income investments, even though there may be some changes to their principal and dividends over time. Fixed income investments are not always secure however. Some people buy mortgages or "junk" bonds that pay very high interest rates but are vulnerable to default.

Annuities

If you buy an *immediate* annuity from an insurance company, you enter into a contract with the insurance company by which they will make fixed monthly or annual payments for a certain number of years (term-certain) or for as long as you live. You can think of it as if you had loaned money to the insurance company and they were paying you back in installments. They also pay back a little bit of the principal each month, so when your final payment comes, the principal has all been repaid. If a person gets a fixed pension from a former employer, it is like an immediate annuity contract, which makes payments of the same amount each year. And every year that passes, those fixed income payments are worth less and less because of the horrible power of inflation. There are other kinds of annuities too, such as deferred annuities, which promise payments starting at a later date. A popular variant is the *variable* annuity. These are like mutual funds where you have a choice of investments up until some time late in life, perhaps as late as age 85, when you must "annuitize," that is, convert to an ordinary annuity with fixed payments. Because you can withdraw your money before being forced to annuitize, variable annuities are not fixed income investments. Until annuitization, they are just a collection of mutual funds that go up and down with market prices.

Equities

Investments that represent ownership are called equities. You probably recognize that term from owning a home. Your equity is equal to whatever is the current market value less your current debt on the property. So that part of the value of your home that you would pocket if you sold it is equity, and the part that your mortgage lender gets is a fixed income investment. Stocks, because they also represent ownership, are also equities.

Securities

Stocks, bonds, CDs, mortgages, annuities, mutual funds, and so on are called securities in the financial world. This is because you hold a piece of paper from a licensed seller that shows you are the owner, and, if necessary, you could use that proof of ownership for a loan. Your investments consist of a group of securities. When I was young, people didn't trust brokers to hold securities, so they actually got the stock or bond certificates. It was easy to relate to the word security when you actually had a tangible piece of valuable paper in your hand. But it was a real pain in the neck, especially for bonds, which used to have coupons attached. When an interest payment was due, you'd take a scissors, clip off the coupon, go to the bank, and exchange the coupon for money. Now interest is much more conveniently deposited directly into your account at a broker, and your records with the broker are your only security.

Mutual Funds

The development of mutual funds really made life easy as an investor. Mutual funds own stocks, bonds, real estate, or other investments, and you buy shares of the fund. You don't have to try and research all of the thousands of possible investments. These funds employ research departments to do that for you. There are more mutual funds than there are stocks on the New York Stock Exchange. That means that many of the stock funds, for example, own many of the same companies in their portfolios. In fact, funds will often "dress up" their funds to include some of the stocks that have done very well in the last quarter by buying those stocks just before they have to publish which stocks they own. When Microsoft was doing fantastically well, it was incredible how many funds reported that they owned Microsoft.

You can buy mutual funds that specialize in almost any imaginable group of securities. You can buy funds with a very narrow focus that will own only stocks in a particular industry, or have certain growth or value characteristics, or companies that are socially responsible, or ones that invest only in real estate investment trusts, or corporate bonds, or government bonds, or municipal bonds, or mortgages, and so on, and so on. Most important, you can buy funds that represent a large groups of stocks, such as the whole stock market, or just large company stocks, or just small company stocks. These are *index* funds that buy stocks (or bonds) in the same proportion as a particular index.

The most popular of the index funds is the one that represents all of the stocks in the 500 largest capitalized companies in the United States. It's called the S&P 500 index after the company named Standard and Poor's that maintains the list, and therefore the index that measures its value. Vanguard Investments started the first of these funds, and it is one of the largest mutual funds in the world today. Every share you buy in an index fund has a very small fraction of a share of every stock that is in the index in proportion to the size of the company it represents. So every share of an S&P 500 index fund has a small piece of 500 companies. Because no further stock selection is necessary, no research is needed, so the costs are very low. Less than one-fourth of all the stock funds do as well as S&P 500 index funds because there is very little cost drag, and, apparently, not many people are able to do better with their own selections, not even professional fund managers. *The Wall Street Journal* often compares the performance of some of the best stock pickers in the world with a group of stocks picked by throwing darts at the list of all of the stocks on the market. It seems that, more often than not, the darts are the winners.

There is one precaution that you should observe for mutual funds that are not in a deferred tax account like a 401(k) or an IRA. Mutual funds usually distribute the gains that they had from security sales within their fund near the end of each year. That's a taxable event in the current year if it isn't happening in a deferred tax account. The amounts of these distributions vary widely, from practically nothing for index funds to sizeable amounts for funds that do a lot of trading or go in and out of popularity. You have to make some allowance for this in your withholding or quarterly tax payments. You can usually get estimates of the forthcoming distribution by calling the fund.

Of course, whenever you take money out of a mutual fund, it too may be a taxable event if the share price has changed since your purchase. Therefore, a checking account in a fund with varying prices can create a real tax bookkeeping problem. That's not true of the category of mutual funds we'll discuss next, money markets, because they keep their per share price at $1.00 per share.

MONEY MARKETS

Money markets are mutual funds that invest in very short term securities, often bonds with three-month maturities. Money markets pay much higher interest than bank accounts, so they are a much better place to hold cash. You can get check-writing privileges, but there may be limits to the minimum size check as well as the number you can write each month. Of course, just as with a bank checking account that pays interest, you have to pay tax on the income earned in the account. However, you can get municipal money market accounts where even the dividends are tax exempt. These are popular as checking accounts for people in high tax brackets.

Investments That Are Like Mutual Funds

The next category of investments we are going to look at is similar to mutual funds because these investments also hold groups of stocks or bonds.

Tax-exempt security trusts are groups of municipal bonds that gradually mature. They pay out both principal and interest with each check, but, though the payment dates are as regular as clockwork, the amounts of the payments are often irregular because they sometimes include the principal of some underlying bonds that matured, and the checks keep getting a little smaller because fewer bonds remain. The trust eventually ends after the shareholders get back their last bit of principal.

Then there are exchange traded funds (ETFs), which are like mutual funds but can be traded any time of the day (mutual funds trade only after the market closes) and also specialize in some particular market index. For example, there are Diamonds that purchase all of the 30 industrials in the Dow Jones Industrial Average. ETFs have a tax advantage because, unlike mutual funds, they are unlikely to give you a surprise gain at the end of the year on which you must pay taxes. These may have funny names like Spiders (for Standard and Poor's Deposit Receipts), which track the S&P 500, Qubes (for their QQQ symbol), which track the NASDAQ over-the-counter stocks, or Webs, which track foreign baskets of stocks.

Higher Growth Rates Mean Higher Risks

When it comes down to it, you can invest in almost anything. You can buy real estate partnerships, oil drilling partnerships, collectibles, commodities, mortgages, precious stones, rare metals, ventures, or almost any other kind of investment you can imagine. You can even gamble and invest in a security where you bet the stock will go up (or down) and someone else takes the bet. The opportunities to invest money are almost limitless. Some are extraordinarily hazardous, and some are either fraudulent or just barely legal. That's the main reason my school teacher friend leaves her money in the bank. She says she just isn't interested in taking the time to learn enough about investing so that she can do better than her bank savings account without losing it to some bad investment or outright fraud.

Older people tend to get into conservative fixed income securities because the income is more stable, and they cannot afford the risk of loosing their principal. Younger people can afford more risk and should have a larger percentage of their savings in stocks or stock mutual funds to be able to make some real gains above inflation. Over the long haul, stocks and stock funds generally have faster growth.

Risk is traditionally measured by the relative amount a security moves up and down over a period of time. You can look at the ups and downs of an individual security or a group of securities in an index to get a layperson's view of risk. If you access almost any financial web site, you can request the historical performance of a security or an index. There are sophisticated measures of risk that are based on statistical analyses of historical price fluctuations, but we're not going to address that here.

The most important thing you need to know when it comes to risk is that individual stocks are much more risky than groups of stocks because groups of stocks benefit from the fact that some stocks are usually going up while others go down. Some people learn this the hard way after buying a particular stock mentioned by a friend, a TV show, or a personal broker. For a short while, they may be elated by the performance, but far too often, it's a short ride that comes to an abrupt end. After losing some money, they at least have a better appreciation of risk as more than a theoretical value. We hope you have already learned those risk lessons and will invest either in mutual funds that have large numbers of stocks or otherwise build a diversified portfolio of stocks that provides some cushioning for the fluctuations of individual stocks in the market. You can also control your exposure to risk by diversifying your investments to include more than just stocks. It's well known that bonds have less volatility than stocks, and short-term T-bills have barely any volatility. However, a bout of significant inflation is really hard on T-bills because they pay so little interest. But it can get worse. People who are the most risk averse and hold a mixture of cash, bank savings, and money market funds with interest rates lower than T-bills are almost sure to fall behind.

Where Do I Start?

There are several basic approaches to determine which investments are best for your situation. All of them require at least some familiarity with financial terms, unless you are willing to turn your entire future over to someone else without really knowing what he or she is doing, which I think is extraordinarily dangerous. If you are serious about such a possibility, or already have a firm in complete control of your investments, at least finish reading this chapter and the one that follows, and then see if you don't feel prepared to get more involved. Remember that you pay dearly to have someone else take responsibility for your investments, and annual charges of 1 or 2% of your investments together with other possible hidden charges can severely damage your investment performance.

Even if you have very little interest in financial matters and want to lean heavily on a professional, it's better to have a little understanding and participate in the decisions. One of the lowest cost ways to obtain some professional help is to employ the advisory services offered by the large mutual fund companies such as Vanguard, Fidelity, T. Rowe Price, and so on. Expect to pay $500 or more to talk to a human being, and expect to get recommendations that largely use the company's own products. A major step up is to select a certified financial planner (CFP) to provide you with more personalized service. You can get names of CFPs in your area by calling the Financial Planning Association at 1-800-282-7526. Ask for *fee only* planners. You can use them for one-time advice and may also want tune-ups in future years, but the principles in this book should help you out appreciably in the meantime.

The most satisfying effort for many people is to study the subject themselves, as you are doing now, and invest their money as they choose. When you need professional help, you'll have better questions and get answers you'll better understand. In any event, don't buy an investment because you heard about it on TV, or a friend recommended it, or you read about it in a financial magazine that said it was the best performer for the last three years, or your broker calls with the best tip ever. *Never.* Only buy securities that meet *your* requirements if and when you need more stocks, bonds, or whatever. Before committing to writing that check, consider some alternatives that will also satisfy your requirements.

While I have your attention about "never" subjects, if you are retired or near retirement, *never* accept either a professional planner's recommended retirement budget or one generated by a computer without at least reading Chapter 6. If you don't feel capable of completing the worksheets there, ask your professional or a friend to do it. Then compare results. Tell your planner you want a projection that accounts for all investment costs (including both the advisor and the funds) and possible adverse times ahead.

Doing It Yourself

Okay, having said that, I'm going to describe some alternatives that are easy to do on your own. We'll describe each of the three key steps in the pages that follow.

1. Probably the most important thing you can do in the beginning is to decide how you want to allocate your investments between stocks, bonds or other fixed income investments, real estate, and money markets.

2. The next step is to decide which investment vehicles (what I often call "trucks," because they carry your investments) are best for you, such as

deferred tax investments, taxable investments, and/or tax-exempt investments.

3. Finally, the last step is to select the particular investments themselves. When you go to a financial advisor, most likely the advisor will take you through the same process in the same order. So even if you decide not to do this yourself, you'll be prepared for what is coming and be able to intelligently question some of the recommendations and ask about alternatives.

The object of all of this is to achieve the largest investment growth possible considering your particular needs for cash as you go along and that is consistent with your tolerance for risk. Keep in mind that you don't know what will happen in the future, so you must have a solid foundation that can withstand some financial shocks. It is unlikely that there will be benign inflation and booming securities markets throughout your retirement, and, if you haven't retired yet, it's even less likely for the still greater number of years ahead of you.

Asset Allocation

Before making investment decisions it is vital that you establish the percentage of stock equity and/or real estate equity you should have in your total investments. Anyone who has compared the results of investing in equities with investments in bonds or other fixed income securities knows that the long-term results are much better with equities, as long as you can afford to live with the way they go up and down in value so quickly. The value of equities is very sensitive to economic conditions.

We will illustrate this with some examples. Let's first look at three people who are trying to save money for retirement. They all have a number of things in common. They started saving $10,000 a year at age 30 and increased the amount by the rate of inflation each year. Each had the same costs: 1.5% for stocks and 1.0% for bonds. All money is deposited in a 401(k) account so there are no taxes on the earnings.

They all started saving in 1950. One of them invested in all large company stocks. Another invested in all long-term corporate bonds. The third had a mix of 50% of each and rebalanced at the end of each year. *Rebalancing* is the term used to describe the process of selling some of the equities and buying more fixed income securities, or vice versa, when the equities are out of line with the percentage your desire, in this case, 50%.

Figure 3.1 shows their investment balances as they progressed toward retirement. These are all inflation adjusted so that a dollar reflects the same purchasing power throughout. (Forty years of inflation would have made the future dollar numbers look astronomical—a common ploy of security sales material.)

The saver with 100% stock could have retired the earliest. The saver with the

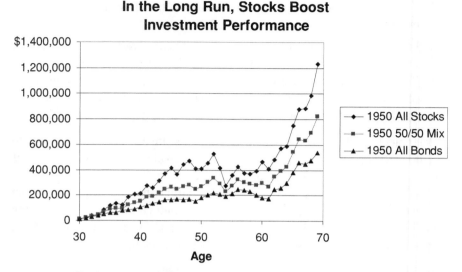

FIGURE 3.1 The investment balances of three different portfolios if saving started in 1950. Values have been adjusted for inflation.

balanced portfolio would have to work for two or three more years than the saver with all stock to achieve the same savings near retirement. The poor fellow with all bonds would wonder if retirement was possible at all and would most likely have to work much longer. However, the person with all stocks would have needed a very strong stomach when he lost about half his investment value at age 54. In fact, the most common thing for people to do at that point is to convert lots of stock to bonds for fear of losing even more.

Results are different if you look at people starting to save in different historical periods. The 1950 case is fairly representative, but if the same three people began saving five years later, as in Figure 3.2, stockholders were not as far ahead. The person with all stock still did the best, but often the person with the balanced portfolio did just about as well. How about the person who invested in all bonds? He or she would have had to wait an extra four to seven years to achieve the same savings as the other two investors.

So, as is true in almost all cases, preretirement savers do better to have substantial holdings in stocks.

After retirement, there are still benefits from significant equity holdings, but there are also more risks. Let's look at what would have happened to three retirees with the same mix of assets as our savers. We'll assume that they all retired at age 65 with $1 million saved and withdrew $35,000 plus 15% tax each year from an IRA. The withdrawals were increased each year by the amount of last year's inflation. Each had the same costs: 1.5% for stocks and 1.0% for bonds. We are not accounting for the IRA's required minimum distribution

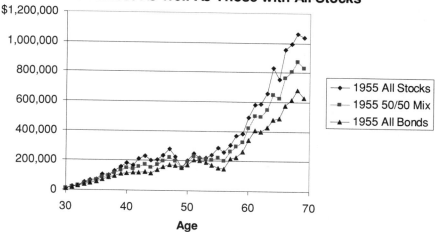

FIGURE 3.2 The investment balances of three different portfolios if saving started in 1955. Values have been adjusted for inflation.

(RMD) requirement after 70½ because it makes little difference in the results as long as the excess distribution is immediately reinvested in a taxable account with the same allocation.

It's not practical to show what happened in each historical period of the past, but we can pick some years that more or less represent good results and bad results. Those who retired in 1955 had a very good future, but those who retired in 1960 had much bleaker prospects. In my own case, I retired in 1989 and enjoyed a tremendous run of a bull market. But my history can't be written yet because the market could go the other way as well, to return to more normal conditions.

Let's look at three people who retired in 1955. The first had all of her investments in large company stocks. Not a lot of retirees had lots of stock in the 1950s, but those who did really got a boost from the market. The second retiree, having worked through the Great Depression, was very conservative and invested only in long-term corporate bonds. The third kept rebalancing at the end of each year to maintain 50% in stocks and 50% in bonds. Figure 3.3 shows what would have happened to their account balances over the years. These balances are shown in inflation-adjusted amounts so that a dollar reflects the same purchasing power each year. All values represent the investment balance at the end of the year, so even at the end of the first year, which began at $1 million in each case, the balances had changed appreciably.

The differences between these three asset allocations are incredible. The person with all bonds would have nothing left if she lived beyond age 85. The person with 50% stock probably would have had a comfortable retirement. The person

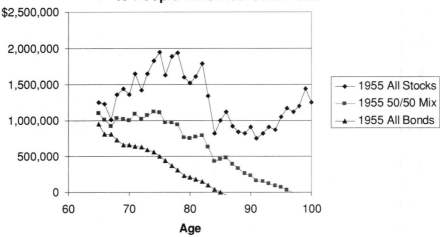

FIGURE 3.3 The investment balances of three different portfolios if retirement started in 1955. Values have been adjusted for inflation.

with all stock would have left something to her heirs but would have undergone a period of severe trauma at age 83 when she saw the loss of more than half of her investments.

Figure 3.4 shows what would have happened to the same three retirees if they retired in 1960 instead of 1955. The retiree with all stocks would have enough money to last until almost age 100. The retiree with the balanced portfolio would run out of money at age 91, and the retiree with all bonds would run out of money at age 87. The differences between Figures 3.3 and 3.4 illustrate an important difference between stocks and bonds in a retirement portfolio. There was little difference for the retiree with all bonds whether retirement started in 1955 or just five years later in 1960. But when a portfolio is heavily weighted with stocks, retirees should anticipate large shocks, and potential heirs should not count their money too soon.

Hedging Your Retirement Bets

These two figures illustrate most of the basic principles of investment allocation. Bonds are stable and sure, but not as rewarding as a portfolio that includes at least some stocks. Allocation is really important—but so is luck. You might retire in a time that is very good for stocks, but there is also a good chance that you may not. At some point, stock portfolios are going to fall appreciably in value. And if you've already gone through a long period of very good times or very bad times, it can certainly color your judgment.

For example, look at the "All Stocks" line in Figure 3.3. Can you imagine the

Stockholders Retiring in 1960 Did Not Do As Well

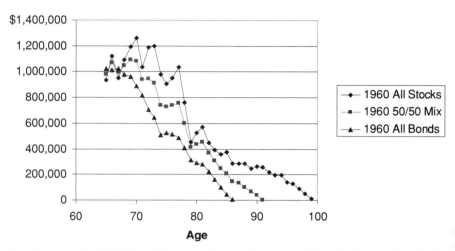

FIGURE 3.4 The investment balances of three different portfolios if retirement started in 1960. Values are adjusted for inflation.

distress of a 79-year-old retiree seeing her investments go from over $1 million to under $500,000 in only two years? Do you think you would have the courage to stay in stocks if you had a similar experience, perhaps just after retiring?

With that in mind, is it possible for a retiree to get the benefits of a stock portfolio when relatively young and still have stability when relatively old? The answer, of course, is yes. All you have to do is change the allocation each year in accordance with your age. Let's work on some examples where we reduce the amount of stock each year by 1%: If you had 50% stock when you were 60, at age 61 you would reduce your stock holdings to 49% of your investments. At 62, you would have 48% stocks, and so on.

We'll have our three retirees start with $1 million and withdraw $35,000 (inflation adjusted) plus 15% for taxes each year. Each will pay investment costs of 1.5% for stocks and 1.0% for bonds. Only this time one retiree will begin with 60% stocks, another with 50% stocks, and the third with 40% stocks. (Again we'll ignore the RMD rule after age 70½ because it does not change the results appreciably if the excess funds are reinvested right away.)

Figure 3.5, which starts in 1955, once again shows that the larger initial stock percentage always does better in this historical period and lasts longer than investments starting with a lower percentage of stocks. The retiree starting with 60% stocks can survive until age 99 without going to the bank, but the retiree starting with 50% stocks runs out of funds at age 95, and the one with 40% stocks at age 92. However, what's really important here is that there was very little lost in this scenario compared with maintaining a constant 50% stock

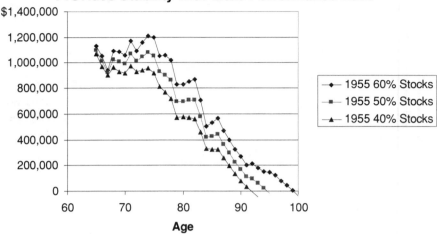

**Reducing Stock Allocation Each Year
Provides Stability with Little Performance Loss**

FIGURE 3.5 Inflation-adjusted balances show the effects of reducing the amount of stock in three different portfolios by 1% each year, beginning in 1955.

allocation as shown in Figure 3.3, which also shows retirement starting in 1955 (compare the middle cases in Figures 3.3 and 3.5). In fact, in the period from age 80 to age 90, the retiree who reduced the allocation of stock every year has about the same investment balances, even though the constant 50% allocation has a slight edge. That slight advantage could easily turn to a disadvantage with a sudden stock market drop.

Let's consider another period of history. We'll start just five years later, in 1960. Again we'll reduce the stock holdings by 1% a year. But what we now see in Figure 3.6 appears very strange. Until late in retirement, it doesn't matter very much whether you started with relatively high or relatively modest stock holdings. Even then, the higher percentage of stock gives you about only one more year to draw on your savings.

By comparing the middle scenarios in Figures 3.4 and 3.6, which both started in 1960, we see there is even less difference between the person with a constant 50% allocation of stock and the case where stock allocations were reduced every year. But the retiree has a lot less risk with the reduced stock allocation.

The retirement autopilot method will stretch your funds even farther than shown in Figures 3.3 through 3.6. All of these figures are based on withdrawing a constant (inflation-adjusted) amount of money each year. The autopilot method, by contrast, will stretch your funds out as you get older by reducing your budget late in life as it senses lower balances and acknowledges that you will probably live longer than you originally anticipated. Nevertheless, these figures make the point very clearly that asset allocation has an extraordinary effect on your future.

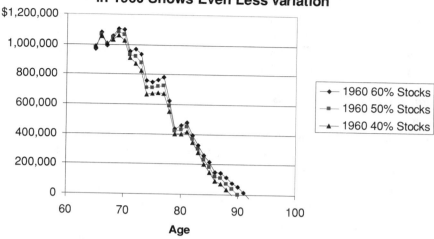

Reducing Stock Allocations for Case Starting in 1960 Shows Even Less Variation

FIGURE 3.6 Inflation-adjusted balances show the effects of reducing the amount of stock in three different portfolios by 1% each year, beginning in 1960.

Some Practical Considerations in Investment Allocation

After seeing the preceding examples, many of you may be ready to run out and buy more stocks. Before you do, though, there are things that you should consider before getting into reallocating your investments, because they may alter your priorities.

1. Make sure that you are not too dependent on the financial condition of your employer when you reach retirement age. Whereas your pension may be funded and enjoy some protection from government investment regulations, things such as company stock, stock options, deferred compensation, consulting contracts, severance contracts, supplemental benefit payments, contracts to return your equity, and the like all depend on your employer's solvency throughout your retirement. I've seen too many people lose so much of their retirement income that they had to return to the workforce when a former employer went bankrupt.

2. Take a look at your debts. If you have high-interest debts, develop a plan to either pay or refinance them before taking any other action. A debt is a negative investment, so every dollar of interest paid is a dollar of gain lost from your investments. Your debt doesn't have to be zero. Debt is great leverage for good real estate investments, and a mortgage provides liquidity when you own your own home. But reducing high-interest loans and credit card debt can be more important than a better allocation of your investments.

3. You don't have to be super precise about changing your allocations around as you age and market conditions vary. Figures 3.5 and 3.6 show that plus or minus 10% allocation from your ideal allocation makes an important difference, but trading securities too often can be costly when taxes are involved. Consider a compromise such as maintaining your allocations within about 5% of your target in such situations.

Allocating Your Investments

So, how can you strike a good balance between growth and stability? Before you can reallocate your investments, you must first know where you are now. Get out a piece of paper and make a list like the one in Figure 3.7. Divide your investments into equities, cash, and fixed income (other than cash).

Your own table will have each of your investments. It could also have the equity in your home, but we'll discuss the pros and cons of this later. Sometimes investments are a mix of equities and fixed income investments, as with so-called balanced funds that maintain their own fixed allocation of stocks and bonds. In that case, divide the balanced fund as in the example with the stock portion under equities and the bond portion under fixed investments, but with your fund's own allocation, of course.

The table includes a "cash" category. Of course, we don't really mean that you would keep your investments in actual cash. That's just the word many money managers use to describe the type of investments that you can convert very quickly to cash. For most people, those investments would be savings accounts or money markets, but if you know you won't need the money for another year or so, you might also meet cash needs with short-term CDs or possibly even a bond fund that invested exclusively in bonds with very short term maturities. There is little volatility in the price of short-term bonds, so the slight additional risk might be worth the slightly greater interest earned.

Once you've seen where your investments are now, you can start to consider if that is the best possible allocation for your current situation. I like to begin with a time-tested way to determine how much equity is appropriate for your age by using a formula in which your percentage of equities equals 110 minus your age. (Twenty years ago, in a more conservative era, the formula was 100 minus your age.) For example, if you are 50 years old, you would have 110 minus 50, which is 60% of your investments in equities. So, if you had $300,000 in investments at age 50, you would begin by looking at 60% in stocks or real estate equity, that is, $180,000 in the example in Figure 3.7.

Be Sensitive to Risk

Until you near retirement, you can tolerate significant market volatility, but unless you are very wealthy, that won't be the case in retirement. It's my feeling that you should ask yourself, "Can I afford retirement if the value of my equities

Your Current
Investment Allocations

Equities	Current Value	Totals
ABC stock	20,000	
XYZ stock	10,000	
Stock fund A	30,000	
Stock fund B	15,000	
60% of $100,000 in balanced fund that maintains 60% in stocks	60,000	
Stock options (Current market value less option cost)	25,000	
Equity in rental property A (Current value less debt)	20,000	
Total equities	180,000	180,000
Cash		
Money market	16,000	
Bank accounts	4,000	
Total cash	20,000	20,000
Fixed Income		
Deferred compensation	30,000	
Government bonds	10,000	
Bond fund	20,000	
40% of $100,000 in balanced fund that maintains 60% in stocks	40,000	
Total fixed income	100,000	100,000
Total Investments		300,000

FIGURE 3.7 Use a chart like this one to list your current investments.

falls 30%?" If not, you will need to reassess the percentage of your investments you have in stocks or other equities.

Since 1926, the real (inflation-adjusted) value of large company stocks dropped more than 10% in about 20% of the years since then, and 20% in about 10% of the years. In almost 5% of the years, the values dropped more than 30%. So-called growth company stocks and small company stocks had much greater declines in bad markets. I don't have any hard data on real estate, but I've seen enough declines during my own real estate investment days to think that the numbers for real estate equity are probably even worse than stocks because real estate investments are almost always leveraged with debt. For example, if the value of the real estate went down from $100,000 to $90,000 and the property had $80,000 worth of debt, the equity went from $20,000 to $10,000, which would be a 50% loss in equity.

If you look at the sample investments in Figure 3.7, you will see that if we had a 30% decline in the $180,000 held in equities, we would have $54,000 of our investments at risk. At age 50, you would probably say you could tolerate that. If you were near retirement, you would go to our planning chapters and make a real test of the numbers by calculating your retirement budget starting with an investment level of $300,000 minus $54,000, to see what would happen.

The formula for calculating equity percentage using 110 minus your age has been fairly well tested by many people. However, if you want to be more conservative and go lighter on equities, you might use 100 instead of 110. On the other hand, there are people who know a lot about equities and have done well with their investments who might want to use 120 instead of 110. If you choose a particular value and stick with it for a number of years, you will be starting with an allocation that offers a good compromise between investment growth and investment risk. As the years go by, your allocations will gradually shift toward fixed income investments. Late in life, the additional stability of fixed income investments will probably be more acceptable than the significant chance of major investment losses in equities.

Need for Cash

But now there is another consideration. Sometimes you might need to withdraw money from your investments for major expenses either before or after retirement. But once in retirement, you most likely will have to withdraw money from your investments for normal living expenses, as well. This is not much of a problem if you are over age 59½ and have most of your savings in mutual funds in an IRA, since withdrawals after that age incur no penalty tax. However, if that is not your situation, you really have to look ahead for about five years to make sure you can get the cash you might need without selling stock or real estate—especially real estate. That's because equities should be very long term investments, in the first place, but more important, there is too much chance that the market will be down when you need to cash them out. If the market is down, that's absolutely the worst time to take money out of equities. That is when you want to be buying equities.

In my own case, once each year I have tried to look ahead at the next five years and ask, "What major expenses do I face that won't be paid with my pension, Social Security, and dividends and interest distributions?" I make a list using current prices and get a total. Then I adjust my investments so that I have at least that much in "cash." Even if this comes to less than 10% of my current investments, however, I always keep at least 10% of my investments in cash to give me a little more ability to rebalance my portfolio or cope with the inevitable unforeseen expenses.

So, if you do the same thing as I do, you'll come up with an amount you should have in cash, that is, money markets or short-term CDs or even short-term bond funds. Suppose your calculation totals $50,000 cash required. Subtract that from your investments: $300,000 minus $50,000 equals $250,000. Then subtract the amount of equities you want to have, as determined either by a formula or your own risk tolerance. In our example, equities are $180,000. So $250,000 minus $180,000 is $70,000. This is the ideal amount you should have in fixed income investments like bonds, bond mutual funds, or CDs.

In this example, we have now established the major allocations: $180,000 in equities, $70,000 in fixed income securities, and $50,000 in cash. Viewed as percentages of the $300,000 total, they are 60% equities, 23% fixed income securities, and 17% cash.

If the sum of your equities and cash requirements exceeds the total amount of your investments, you'll have to reduce the amount of equities so that your only investments are cash and equities. There will be no room for fixed income investments.

What about the Equity in Your Home?

It is probably tempting to include the equity in your home in your asset allocations. My advice is, "don't!" Unless you sell your home, downsize, or become a renter, the house is not a source of retirement money. The reality is that if you are a home owner now, it is likely you will be a home owner during most of your retirement. Further, even if you don't stay in your current house, retirees often get new homes, sometimes to relocate, and, believe it or not, often to buy a larger house. This happens frequently, so instead of your house being an investment, it is really a down payment on another house instead of a source for retirement funds. However, *if* you are very confident that you are going to sell your home and become a renter, by all means, include your home equity as part of your assets. Also, if you think you might get a reverse mortgage to help finance your retirement, include part of your home equity as an investment. A rough approximation of the amount you would be able to get in that situation is about 40% of your current equity. If you are confident that you will downsize, that is, sell your home and purchase a less expensive one, include the difference in prices as an investment.

Allocation Control

It's not practical to control allocations too strictly. I try to keep my equities within about 5% of my target; for example, at age 67, my target is 110 minus 67, which is 43% equities. If my equities go over 48%, I sell some and buy bonds until I'm back at my target. If my equities fall below 38%, I would buy more equities after selling some bonds. I only look at my actual allocations a couple of times a year. That's plenty, because in general you should probably only need to rebalance your investments once a year, and sometimes only once every other year. It's interesting to note that when the market has fallen, rebalancing makes you buy stocks when their prices have fallen, and sell them when they have risen. That's a practical implementation of the "buy low, sell high" theory of financial success.

If you do this allocation analysis the first time, or an investment advisor does it for you, you will undoubtedly have to transfer some of your investments around to match the desired targets for equities, fixed income investments, and cash. You don't have to do this all immediately. You might take up to a year to make the transition, or you might do part of it each month. I seldom take precipitous financial actions. If you don't have enough stocks, slow movements give you the benefit of dollar cost averaging.

It's much easier to rebalance your investments inside a deferred tax investment than a taxable investment, so you should really look there first. That's because you can switch things around all you want in a deferred tax plan without any tax consequence or reporting. However, you may not be able to use this option if you are like me. A number of years ago I ran out of this flexibility because my stocks outside the deferred tax accounts grew so much that I no longer had any stocks left in my deferred tax accounts to work with. Now, rebalancing when stocks grow faster than bonds means I periodically have to take the tax and bookkeeping consequences.

Subdividing Your Allocations

So far we have talked about what investment analysts often call *classes* of investments, namely, equities, fixed income investments, and cash. The subdivision of these classes into subclasses is also important. You can do it very simply or you can add in a lot of sophistication that may or may not give a better result. My own equity subclasses are large company stocks, small company stocks, growth company stocks, and real estate equity. (Financial advisors would say I should have some foreign stocks too, but I'm happy with my choices.) My fixed income investment class is limited to intermediate-term municipal bonds that I always keep until they mature or are called. Add my money markets, and that's it. I don't worry much about rebalancing the subclasses, but a person can't go too far wrong by dividing the subclasses equally within the class and considering rebalancing subclasses only every third or fourth year.

Please understand that serious financial advisors are generally not as cavalier as I am about a regimen of selecting and controlling subclasses. In the extreme, some people might think they have to reallocate when a growth company is bought by a value company. That kind of event doesn't bother me a bit because I buy mostly mutual funds where what happens to one company has little effect on the whole fund.

Sophisticated investors create many asset subclasses from categories such as large company growth stocks, large company value stocks, small company growth stocks, small company value stocks, international growth stocks, international value stocks, short-term bonds, intermediate-term bonds, long-term bonds, U.S. government bonds, industrial bonds, municipal bonds, retail real estate, industrial real estate, office real estate, apartment real estate, real estate in different parts of the country, precious metals, cattle, commodities, ventures, collectibles, and so on, and so on. The possibilities are endless. But finally it always comes down to picking a real investment, not just setting up an asset class. Many professionals are fond of saying that the selection of a particular investment within a class is not as important as the asset class. That's true—until you select a real dud as the particular investment. And you may find that it's impractical for you to buy many of the asset classes because, for example, your 401(k) mutual fund choices don't include any investment within that class.

Of course, everyone would like to own the highest returning assets in any period. Since we can't foresee what those assets will be, we compromise. We hope we will find a mix that has more items that increase in value than ones that fall. However, it's not easy to find securities that obviously go up when other securities go down. Many years ago they used to say that bonds were a good alternative to stocks when stock prices are falling. That's true if you bought the bonds when the stocks started to fall, and they had a maturity date that would correspond to the time when stocks started to go up again. Unfortunately, there are lots of times when stocks and bonds behave badly just at the same time.

Like many people before me, and many that will come after me, I did statistical analyses of various kinds of classes to find some kind of counterbalance to stocks in various subclasses. The idea is to find some other kind of investment that consistently goes up when stocks go down. Unfortunately, the investment that does that well doesn't yet exist. When large company stocks really go south, so do small company stocks, and even the bond results get poorer.

Everyone also searches for a class of investments that thwarts inflation. Except for Social Security and those fortunate few who have pensions with cost of living adjustments (COLAs), almost everyone suffers when inflation goes on a rip. People in money markets get hurt badly, as do bond holders and those with fixed payment annuities. Small cap stocks seem to have done better than large company stocks occasionally in periods of great inflation in the United States. Fortunately, U.S. inflation has not hit the 100% or 1,000% a year mark as it has in some other countries. Those inflation rates reduce almost everyone to paupers.

Probably the best investment during periods of high inflation is real estate. Then it can be an incredible investment. Not only may the value increase with inflation, but any debt gives you some leverage to effectively increase your profitability. That debt is held by one of those losers in a highly inflationary environment. It's just another good reason not to pay off the mortgage on a home too quickly.

It will be interesting to see how real estate investment trusts (REITs) behave during periods of high inflation. These investments fall someplace between stocks and directly owned real estate. They are shares that anyone can buy just like a stock. Precious metals and collectibles are the classic hedges against inflation. But neither of these pay any dividends or interest, and they can be terrific duds at all other times.

Modern Theories on Allocation

There are many scholarly people, statisticians, professors, students preparing a thesis, and others who study the historical performance of various asset classes. They often believe that they can pick an optimum allocation of asset classes, sometimes as finely divided as many of the categories previously mentioned. Their goal is to give you an optimum percentage of each of these asset classes. In their lingo, this is the "efficient frontier."

I am neither a supporter of these scholarly views nor a person who denies them. I believe there is value in the diversification they propose, but I'm always skeptical about any fine-grained allocation, especially when the studies ignore asset classes other than stocks and bonds. As a practical matter, it frequently is not easy to change allocations even if you think they should be different. Getting out of real estate is something that can test your patience. Selling a stock or fund with large unrealized capital gains is, at the least, uncomfortable. Buying stocks in a declining market takes real courage. And, except for deferred tax accounts, you will have to make and keep records of these transactions, so you can report them to the IRS. It is easy to change your allocations of stocks and bonds within the choices available for a 401(k), IRA, variable annuity, or other vehicle that has deferred taxes. Of course you are limited to the choices provided by the investment firm that administers your deferred tax account unless you are one of those few people who has a self-administrated IRA that allows you to select virtually any kind of an investment. With deferred tax accounts, most often, all you have to do is pick up the phone or log on to the Internet, identify yourself, and say what you want done. You don't have to worry about the taxes or bookkeeping. These reasons alone should be a good incentive to keep most of your stock holdings in deferred tax accounts unless you have really substantial investments in taxable accounts.

NOTE FOR HIGHLY TAXED PEOPLE

If you are in a high tax bracket, you probably recognize that investments in deferred tax accounts are not worth as much as in taxable accounts. That's because they are subject to ordinary income tax rates on withdrawals. You could allow for this in your calculations by looking at your allocations on an after-tax basis. This is a waste of time for people with low tax rates, and it's also a waste of time if the majority of your investments are either in deferred tax accounts or in taxable accounts. However, if this applies to you, one way to move your calculations up a notch in accuracy without going to a lot of effort is to reduce the value of any investment in deferred tax accounts by your net tax rate. So, if you had $500,000 in stocks and your net tax rate was 20%, you would reduce the value of your stock in the example by 20% times $500,000, which equals $100,000 for a net after-tax stock of $400,000.

Summing Up Allocations

My own feelings about asset allocations are simple and old-fashioned. There is no perfect allocation formula. Of course you want both maximum growth and maximum stability. That investment doesn't exist, so you choose some classes that will do the former and some that will do the latter. This has to be blended with reasonable diversification, practical administration, and liquidity to satisfy short-term needs. Here is a summary of the steps we've discussed that lead to a good allocation:

1. Make a list of your current investments in three separate categories: equities (stocks and real estate), fixed income (bonds, deferred compensation, loans owed to you), and cash (money markets, savings accounts, checking accounts). If you are in a high tax bracket, consider doing this analysis on an after-tax basis. Total each category and add these to see your total investments.

2. Determine how to pay off or refinance any debts that have high interest rates before you start taking any action on the steps that follow.

3. Determine the percentage of your investments that should be in stock and real estate equity with a formula like 110 minus your age. Multiply this percentage times your total investments to determine how much of your investments should be in equities. Consider whether you could afford a 30% drop in stock value. If not, reduce this equity target to something you can tolerate.

4. Unless you are over 59½, and want to take the money from an IRA, put most of the amount you anticipate you will need for cash in the next five years into a money market account, short-term CDs, or a short-term bond fund. If this is not at least 10% of your investments, increase this cash target accordingly.

5. Add equity and cash targets, then subtract that total from total investments. This is the amount that should be in bonds or other fixed income investments. (If the total of your equities and cash targets exceeds your total investments, make equities equal to total investments minus cash needs.)

6. Subdivide your equities into real estate and stocks. There is no perfect division here. It's just a matter of your own personal judgment and where you feel the most confident. For more diversity, divide the stocks into approximately equal parts of large company stocks, small company stocks, growth stocks, and foreign stocks (if you want). Or use a reference with more sophisticated tools. If you are just starting and have very little stock equity, consider either an index fund for the total stock market or a group of index funds, each one of which represents your preferred asset classes.

7. Don't let yourself become vulnerable by having a high percentage of your retirement prospects, such as deferred compensation, stock, stock options, or a contract to buy your interests, depend on one factor, like your employer's solvency.

8. Compare your target allocations with your current allocations. See how much you have to sell and how much you have to buy to reach your target allocation.

9. You don't have to reallocate your own investments into your new classes immediately. First study the following material on vehicles. Then determine which vehicle would be best for each.

10. Review your intentions with a professional who has no interest in managing your investments. Then take up to a year to implement the changes.

Vehicles

New investors frequently get confused about the difference between investments and vehicles, and before we go too far, perhaps at this point it's worth discussing what they are exactly. A vehicle is something into which you put investments. In a sense, they are like trucks that carry mutual funds or other investments. For instance, an IRA is a vehicle that carries investments, usually mutual funds, for you. What kind of investments they are is up to you. There are, of course, different types of vehicles, and each has its own characteristics. Congress invents new ones all the time.

Vehicles with Tax Deductions

These are the most popular retirement vehicles for mutual funds of various kinds. They include plans such as a 401(k), 403(b), Keogh, IRA, and other similar government-approved plans. Unlike other vehicles, you can deduct contributions to them from your income on your tax return. Further, your savings grow without your paying any tax on interest, dividends, or capital gains distributions. Only when you take money out do you pay income tax, and the only amount taxed is the amount you withdraw. (But that withdrawal is taxed at ordinary income tax rates, not at lower capital gains rates.) The bookkeeping is extraordinarily simple for the employee, but not necessarily for the employer. Most employer savings plans are in this category; often the employer will match a certain part of your savings. Matching funds are not taxed either until you actually make a withdrawal.

There are, however, strict rules for withdrawals. Except for unusual cases, you cannot withdraw money until after age 59½. After age 70½, the government requires you to withdraw a certain RMD that is dependent on your age at the time, or suffer sever penalties. It's possible to borrow money from these plans, but the terms are so onerous that such loans should only be used as a last resort—especially if you expect to leave your current employer before the loan is repaid.

Some companies permit you to buy stock in plans of this type. There is a way to get the stock itself and pay only capital gains taxes on the subsequent growth, but you should explore the details of that with your employer and/or accountant.

Employer-Sponsored Tax-Deferred Vehicles

The principal plans here are deferred compensation plans, supplemental benefits for highly compensated employees (which allow them to make deposits that exceed what otherwise would be the annual limit on 401(k) contributions), severance payment plans, and stock options. They are all subject to income taxes on distribution, but some stock option growth can be considered capital gains. Severance pay is also subject to the Federal Insurance Contribution Act (FICA) and Medicare tax each year. The supplemental benefit is the only one of these where you may be able to select mutual funds. Deferred compensation and severance payments are contract commitments between the employee and the company. They all depend on the company's solvency.

Nondeductible IRA Vehicles

These are another popular retirement vehicle for various kinds of funds. They differ from the deductible tax-deferred vehicles because your savings contributions are not a deduction from your income tax. As a consequence, your contributions are not taxed when you make a withdrawal. Instead, you pay taxes only on the growth you earned from them over the years. The principle vehicle here is the self-funded IRA. It has the same kind of withdrawal rules and taxes as a regular IRA.

Roth IRA Vehicles

Contributions to Roth IRAs are not deductible either. However, their great benefit is that the withdrawals are not taxable and there is no required minimum distribution requirement after age 70½, so it is an excellent vehicle for funds you want to pass on to heirs. Roth IRAs are not available to high-income people.

Variable Annuities

Variable annuities are like a truck with a trailer attached. The truck carries mutual funds of your choice as well as a little bit of insurance, for which you often pay dearly. These are sold by insurance companies and major mutual fund companies that get an insurance company to back them. Generally there is only enough insurance to let the vehicle slip under the laws that benefit insurance companies. For example, they may provide only enough insurance to allow you to get back your original contributions, not their growth to some subsequent higher value. You can make contributions at any time in virtually any amount. The rules for variable annuities are much more flexible than IRAs up to a point, and that's where the trailer comes in. You can withdraw as much as you like in any year, although some impose a penalty for withdrawals within the first few years. After you get to a specified age, usually between age 65 and 85, the policy demands that you either withdraw any remaining funds or convert to an annuity that makes payments for a fixed number of years (term-certain) or for your lifetime.

Variable annuities are often loaded with insurance, commissions, and administrative costs. They are usually a very profitable product for financial advisors. There are only a few that have relatively low costs and offer a selection of low-cost mutual funds. Look carefully!

Charitable Vehicles

Several major mutual fund companies offer charitable trusts. You can donate either cash or appreciated securities, get a tax deduction, and subsequently direct the trust to invest the money in some of their funds. You no longer can use the money for your own income, but you can, at any time, direct the trust to mail checks to legitimate charities of your choice. It's a way of getting more out of your charitable contributions because the money can grow tax free until you're ready to make contributions. It also gets the money out of your estate before your death, which will reduce estate taxes. Alternatively, if you have lots of money, with the help of an attorney you can set up your own trust just for giving, or establish a charitable remainder trust that will give you income, or a charitable lead trust that will return your principal. These are great for helping charitable organizations and provide varying degrees of deductibility.

Also, in any of these charitable vehicles, if, for your donation, you transfer stock or other investments that have grown in value, you don't have to pay the capital gains tax that would be due if you first sold the investment and then donated the cash. Often, they are excellent places for higher-risk investments if you know that you will ultimately give them to charities because you are not risking money that will be future income for you. You are risking how much the charities will get. Finally, these vehicles will let you make donations anonymously so you won't be harassed with subsequent solicitation notices.

Your Own Accounts

Besides the preceding vehicles, there is the ordinary account you can establish with any broker, agent, bank, or mutual fund, or it can be self-administered, as, for example with online trading. It can contain EE savings bonds and I (inflation) bonds, both of which allow you to defer taxes. It can contain tax-exempt securities such as municipal bonds, municipal bond mutual funds, tax-exempt security trusts, and municipal bond money markets. It can contain stocks, bonds, or funds of almost any description. You can sell or buy whenever you want. You can buy insurance products such as instant annuities that start making payments right away. You can get life insurance to help pay estate taxes. There are lots of opportunities, hazards, and benefits, but you are in control.

You are also in control of the tax situation. You can gift appreciated securities and escape taxes on the growth. If you buy a stock or fund, you can hold it for many years, thereby not only getting tax deferrals but also benefiting from capital gains tax rates on the sale instead of higher ordinary tax rates. (These lower rates apply only if you hold the investment for more than one year.) That's why this deferral doesn't work for many funds that buy and sell stock so quickly that they declare most of their capital gains several times a year. (Such funds are called high-turnover funds. A low-turnover fund might turn over only 10% of its portfolio a year, while a high-turnover fund might turn over 100% or even more.) So there are many things you can do to achieve better after-tax performance if you choose good vehicles and then good investments for them. Let's take a look.

Finding the Best Vehicles

So what are generally the best vehicles? Probably the best of all is that part of an employer's savings plan that is matched by the employer's contributions. It's important to put as much money that you can into these, at least up to the point where your employer stops matching. Effectively, you'll get a return on your savings that is extraordinarily high. If your employer matches your savings by 50% and your return on the underlying investment is 10%, you've made a 60% return on that savings in the first year. And, ever after, you've got 50% more principal than you would have without the matching contribution. That's a deal! Don't miss this opportunity even if you have to borrow money occasionally to be able to make these savings.

The second priority vehicle should be the Roth IRA for many people. Unlike many other deferred tax plans, your contributions are not tax deductible, so it's a little harder to add to your savings each year. However, since withdrawals from Roths are not taxed, you benefit when you start to withdraw the money. If you expect your net tax rate to be the same or higher in retirement than while working, this is a fantastic opportunity. There are some limitations on withdrawals before age 59½, but I've always felt that if you have to rely on such withdrawals before that age, except in some very rare circumstances, you shouldn't be retiring anyway or you must have a lot of other money stashed away. Unlike regular IRAs, there is no required minimum distribution after age 70½. This too can be a real blessing.

You can establish a Roth account at almost any financial institution such as a brokerage firm, or a mutual fund company, or even some banks. Compare costs, especially if considering a bank. Pick one that will give you a decent set of choices within the account so that you can reallocate your investments as you get older or your circumstances change.

Roth IRAs are so good, in fact, that you should consider converting a regular IRA to a Roth IRA. You must be able to meet the current minimum income requirements, which you can get from your mutual fund firm or accountant. Don't make the conversion if any of the following apply to you:

- You will need any of the money in less than five years.
- Your tax rate will be lower in the future than now.
- You can't pay the taxes due on conversion with funds outside your IRA.
- You have to get a loan to pay the taxes due on conversion.

The third highest priority is usually an employer's savings plan, like 401(k)s, even if no matching funds are available, or an IRA where your contributions are tax deductible. To do better than these first three choices of vehicles, you would have to find investments that have an after-tax return significantly greater than the return on investments in these vehicles. That's very hard to do. For example, if you can get a 10% return on a stock fund in one of these vehicles, you would need to get the equivalent of a 10% after-tax return from a taxable account. This translates to more risky returns of about 12% at a 15% tax rate, 14% at a 28% tax rate, and 17% at a 40% tax rate. Sustaining those kind of rates for many years is probably impossible.

Employee savings plans have a great benefit that's often overlooked. They provide for automatic savings from your paycheck. This means that you are not tempted to spend the money because it never shows up in your take-home pay. For that reason alone, I think that people should save the maximum in their employer's savings plan even if they think they might ultimately get greater after-tax results from another investment.

Beyond these three priority vehicles, there is no vehicle that is always going to be better than all of the rest. Investments in taxable securities, tax-exempt accounts, or real property can be better than deferred tax vehicles where the original savings are not tax deductible, as with variable annuities and some IRAs. People who buy and hold securities for many years get even better tax deferrals than they would in a nondeductible IRA. That's because if you hold these securities long enough, there is no tax until they are sold. Then they are taxed at the lower capital gains tax rate, while IRAs are taxed at higher ordinary income tax rates.

So what is the worst vehicle? That's a truck within a truck, that is, a variable annuity within an IRA. The advisor gets a lot of money, and the investor is saddled with high fees and mandatory IRA required minimum distribution rules.

That said, there are some good applications for low-cost variable annuities. These include cases where no withdrawals will be taken for a large number of years. Also, they may be a benefit to someone very late in life who does not want to be bothered by investments, is willing to receive lower returns, and wants to convert the investments into an ordinary annuity with regular monthly or annual payments.

Another good application for a low-cost variable annuity is for older parents who want to gift money to adult children for the children's ultimate retirement. The children can't take the money out without a penalty before age 59½. However, if the child is willing, and the parents ultimately need some of the money, the children can withdraw some funds (with a 10% penalty if they are not yet 59½) and gift it back to their parents.

Taxable or tax-exempt investments do hold a major edge over IRAs and other tax-deferred accounts in one important area: legacies to heirs. That is because the cost basis in nondeferred accounts is marked up to the market value on the day of death. This statement, seemingly mysterious to many, can be very important to a surviving widow or widower who would be much better off inheriting highly appreciated stocks or mutual funds or even real estate than money in an IRA. That's because the survivor can sell such securities immediately without paying any tax. On the other hand, an IRA will be taxed at ordinary tax rates forever, and, on the death of the surviving spouse, be subject to any estate taxes as well. That really adds up—and probably means that even if there is money left in your IRAs after you and your spouse die, the IRS may get far more of it than your heirs.

Measuring Your Vehicle's Value

The vehicle you choose for your investments makes a tremendous difference in the value of your investments when you get around to cashing them in. That's largely because of tax differences, so one thing we want to be able to measure is a vehicle's effectiveness as a tax shelter. We'll do this both for low- and high-taxed individuals, because at lower tax rates, the choice of vehicle may be less important than other factors.

High-turnover funds, such as aggressive growth funds, are those that do a lot of stock trading and therefore sell a large part of their portfolio each year. This means that most of your gains are ordinary gains instead of long-term capital gains. They also distribute long-term gains each year, and, though they are taxed at a lower rate, you lose the benefits of deferring these taxes for many years. Very low turnover funds like index funds seldom distribute their long-term gains. High-turnover funds often look good in a prospectus that does not show what the results would be on an after-tax basis. Additionally, if you switch between funds frequently, you'll lose many of the benefits of capital gains deferrals. In effect, you've made what might otherwise have been low-turnover funds into high-turnover funds because you just turned over 100% of the fund with your sale and purchase of another fund.

If you have your investments in deferred tax vehicles, all of your gains, whether ordinary or long-term capital gains, are taxed at ordinary rates, but you don't pay the tax until you make a withdrawal. This makes it extraordinarily tough to think through which might be the best vehicle for a particular kind of investment. That's why we prepared Figure 3.8, which will help us solve this puzzle.

Stock Funds

Figure 3.8 is for stock funds, all of which can be purchased in any of the vehicles shown. The figure displays how $1.00 would grow over 20 years for a fund with a 10% total return, which includes an annual 2% distribution of dividends. The numbers are tabulated using a modest inflation adjustment of 3% per year so that they reflect today's dollar values. Different inflation rates would not change the relative ranking.

There are two columns, one for a low-taxed person and the other for a high-taxed person. Low taxes here mean a 15% ordinary tax rate and a 10% capital gains tax rate. High taxes mean a 40% ordinary tax rate and a 20% capital gains tax rate. Depending on your own tax rate, you will be more interested in one of these columns than the other. You will reach the same basic conclusions for each tax rate, but at the lower tax rates, you might decide that other factors are more important. For example, your IRA might not offer a fund as attractive as one you can get outside your IRA.

On the left we list the various kinds of vehicles. Let's look at the most important point first. At the top of the column are the 401(k)s with matching employer contributions. Remember, we said that you never wanted to pass up the opportunity to save at least as much as your employer would match. The $1.00 would grow to $6.33 for the low-taxed person and $4.47 for the high-taxed person with 100% employer matching. That's pretty spectacular in either tax bracket. Nothing else comes close.

20-Year Ride for $1.00 in Stock Funds

(After 3% inflation)

	Low Tax	High Tax
Deferred Tax Vehicles		
401(k) with 100% matching	$6.33	$4.47
401(k) with 50% matching	$4.75	$3.35
401(k) or deductible IRA	$3.17	$2.23
Above with tax savings invested	$3.72	$3.72
Nondeductible IRA	$3.25	$2.46
Variable annuity with 1% costs	$2.64	$1.86
Variable annuity with 3% costs	$1.82	$1.29
Currently Taxable Vehicles		
No capital gain distributions	$3.32	$2.78
Turn over above fund every five years	$3.15	$2.51
Capital gains distributed every year	$3.05	$2.40
With all ordinary gains	$2.83	$1.78
Tax-Exempt Vehicles		
Roth IRA	$3.72	$3.72

FIGURE 3.8 Growth of $1.00 with stocks invested in various kinds of vehicles.

A Roth IRA is the next best vehicle. You could get the same performance from a regular IRA if you would also save the reduction in taxes you get from a deductible IRA. For example, if you put $1,000 into a deductible IRA and you were in a 40% tax bracket, you got an extra $400 in your pocket because of the tax deduction. Suppose you invested that instead of spending it. People seldom think about that, and you may not be able to do so if you are already near whatever is the maximum annual contribution you can make to your 401(k) or IRA. So a Roth IRA is the second best vehicle if you qualify for it.

Figure 3.8 shows that the third best vehicle is a stock fund that makes no capital gains distributions and one that you do not sell during the 20-year period. You can buy funds that would allow you to come very close to this objective. They are called tax-managed index funds. Many people can't resist the temptation to sell funds once in a while, particularly if they have an advisor who will get a fat fee for encouraging them to make a trade. I've held on to just plain index funds that are just about as good as tax-managed funds if you keep them for long periods like that. In fact, it's entirely possible that I may own those funds for 40 years and pay no capital gains on them at all, because capital gains taxes generally are forgiven on the day you or your spouse dies.

The same principle applies to real estate investments. There are people who, after selling their investment properties, reinvest the funds immediately in another investment property and take advantage of what's known as a 1031 exchange that's allowed only on real estate sales. Then no taxes are paid on the sale, so the real estate investments continue to grow free of capital gains tax. On the death of either spouse, all of those taxes generally are forgiven, as is the accumulated depreciation that would otherwise be taxed. It's a heck of a deal for the surviving spouse or heirs. When you hear about wealthy people who pay no income tax, they are usually in these kinds of investments.

However, let's suppose that you can't resist the temptation to trade funds and sell them every five years, or suppose that your mutual fund effectively does the same thing with their own trading, which is typical of some stock funds. Then Figure 3.8 shows you lose a little, and you are in the same ballpark as a nondeductible IRA. You lose even more if the capital gains are distributed every year, and even more than that if the gains are taxed at ordinary rates, as happens with high-turnover funds.

This brings us down to variable annuities. There are a sparse number of variable annuities with costs lower than 1%. There are a large number of variable annuities with costs over 3%. At 3%, a variable annuity is about the worst investment you can find in this situation. When the costs are 1%, they still don't look very good, but for longer periods and for special conditions, a low-cost variable annuity may be attractive to some people. Unfortunately, these vehicles are so profitable to the sales agents that they are often pushed very hard.

Bond Funds

Let's now look at bonds in Figure 3.9. This figure is similar to Figure 3.8 in many respects, but you'll notice some differences. There are no rows for "No capital gains distribution," "Turn over above fund every five years," or "All capital gains distributed every year." The reason is that all of these vehicles are taxed at ordinary income tax rates. Capital gains taxes are very small for bond funds except in extraordinary conditions.

Also, we added a couple more taxable accounts for some other fixed income investments to this table to show how they would compare, namely, a 4% CD and a 2% bank account. Note that a 2% bank account not only doesn't gain you anything over 20 years, but you actually lose. That would also be true with a 3% account. It could be worse, I suppose; you could put the actual cash under a mattress.

The other major difference is that there is an extra row added for "Tax-exempt muni bonds." Municipal bonds, most often called *muni* bonds for short,

20-Year Ride for $1.00 in Bond Funds

(After 3% inflation)

	Low Tax	High Tax
Deferred Tax Vehicles		
401(k) with 100% matching	$3.02	$2.13
401(k) with 50% matching	$2.26	$1.60
401(k) or deductible IRA	$1.51	$1.07
Above with tax savings invested	$1.78	$1.78
Nondeductible IRA	$1.59	$1.29
Variable annuity with 1% costs	$1.25	$0.88
Variable annuity with 3% costs	$0.85	$0.60
Currently Taxable Vehicles		
6.0% bond	$1.50	$1.12
4.0% certificates of deposits	$1.08	$0.89
2.0% bank account	$0.78	$0.70
Tax-Exempt Vehicles		
Roth IRA	$1.78	$1.78
4.5% tax-exempt muni bonds	$1.34	$1.34

FIGURE 3.9 Growth of $1.00 with bonds invested in various kinds of vehicles.

pay a lower interest rate than taxable bonds because their interest is tax-exempt. In the example, the interest rate on a taxable bond fund is assumed to be 6% before tax. On the other hand, the interest rate on the muni bond fund example is 4.5%. Even though this is a lower rate, it's a better deal for a highly taxed person. We can see that by comparing the growth of the muni bond in the last row with the row labeled "6.0% bond." For either a high- or low-taxed person, the muni bonds would grow to $1.34 over 20 years, but a taxable bond, even though it is at a higher interest rate, grows to only $1.12 for the highly taxed person. The muni bond is not a good deal for the low-taxed person because she can get $1.50 from the taxable bond.

Even with bonds, the best performance would come when your employer matched your savings with some amount. Again, this would be the very best possible situation. But you wouldn't want to displace stocks with bonds in such an account if you still had some more stock to allocate to this vehicle.

If you had a Roth IRA, you would never buy a muni bond in it, because you can buy a taxable bond at a higher interest rate and still pay no tax on it. Once again, the Roth IRA is the second best vehicle, although, in those situations where you can reinvest the tax savings from your tax deductions, you would get the same performance.

The last observation about Figure 3.9 that I would like to make is that it would be the height of bad judgment to buy a bond fund in a high-cost variable annuity, especially if you are highly taxed. A variable annuity with a 3% cost is only pennies away from what you would lose if you literally stuck cash under your mattress! What this says is that, if you pay attention to the findings in the figure, you would never want to own *only* a variable annuity, because your allocation analysis undoubtedly showed that you should have some bonds or other fixed income investments. If there is an intelligent step to take in this situation, it would be to put your stocks in the variable annuity and buy your bonds directly or in some other vehicle.

Allocating within Vehicles

We have just seen that it would be very unlikely you would want to put any of your fixed income allocation into a variable annuity. But what about all of the other possibilities in other vehicles?

First, construct a table similar to that in Figure 3.10, which provides the tools we need to determine a distribution that satisfies both the class allocations and our current vehicle distributions. This table is designed so that it has the highest return vehicles at the top and the lowest at the bottom. In the column "Current Vehicle Balances," enter the current balance you have for each existing vehicle. In the bottom row, enter your target total allocations for each class. If you have subdivided equities into subclasses, you would have a column for each subclass. We have only two equity subclasses: real estate and stocks. Now you are ready to divide your resources to get the best possible distribution of your investments.

You might ask why there are no 401(k) matching vehicles on this table. The reason is that once you and your employer have made the contributions the matching funds are no longer distinguishable from the unmatched funds in the balance of those accounts that we show here. Remember, the amounts in this table are the total current amounts in your accounts. Later we'll talk about a similar table for your *new* contributions. Such a table would have your 401(k) matching opportunity at the top of the list.

Now, we'll begin the job of spreading the allocations among the various vehicles. The first step is to enter real estate equity under the equities column. See Figure 3.11. The next step is to fill in the remaining vehicles. Since we have ordered the best vehicle performance from top to bottom, it's easy to fill out the equities. Use the most that is available in the current balances for equities until

Current Balances and Allocations

Vehicles	Current Vehicle Balances	Allocation Classes			
		Equities		Fixed Income	Cash
		Real Est.	Stock		
Roth IRA	10,000				
401(k)/deductible IRA	200,000				
Nondeductible IRA	0				
Taxable or tax-exempt	90,000				
Variable annuity	0				
Total allocation	300,000	20,000 / 180,000	160,000	70,000	50,000

FIGURE 3.10 Begin by listing balances for current vehicles and desired allocations.

you reach the equity class limitation, in this case $20,000 real estate and $160,000 stock for a total of $180,000.

Then go to the cash column. Since cash is determined by what you need in about the next five years, and it was defined as only those needs that wouldn't be satisfied with withdrawals from deferred tax investments, the cash entry belongs in "Taxable or tax-exempt." Remember that your cash needs were calculated on the basis that either you are too young to be able to get money from deferred tax accounts for a number of years yet without incurring an early withdrawal penalty, or you chose to select a taxable investment anyway for your cash needs.

That only leaves fixed income, which is now easy to fill in so that the entries match the totals in the fixed income class.

With regard to *new* savings for this year and the future, make a table just like Figure 3.11. Divide your new savings so that they match your allocation class needs, and put them in the highest return vehicles that are appropriate. If your employer offers 401(k) matching funds, that vehicle should be on the top of the list. You go through exactly the same process, but the numbers are now annual savings deposits instead of the current balances. It's really easy!

You now have a framework that will give you the best possible investment

Allocate Your Resources

Vehicles	Current Vehicle Balances	Allocation Classes			
		Equities		Fixed Income	Cash
		Real Est.	Stock		
Roth IRA	10,000		10,000		
401(k)/deductible IRA	200,000		150,000	50,000	
Nondeductible IRA	0				
Taxable or tax-exempt	90,000	20,000		20,000	50,000
Variable annuity	0				
Total allocation	300,000	20,000	160,000	70,000	50,000
		180,000			

FIGURE 3.11 Now, distribute your vehicle balances to your allocation classes until they match the totals at the bottom of the columns.

performance that fits your risk tolerance. You're ready for the final step: selecting the best investments for each class in each vehicle.

Making Smart Investments

Now that you know something about allocations and vehicles, you can address what kind of investments you should select. You won't always be able to use the best investments in every area on your allocation table because your selection may be limited to the funds offered by your company savings plan, for example. However, many of these plans now give you a wide range of choices. Of course, once you start investing outside of these plans, you can invest in almost anything you want.

You'll Make Mistakes

First, though, let's look at some of the pitfalls you may encounter along the way. Maybe we can help you avoid some of them. The truth is, even when you have a large number of choices, you are going to get some investments that will turn out to be real dogs, because there will be things beyond your control. In my own case, I got stung on real estate investments. That was because of a change in the tax law in 1986 that greatly reduced the losses that could be claimed from real estate partnerships. This drove investment real estate prices down severely.

Also, I certainly learned some painful lessons much earlier in my career. One of these was to be wary of the products pushed by my brokers and a good part of the financial media. I'd get a call from a broker who would tell me about this *must have* investment. Many times I'd yield to the enticing pitch and get my wallet out. As I recall, in most of those cases I lost money.

I've learned from my mistakes as well as my successes. I've spent years on the computer making theoretical comparisons of various alternatives, and my research has been mentioned in numerous national financial publications. I'm not a registered investment advisor, and I don't sell any securities, but many who have such credentials often use my work to advise clients. Unlike most planners, I have actually owned, not just read about, a large number of the investments discussed in this book. Experience, not theory, often gives you a different perspective. Perhaps the following considerations will help you avoid some of the scams, reduce your bookkeeping chores, and get better investment results.

Be Wary of the Media

Virtually all of our financial information comes from some sort of media, so I don't want to throw the baby out with the bathwater. But there is an awful lot of financial trash out there. After retirement, I probably subscribed to 20 financial news products, ranging from pure pulp to scholarly publications for profes- sional planners. In the morning, I always did (and still do) watch CNBC—for entertainment. I'm amazed at the vitality and sincerity of the guests who are spotlighted. Unlike me, these people are articulate and fast on their feet. Some back up their views with charts cluttered with moving averages, relation to the general market, or other information. In their particular specialties, I know they know a lot more than I do, but I know something that they can't admit or no one will invite them to be on TV anymore. That is that no one can predict the future. The only thing you can say for sure is that tomorrow the market will be either higher or lower.

I know another thing. Many of these people are paid incredible sums for their work. Their offices and homes are often in the most expensive real estate dis- tricts in New York. I know that the fees people pay to buy and sell securities most often do more for these executives' lifestyles than for their investors' returns. In fact, low-cost funds with lower compensated managers often do bet- ter than the ones with all the glitz around them.

These TV personalities never mention that other silent partner in your investments who also takes a cut. This partner sucks money from the underly- ing companies you invest in, then from the dividends the company pays you, then from the gains you may glean over the years, and finally takes a percentage of whatever is left of the investment on death. That silent partner is, of course, Uncle Sam. Many times, these TV stories would be different if their results were shown on an after-tax basis.

Getting Started with Mutual Funds

If you know nothing about investing, the best thing to do for most people is to buy a no-load mutual fund that includes both stocks and bonds. No-load funds are the ones that do not charge a fee when you buy them. The fund can still have high internal costs, but, if you stick with the really large investment firms and avoid insurance companies and banks, you'll probably be all right. You won't be able to fine-tune the numbers much, but you can find funds that will suit a variety of circumstances. Some funds invest about 60% of their funds in stocks, which is not a bad distribution for a working person. Others invest about 40% in stocks, which is not a bad distribution for a retired person. Since the funds are continually rebalanced, you get the advantage of some of that buy low, sell high action that everyone would like to achieve.

Some of these mixed funds have very good bond trading departments for the fixed income part of their portfolios. They'll probably do a lot better than you'll be able to do on your own with the nonstock part of your portfolio (unless you are a careful buyer and hold bonds to maturity to avoid additional fees).

A Better Approach with Stock Mutual Funds

You can often improve your performance by selecting one or more stock mutual funds and one or more fixed income investments instead of using balanced funds as discussed previously. We'll later cover fixed income investments, but let's talk about stock mutual funds now.

The lowest-cost stock funds are index funds. You can buy them directly from most of the large investment firms, and you may find them in the list of funds available in your employer's savings plan. The most popular index funds are those that try to duplicate the performance of the S&P 500 index. There are also total market index funds that try to represent the performance of about 5,000 companies in proportion to the current value of the total stock outstanding for each company. That's a good choice for someone who wants to buy only one stock fund. Some people buy a fund representing only small companies and, to spread the risk, put perhaps two-thirds of their stock allocation into the S&P 500 and one-third in the small company index fund. You can't go very far wrong with any of these choices. Many studies show that these approaches using index funds do better than an individual selection of stocks even when selected by a professional. I distinctly remember a trip where I sat next to the chief financial officer of one of the biggest companies in the country. He said he was tired of his money managers who continually failed to get up to the market averages. He was on his way to fire them and invest exclusively in index funds.

If you work with an investment advisor, you will probably move a step up in complexity. You may have a chance of doing slightly better at certain times with the help of expert advice, which is not unimportant to a retiree, but over very long periods, you may not do much better than you would with the preceding simple approach. The advisor may recommend either a foreign or a global fund, both large and small company value funds, as well as both large and small company growth funds. Many of these funds are relatively low-cost index funds, but some are laden with fees and hidden costs. You'll have to ask because it's the kind of information that does not come out voluntarily.

Fees, Loads, and Taxes Can Be Painful!

Unless you are very careful, mutual companies, brokers, money managers, and the government will get more from your investment than you will, especially if you subtract inflation from your after-tax return. It's not always easy to get your fair share. I personally do not like to buy funds through a broker or other intermediate firm or person, and, with few exceptions, I try not to get involved with load funds and/or funds with large portions of their returns subject to ordinary income tax. It's too easy to lose enough points so that the real returns can be negative.

Don't let this discourage you from investing in mutual funds. It's tough to buy or sell anything without paying fees and taxes, and there is no way to escape inflation's devastating effects. The thing that you've got to do is try to make gains penny-by-penny. This means looking carefully at risk, fees, and the tax consequences.

Purchasing Individual Stocks

If you are just getting into investments and want to buy a couple of stocks, my own recommendation is, "don't!" unless you want to consider this play money. Ownership of individual stocks is for people who can obtain significant tax gains and have the time and money to select both a diversified stock portfolio and a fixed income portfolio with proper distribution for their needs. Unfortunately, most people today don't buy a stock for the intrinsic value of the company itself. They buy it because a friend bragged about it or the media touted it or because its recent history looks good.

As a buyer of individual stocks, there are some fundamental things to keep in mind. One of these is that there are as many people who sell at the bottom as who buy at the bottom. There are also as many people who buy at the top as sell at the top. This has to be so because for every buyer there must be a seller. This tells you that 50% of the people are going to be doing the wrong thing in the stock market at any given time. Of course, you hope that your research (which is probably exceeded by staff work in the large investment houses) and your unique signals (which are probably already used by millions of people) will put you in the 50% that sells at the top and buys at the bottom. Good luck! After accounting for costs, only a very small number of people do better than the stock market average, and they usually don't do so for many successive years.

Exchange Traded Funds

There is a new kind of vehicle on the market that is a cross between an individual stock and a mutual fund. It actually may turn out to be better than either. These investments are known as exchange traded funds, or ETFs. The first of these to gain any popularity was the Spider, short for Standard and Poor's Depository Receipts. You can buy these from your broker. Like an S&P 500 index fund, Spiders are baskets of stocks representing the 500 largest companies in the United States.

The big advantage is that you do not have a buildup of unrealized capital gains as happens with mutual funds. This is not very important unless there is a market meltdown when everyone wants to sell. Then the mutual funds, but not the ETFs, must distribute large parts of those capital gains to the remaining fund holders even though those who continued to hold the fund did not sell anything. There is a secondary benefit for people who like to sit at their computer and try to take advantage of what may happen minute to minute. ETFs can be traded any hour of the day, while you can only trade mutual funds at the closing price for the day. The disadvantage of the ETF is its trading cost, which can be higher than a good low-cost index fund.

You can now get ETFs for a significant number of selected market areas, including foreign baskets of stocks from individual countries. Keep in mind, though, that the narrower your focus, the higher the volatility. These are great for those who like to chart stocks and stick by their computer for formula-driven signals to sell or buy, but only a small fraction of people make money doing this.

Fixed Income Investments

If you have less than $100,000 to invest in fixed income investments, look into no-load mutual bond funds. You can get these in short-, intermediate-, and long-term varieties. You can also get these in bond index funds, which are attractive because they have lower costs. Costs for bond mutual funds have to be significantly under 1% or they will badly damage the ultimate value.

If you are in doubt about whether to buy a bond fund that is short, intermediate, or long term, consider intermediate. Short-term bonds have, of course, much lower interest rates. But an intermediate-term bond's interest rate is not that much lower than the long bond's, and it's more resistant to economic interest rate fluctuations. Short-term bond funds are good for money you might need in the near term, but even if you can get checking privileges, you don't want to try and use it as a checking account or you will have far too much work when tax returns are due.

Another kind of mutual bond fund worth comparing to intermediate no-load mutual bond fund is a Government National Mortgage Association (GNMA) fund, which may have competitive interest rates. The underlying securities are home mortgages for which the government guarantees interest and principal payment. That guarantee doesn't mean that you'll get all of your principal back, however, because when new mortgages are added and old ones are paid, your fund's value will gradually change either up or down. Also, any bond fund will change value when national interest rates change.

An alternative to a mutual bond fund is a unit trust or tax-exempt security trust. These are securities that hold baskets of bonds, often with similar maturities. Like ETFs in the stock world, you will not get any surprise from an unforeseen large capital gains distribution. You will get checks for the interest on a regular basis, and, over time, you will gradually get your principal back as the underlying bonds mature or are called. As this happens, your interest checks get smaller, and after the last bond in the trust is gone, your checks stop. The bookkeeping is largely up to you. You won't get as much information as you would from a mutual bond fund.

Purchasing Individual Bonds

For the fixed income part of your taxable account allocation, quality bonds are worth the effort if you have over $100,000 to invest in them. Maturity dates should coincide with your need for cash and should be staggered timewise ("laddered") so that your bonds mature in different years, even if you plan to reinvest the proceeds in more bonds. As tempting as very long term bond rates may be, it's not wise to invest everything in the same maturity. Interest rates will change as economic conditions change, sometimes for the better and sometimes for the worse. It's better to just roll with the punches, that is, buy new bonds when old ones mature and not try to second-guess future interest rates by trading in and out of bonds.

Purchasing bonds directly from a broker is attractive if you are pretty sure that you can hold them to maturity or the call date. Remember that the call date gives the issuer of the bond the right to cash out your bond on that date, and they will do this only when it is to their benefit, and therefore not yours. It's virtually impossible to know how much of the bond's original cost is going into the broker's pocket unless you buy *original issue* bonds. If you ask your broker to confine the search for a bond to original issues, that's the best way to ensure that you got a low-cost purchase. If you hold the bonds until they mature, or are called, you will have no broker's cost on the back end at all.

You want to spread your bonds so that they come from different sources in case an issuer should have financial problems. I buy only bonds that have a high-quality rating (aa or better), and I tend to select bonds that have a high-quality rating on their own without needing insurance to achieve that rating. It is also a good idea to diversify with bonds issued by different industries or government bodies.

Don't try to keep the bond certificates yourself. Hold them in a broker's account so that all of the interest and bond proceeds automatically go into a money market. I learned this lesson the hardest of ways back when you clipped coupons for interest—which in itself was a big pain for both me and the bank. When the bonds were called, it took me six months to discover that they owed me the principal, and then I had to go through all of the mechanics myself to get the money from the issuer. A broker's account will do all of this for you quickly without your effort, and it won't cost you any more.

A relatively new and often unrecognized bond is the federal government's inflation-adjusted I bond, which you can buy from your local bank just like you can buy an EE savings bond. These inflation bonds help you make money from inflation because the interest rates increase with inflation. They also pay better interest than EE bonds. For all practical purposes, you don't have to worry about maturity dates or being called. You pay tax on the income only when you redeem the bond, which you can do at your local bank.

Municipal Bonds

You should not buy municipal bonds (usually called muni bonds) at all unless you are in a high tax category. The general rule of thumb is that the interest rate on muni bonds (or muni bond funds) must be higher than the after-tax return you can get from taxable bonds (or taxable bond funds). For example, if taxable bonds have 7% interest and your marginal tax rate is 40%, your after-tax interest rate on the bonds is $7\% \times (1.00 - 0.40) = 4.2\%$. In this example, if you can get munis of the same quality with rates above 4.2%, consider buying them. If you are in a tax bracket that can benefit from muni bonds but you don't have more than $100,000 for bonds, you may do better buying a good intermediate muni bond fund than trying to buy muni bonds directly.

Incidentally, don't think that muni bond funds are always tax free. You may have some state tax on interest from bonds issued in states other than your own, and periodically you may have capital gains distributions if you have bond funds. In my experience, the worst situation is when the price of bonds falls abruptly. Not only does the value of your fund go down, but also you may have to pay income tax on a capital gains distribution because the bond fund had to unload some of its bonds to meet redemptions that, in turn, triggered capital gains. High muni bond interest can also trigger alternative minimum taxes or taxes on Social Security.

For the Richer Set

For most people, it's better to have stocks in deferred tax accounts than taxable accounts. However, if you have substantial taxable investments and want to leave funds to your heirs, I believe that it's better to have your stocks in the taxable accounts and your bonds in deferred tax accounts. But be aware that rebalancing taxable accounts is usually not tax efficient unless you have some offsetting losses or enjoy gifting stock either to charities or heirs.

Look into tax-managed funds. These require that the fund manager try to off-set gains with losses when selling securities in his or her funds, as well as other practices designed to reduce any taxable distributions, such as charging fees to people who try to get in and out too quickly. These are great vehicles to have in your estate when you die.

You may be tempted by hedge funds and venture capitalists. If you partici-pate, consider it play money, and don't use money that would otherwise be important to your heirs or a charity. If you really want to give money away, con-sider giving money to a charitable gift fund. Donate highly appreciated securi-ties to avoid paying capital gains tax on them. If you do it in large enough bites, say enough money for several years' worth of contributions, you will get bigger tax reductions because of the IRS's mechanization of the "phase out of deduc-tions" for higher-income people.

Real Estate

There are so many real estate investment possibilities that it is hard to make any general comments. I'll tell you about some of the lessons I've learned over the years, though, and later in the chapter we will talk about your home as an investment.

Real estate is practically never a liquid investment; that is, you can't just get cash for it when you want—unless you are willing to take a severe trouncing. The only real estate investments that are really liquid are REITs, or real estate investment trusts. These are publicly traded securities that you can buy through your broker. It is better to buy them in a mutual fund than on an indi-vidual basis because then you get some diversity. Such funds, however, are usu-ally listed as specialty funds that track a very narrow market and therefore can be quite volatile. But they are the easiest way to get a toe into the real estate market.

Personal investments in raw land can be a real bummer, especially if it is not zoned properly or has some other underlying problem. There are almost an infi-nite number of potential problems, including local codes, easements, future use of adjacent land, environmental law violations, covenant restrictions, suscepti-bility to impact fees, assessments, and property tax increases. And even without these kinds of problems, the appreciation on the property often lags behind the cost of ever increasing property taxes. When you go to sell it, it's hard to find a buyer who saw all of the value that you envisioned.

Probably the least liquid part of the real estate market is rental property owned in a partnership. I have a neighbor who not only couldn't sell a partner-ship, but had to work very hard to give it to a charity because most charities would not accept a partnership as a gift. After finding a willing charity, he then had a difficult (and expensive) time getting a value to report on his tax return. Partnership ownership is also a tax headache. The loss limits and tax loss deferrals are too complex to handle here, but they are not favorable to you. Frequently the tax report that you need from the partnership in order to file your own return is so late that you have to file for an extension. And, if your partnership owns real estate in other states, you may have to file income tax statements in several states. Consider such investments very carefully. The salesperson won't offer to tell you about any of these problems.

If your investment is in income-producing real estate that you own directly, at the very least you have a lot of bookkeeping, and, most often, you have maintenance and rent collection problems of some sort. This kind of investment is not for remote owners who don't want to get their hands dirty. If you pass off the management job to professionals, as you might in a resort area condominium, for example, you may lose half of your rent to the management firm. This is an indication of the amount of work involved in managing rental property.

There is a common belief that real estate is a safe investment because property will always appreciate in value. Unfortunately, this isn't necessarily so. I have a former business associate who, earlier in his career, had been an officer of a major industrial company and at one point was worth several hundred million, on paper. He invested substantial amounts in rental properties. There was a severe downturn in the real estate market at the same time he had other demands for cash. He could not sell enough property at a price high enough to make his loan payments or pay the income tax due on all of the accelerated depreciation he had accumulated. Suddenly his several hundred million dollars of assets turned into nothing but debt to the government.

More likely, though, your investment in real estate will be a vacation home. If you rent it out when you aren't using it, there are two good tax positions. The first is if you only use the property yourself for two weeks or less and otherwise rent it. The second is if you rent it out for two weeks or less and then use it yourself the rest of the time. In this latter case, you don't have to pay any income tax on the rent. In between these two extremes, the tax situation isn't so attractive. Also keep in mind that you may have to file a state income tax return if your real estate is in another state, and when you die, you may have to go through probate in that state. Did the salesperson mention those little things? One alternative is to hold the property in a corporation or trust to avoid out-of-state probate. The tax and valuation problems remain, but your shares of corporate stock are what is probated, and only in your state.

Your Home as an Investment

Almost any of the major retirement planning computer programs has an entry for the value of your home and your estimate of its appreciation rate. Before you enter any values here, you want to think about the implications. Counting your home as an asset may mislead you into saving too little or to spending too much.

Middle-aged people who have not saved enough money often say that their home is their major retirement investment. This is much better than saying that their major retirement investment is the weekly purchase of state lotto tickets, but is your home truly a retirement resource? You have to answer this question from your own perspective, but even the most foresighted people can't predict all of the twists and turns ahead in their lives nor the emotional and financial considerations that will apply in the future.

Furthermore, a home is more than something you can just trade in for another investment. You have emotional ties to it, and it meets certain family needs. It is in a neighborhood that you like, or your close friends are nearby. It represents years of your effort in tailoring it to meet your tastes. The furniture, decorations, mementos, and even quirks are things that you have learned to enjoy. Often, it is part of a community that provides a support system to help you when you are in trouble.

A home is a peculiar financial resource. It has no liquidity, and you can't just go out and raise money by selling off a corner of the lot or marketing a room that you think you can do without. You must either sell the whole house, or not sell it at all, although you might be able to take in a renter or borrow on it. After you sell, you must either buy a new home or become a renter. If you are buying, you will probably increase your indebtedness with a larger mortgage than you had before.

Selling a home and buying a new home is always a traumatic experience, but the level of trauma increases as you get older. It's harder to part with things; your living habits get more inflexible, and you must find and get used to new services in your new location, including doctors and medical support facilities. Both my wife and I have gone through these experiences a number of times with our parents. The situation was quite different for her parents than mine, but there was always lots of emotion and trauma.

My parents sold their home several times both to gain some funds from downsizing and to stay close to my sister and her children. My sister was great at setting up all of the mechanical things in advance, such as finding affordable houses to look at, getting lists of local doctors, and so on. But it was a lot of work for her, and the moves were very hard on my parents. Eventually, my mother died; my father sold the last house, and moved into an independent care facility. The downsizing gave him a precious few extra dollars for investment as a practical matter, and the proceeds from the final sale ultimately paid for some of the additional costs at his independent care facility.

My wife's mother raised two daughters on the salary of a waitress and managed to buy a small home at the same time. Needless to say, it was very hard for her mother to consider selling something that had been such a large part of her life and something she had worked so long to achieve. She finally conceded to the pressure of harsh winters and the need for increased medical and personal care assistance and home maintenance work she could no longer do herself. Again, the money she realized from her investment in the family home went into independent and, later, assisted care.

These two cases have something in common: Neither my parents nor my wife's parents used their homes as a source of funds for ordinary expenses. Rather, they were a reserve for things unforeseen.

If you've already retired, what are some things that you can do to realize some return from your home that you can use as a source of funds? A very practical option is to rent out a room. If the home owner is elderly or disabled, it may be a fair trade to provide free or reduced rent in exchange for some home care assistance.

Another option is to take out a home equity loan or refinance the home. Of course the problem with this is that these loans are accompanied with an increase in monthly expenses to make the payments. You're either betting that, on an after-tax basis, you can get more from investing than the lender can get from the interest on the loan, or you're betting that you will die before the whole amount is due, so the remaining debt will be someone else's problem. Unfortunately, you may well lose the bet on both counts and be left with no more options than the probable loss of the home in a sheriff's sale.

Still another option is a reverse mortgage. However, there is no way you can come close to recouping the value of your home this way. The lender has to assume that you will live longer than the average person when setting up the terms. And you will have to pay loan fees. If you are not yet retired and your future plans are based on this option, you might use only 40 to 50% of your home equity (current market value less debt) as an asset in your retirement expense calculation.

If you need some equity from your home for retirement, you may be better off to bite the bullet as early as possible, even before retirement, and really downsize to whatever is the least expensive arrangement you can live with. Then invest the money and meter it out slowly and conservatively over your retirement years. I've seen too many people who wished they had taken these draconian actions earlier.

Investing in a House: Some Economic Facts!

Virtually everyone has to make a decision about investing in a house at some point in life. Early on, it may be the decision to invest in your first house. Sometime along life's way, it may be the decision to buy a vacation home. Late in life, it may be the decision to sell a house and become a renter. Although these choices are often more emotional than analytical, almost everyone tries to put some numbers down to try and quantify the comparisons.

You can use the autopilot methods in Chapter 5 before retirement or Chapter 6 after retirement to help in this decision. For example, if you are trying to decide whether to sell your home and rent when in retirement, you can plug the amount of cash you will get from the sale of your home into the autopilot method and find out whether the increase in your budget will cover the rent you might expect to pay. Or, for a vacation home, you can reduce your investments by its price and see if the budget reductions are more or less than the annual rent you would have to pay a resort for a couple weeks or months of relaxation.

If you use one of the few comprehensive computer programs that are designed to help in these decisions, the most important input you'll need is the appreciation rate assumption. You'll just have to guess at this, but if the appreciation rate must be much more than inflation to justify your decision, you are unlikely to justify the purchase on economic grounds. You've heard of the expression that there are only three things that count in selecting real estate, and they are location, location, and location. Of course, what this really boils down to is appreciation, appreciation, and appreciation.

It's relatively easy to put together some numbers that show a home is a good investment compared with renting an equivalent place for long periods of time, unless, of course, you paid too much or prices are really low when you get ready to sell. In fact, the home becomes a better investment with each year of ownership. That's especially true in times of high inflation.

On the other hand, it's very hard to justify buying a vacation home as an investment unless you use it just a little and rent it a lot. If it is idle most of the year, the appreciation rate has to be much higher than inflation because of the constant drag of property tax, utilities, and maintenance costs. From an investment perspective, an idle house is worth less than money under your mattress. There is practically no way for appreciation to overcome the continual cost drag unless, within a very short period, someone with money to burn makes you an offer you can't refuse.

For the same reason, a house that is much larger than your needs is not a good investment. Yet that's a very common mistake retired people make. They either hold on to a large house in the hopes that their children and families will occasionally visit, or worse, they intentionally buy a larger house for that purpose. Unless you have abundant retirement funds, such actions are very costly.

Overall, the best course for financial planning is not to consider the equity in your home as an investment unless you plan on a sale within a few years— either to downsize to a less expensive place or to rent forever after.

But I Want to Relax!

Those of you with substantial resources who are determined to get good performance from your investments are probably already significantly involved in managing your money and will probably remain so until the time comes when you are willing to pay the price for convenience. I'm one of those people who enjoys managing investments, but I hate the associated tax-accounting work. Even for me, the time may come for a simpler life. This point becomes very important as your age increases, your eyesight dims, and your energy level falls to a fraction of its former self. Then you start looking for someone to manage your money for you.

Alternatives to Paying for Convenience

People who opt for extreme convenience either buy annuities or pay others to manage their money for them. This convenience comes at such a high cost that before doing either of these things in your quest for the simple life, give serious consideration to just getting a good balanced fund and designate that the dividends and capital gains distributions go to a money market fund. As you liquidate, the bookkeeping will be pretty easy, and you'll probably be a lot further ahead. Or, for just a small step up in complexity, buy Standard and Poor's Depositary Receipts (SPDRs) for your stock allocation and I bonds from your bank for your fixed income. Think of it as your own tax-managed mutual fund with you as its highly paid fund manager.

Turning Your Portfolio Over to Someone to Manage

If you're going to pay for convenience, make sure you know how much it is going to cost. If it's costing 2% of your assets each year, you should expect to get an incredible amount of service and performance. If, in addition, you are paying hidden fees for mutual funds or brokers, you start off by giving away the majority of your inflation-adjusted earnings. Elicit some other opinions first from an accountant or certified financial planner.

Fixed-Term or Lifetime Annuities

If you choose to buy an immediate annuity or convert a variable annuity to an immediate annuity, shop around. Rates and quality of insurance vary, so you may be able to get a better deal from a different investment source. (Often you can make a tax-free exchange with another firm using a 1035 exchange. Ask the new firm to help you with the mechanics.) Don't let the salesman imply that your return on investment equals your annual payments divided by your initial investment. Your annual payments are a return of both interest *and principal.* I have a close friend who purchased two immediate term-certain annuities, which then made payments over 20 years. He had been misled about the return to begin with, and to make matters worse, he outlived the date of the last payment by many years, and ended up with nothing. Unless you live significantly longer than your current life expectancy, and you have an annuity that guarantees you payments for life, you can generally do better financially by owning a balanced mutual fund.

Variable Annuities

There are only a few variable annuities that have attractive enough results to consider as reasonable candidates for your money. The best candidate to own a variable annuity is a person who currently is in a high tax bracket; expects to leave the money untouched for a very long period, and cashes out; or annuitizes (converts to a series of fixed payments) many years later when he or she is in a lower tax bracket. If you don't fit this model, make sure you understand why you are making this investment, and then do a lot of comparison shopping. Also keep in mind that it is a lousy investment for highly taxed people to leave to their heirs, who will have to pay not only estate taxes but also income taxes. Not much will be left.

Some Investments to Avoid

I know there are many people who believe that I am dead wrong about some of these, but let me tell you some of the investments that I avoid like the plague at this point in my life: partnerships of any kind, oil drilling, precious metals and gems, collectibles, commodities, any living creature, almost any form of leverage, speculation or gambling, securities with tax complications, anything that cannot easily be sold, and anything that would take much work on my part. No matter what you may tell your spouse, lottery tickets, jewelry, automobiles, boats, and vacation homes are not investments.

The Ultimate Easiest Way

Marry someone younger with good looks, intelligence, energy, and a lot of money. Love and a good personality would be real pluses. If that's not feasible, engage a professional planner or accountant on a fee only basis once a year to look over your investment allocations and living expenses. Go to the appointment with a trusted relative who you believe has some appreciation for the principles in this book. Then have the relative assist in carrying out the professional's recommendations, but keep all of the accounts in your name for your own authorization, and you sign the checks.

CHAPTER 4

Return on Investments

If you want to know the value of money, go and try to borrow some.*

eturn on investment is a very simple concept in principle. It's the practical application of the concept to real-world conditions that provides opportunities for misunderstanding and therefore misrepresentation. We're going to examine a number of details about returns so that you will do a better job of your own planning. This includes some education on how returns are calculated. We will begin with the technical definition of return on investment. Then we'll show you how to measure your own past performance and better estimate what may happen in the future. We'll provide you with returns that you can use in the planning chapters ahead. And, we'll show you some of the tricks used in the finance business to make you think you'll do better than is likely.

Return on investment, or *return* for short, is the remaining key element for your future planning. It's even more important than how long you will live, your future net tax rate, and an accurate estimate of the total value of your current investments or the new amount you will save this year. It is completely dependent on your asset allocation, vehicles, and particular choices of investments— all subjects that we've already covered and are the foundation of your retirement plan. Returns are more important than your other inputs because they are the basis for forecasting your future, and those forecasts will change considerably with just a small change in a return.

Think of returns as the engine that powers your investments. It's like a horsepower measure for an automobile or truck. With too little power, you lag behind. Considering the actual return of a retirement portfolio, a return of 4% is

*Benjamin Franklin.

anemic, sort of like having only 50 horsepower to power a 3,000-pound automobile. People with balanced portfolios might have returns of 6 to 8% over long periods of time. That's about 150 horsepower, or what might be a good trade between power and gas consumption for an automobile. By historical standards, long-term returns of over 10% for a balanced portfolio would be remarkable, more like a 400 horsepower engine in a small car.

Let's start by defining our terms.

What Is Return on Investment?

In its simplest form, return on investment is the same as growth of an investment. Perhaps it's easier to understand if you consider something analogous to a situation you may recognize from your past. Suppose you decided to buy a decorative tree for your backyard. There was one in the nursery about 8 feet high that looked just about right. There wouldn't be many leaves to rake in the fall, and it would fit fine between your house and the fence. The salesman said it would grow only about 10% a year. That didn't seem like much, so you bought it. Let's assume it was 100 inches tall right then. The next fall, it grew 10 inches, just like the salesman predicted. In the second year, still growing at only 10% a year, it added another 11 inches and now was 121 inches tall, or about 10 feet. By the third year, it added 12 inches and now totaled 133 inches high. There are noticeably more leaves to rake. By the tenth year, the height is 259 inches (over 21 feet), and the leaves are definitely irritating. Now 20 years have gone by, the tree is 673 inches (56 feet) tall, and, not only does it seem that you are raking leaves forever, but the branches are now extending over your roof and that of your neighbors.

So it is with returns, except that the growth percentages relate to the growth of your investments where bigger truly is better. Bonds might have a 6% return and stocks a 10% return. One hundred dollars invested in stock at 10% return would be worth $110 at the end of the first year. At the end of the second year, it would be worth $121, just like the tree's height. In 20 years that amount would compound to $673 with a continuous 10% growth.

In real life, neither the tree nor the investment would grow the same percentage each year. However, if we know the beginning number, the end number, and the number of years, we can get an equivalent annual rate that would have produced the same results. That compound rate is what the financial media and mutual funds report for 5 and 10 year results when they cite the performance (think horsepower) of their investments over a period of time. Then they often compare their own performance to the performance of an index calculated the same way.

There's nothing complex or mysterious about how they get the number. They either use a financial calculator, a computer, or a table such as is shown in Figure 4.1. In the case of our examples, the ending value after 20 years was 673 and the beginning value was 100. The growth factor was 673 divided by 100 or 6.73.

Look in the row for 20 years at 10% growth in Figure 4.1, and that's the number you'll see. Consider another example. Suppose someone said that their mutual fund increased by 50% over 10 years. That sounds pretty good, doesn't it? What it really means is that the ending value divided by the beginning value is 1.50. Look in the 10-year row and find the nearest number to 1.50. That's 1.48 in the 4% column. That means the investment grew at a compound rate of about 4%. Not quite as impressive. That's the 50 horsepower car.

There's a reason that I used the horsepower analogy to show the similarity to returns as a measure of power. That's the power of compounding that is illustrated beautifully in Figure 4.1. Let's compare what happens with three examples—an anemic 4%, a representative 8%, and a powerful 12%—by looking at how much an investment would grow over 30 years in each case. So look at the year 30 row of Figure 4.1 and imagine how $1.00 would grow. The 4% investment compounds to $3.24. The 8% investment compounds to $10.10. And the 12% investment compounds to $30.00. Return is a measure of the power of your investments.

Various financial publications call this compound rate various names such as annualized returns or average returns, or sometimes they just call it the return. I don't like to call it an *average* return because it is not the way most people define average, which is the sum of the values divided by the number of items in the group. For example, suppose you had a stock with returns that were +30%, −30%, and +30% in three successive years. The average of those three returns is (30% − 30% + 30%) / 3, which is 10%. But that's not even close to the compound return. In the first year, 30% growth of $1.00 would add $0.30 for a total of $1.30. In the second year, 30% loss would subtract $0.39 leaving $0.91 at the end of that year. In the third year, 30% growth would add $0.27 (rounded) so the ending balance after three years would be $1.18. That's a compound return of under 6% from Figure 4.1. So the 10% average return is considerably higher than the compound (or annualized) return of 6%. That's why I always raise my eyebrows when I hear the word *average* from a financial salesperson. He could be trying to mislead me.

Calculating a Return

Whether you have just a simple savings account or a complex portfolio with many different kinds of investments, return is defined the same way. It's the percentage growth in one year. The tree grew 10% a year. The investments grew 10% a year. If you don't have any deposits or withdrawals during the year, there is a very simple equation that defines return:

$$\frac{\text{Year-end balance} - \text{Start of year balance}}{\text{Start of year balance}}$$

Let's illustrate the equation with the same numbers we used previously. For example, if you started a year with $100 in savings and ended up with $110 at

Growth Factors for Compound Returns

Years	1%	2%	3%	4%	5%	6%	7%	8%	9%	10%	11%	12%	13%	14%	15%	16%	17%	18%	19%	20%
1	1.01	1.02	1.03	1.04	1.05	1.06	1.07	1.08	1.09	1.1	1.11	1.12	1.13	1.14	1.15	1.16	1.17	1.18	1.19	1.2
2	1.02	1.04	1.06	1.08	1.1	1.12	1.14	1.17	1.19	1.21	1.23	1.25	1.28	1.3	1.32	1.35	1.37	1.39	1.42	1.44
3	1.03	1.06	1.09	1.12	1.16	1.19	1.23	1.26	1.3	1.33	1.37	1.4	1.44	1.48	1.52	1.56	1.6	1.64	1.69	1.73
4	1.04	1.08	1.13	1.17	1.22	1.26	1.31	1.36	1.41	1.46	1.52	1.57	1.63	1.69	1.75	1.81	1.87	1.94	2.01	2.07
5	1.05	1.1	1.16	1.22	1.28	1.34	1.4	1.47	1.54	1.61	1.69	1.76	1.84	1.93	2.01	2.1	2.19	2.29	2.39	2.49
6	1.06	1.13	1.19	1.27	1.34	1.42	1.5	1.59	1.68	1.77	1.87	1.97	2.08	2.19	2.31	2.44	2.57	2.7	2.84	2.99
7	1.07	1.15	1.23	1.32	1.41	1.5	1.61	1.71	1.83	1.95	2.08	2.21	2.35	2.5	2.66	2.83	3	3.19	3.38	3.58
8	1.08	1.17	1.27	1.37	1.48	1.59	1.72	1.85	1.99	2.14	2.3	2.48	2.66	2.85	3.06	3.28	3.51	3.76	4.02	4.3
9	1.09	1.2	1.3	1.42	1.55	1.69	1.84	2	2.17	2.36	2.56	2.77	3	3.25	3.52	3.8	4.11	4.44	4.79	5.16
10	1.1	1.22	1.34	1.48	1.63	1.79	1.97	2.16	2.37	2.59	2.84	3.11	3.39	3.71	4.05	4.41	4.81	5.23	5.69	6.19
11	1.12	1.24	1.38	1.54	1.71	1.9	2.1	2.33	2.58	2.85	3.15	3.48	3.84	4.23	4.65	5.12	5.62	6.18	6.78	7.43
12	1.13	1.27	1.43	1.6	1.8	2.01	2.25	2.52	2.81	3.14	3.5	3.9	4.33	4.82	5.35	5.94	6.58	7.29	8.06	8.92
13	1.14	1.29	1.47	1.67	1.89	2.13	2.41	2.72	3.07	3.45	3.88	4.36	4.9	5.49	6.15	6.89	7.7	8.6	9.6	10.7
14	1.15	1.32	1.51	1.73	1.98	2.26	2.58	2.94	3.34	3.8	4.31	4.89	5.53	6.26	7.08	7.99	9.01	10.1	11.4	12.8
15	1.16	1.35	1.56	1.8	2.08	2.4	2.76	3.17	3.64	4.18	4.78	5.47	6.25	7.14	8.14	9.27	10.5	12	13.6	15.4
16	1.17	1.37	1.6	1.87	2.18	2.54	2.95	3.43	3.97	4.59	5.31	6.13	7.07	8.14	9.36	10.7	12.3	14.1	16.2	18.5
17	1.18	1.4	1.65	1.95	2.29	2.69	3.16	3.7	4.33	5.05	5.9	6.87	7.99	9.28	10.8	12.5	14.4	16.7	19.2	22.2
18	1.2	1.43	1.7	2.03	2.41	2.85	3.38	4	4.72	5.56	6.54	7.69	9.02	10.6	12.4	14.5	16.9	19.7	22.9	26.6
19	1.21	1.46	1.75	2.11	2.53	3.03	3.62	4.32	5.14	6.12	7.26	8.61	10.2	12.1	14.2	16.8	19.7	23.2	27.3	31.9
20	1.22	1.49	1.81	2.19	2.65	3.21	3.87	4.66	5.6	6.73	8.06	9.65	11.5	13.7	16.4	19.5	23.1	27.4	32.4	38.3

21	**1.23**	1.52	1.86	2.28	**2.79**	3.4	4.14	5.03	6.11	**7.4**	8.95	10.8	13	15.7	**18.8**	22.6	27	32.3	38.6
22	**1.24**	1.55	1.92	2.37	**2.93**	3.6	4.43	5.44	6.66	**8.14**	9.93	12.1	14.7	17.9	**21.6**	26.2	31.6	38.1	45.9
23	**1.26**	1.58	1.97	2.46	**3.07**	3.82	4.74	5.87	726	**8.95**	11	13.6	16.6	20.4	**24.9**	30.4	37	45	54.6
24	**1.27**	1.61	2.03	2.56	**3.23**	4.05	5.07	6.34	7.91	**9.85**	12.2	15.2	18.8	23.2	**28.6**	35.2	43.3	53.1	65
25	**1.28**	**1.64**	**2.09**	**267**	**3.39**	**4.29**	**5.43**	**6.85**	**8.62**	**10.8**	**13.6**	**17**	**21.2**	**26.5**	**32.9**	**40.9**	**50.7**	**62.7**	**77.4**
26	**1.3**	1.67	2.16	2.77	**3.56**	4.55	5.81	74	9.4	**11.9**	15.1	19	24	30.2	**37.9**	47.4	59.3	73.9	92.1
27	**1.31**	1.71	2.22	2.88	**3.73**	4.82	6.21	7.99	10.2	**13.1**	16.7	21.3	27.1	34.4	**43.5**	55	69.3	87.3	110
28	**1.32**	1.74	2.29	3	**3.92**	5.11	6.65	8.63	11.2	**14.4**	18.6	23.9	30.6	39.2	**50.1**	63.8	81.1	103	130
29	**1.33**	1.78	2.36	3.12	**4.12**	5.42	7.11	9.32	12.2	**15.9**	20.6	26.7	34.6	44.7	**57.6**	74	94.9	122	155
30	**1.35**	**1.81**	**2.43**	**3.24**	**4.32**	**5.74**	**7.61**	**10.1**	**13.3**	**17.4**	**22.9**	**30**	**39.1**	**51**	**66.2**	**85.8**	**111**	**143**	**185**
31	**1.36**	1.85	2.5	3.37	**4.54**	6.09	8.15	10.9	14.5	**19.2**	25.4	33.6	44.2	58.1	**76.1**	99.6	130	169	220
32	**1.37**	1.88	2.58	3.51	**4.76**	6.45	8.72	11.7	15.8	**21.1**	28.2	37.6	49.9	66.2	**87.6**	116	152	200	262
33	**1.39**	1.92	2.65	3.65	**5**	6.84	9.33	12.7	17.2	**23.2**	31.3	42.1	56.4	75.5	**101**	134	178	236	311
34	**1.4**	1.96	2.73	3.79	**5.25**	7.25	9.98	13.7	18.7	**25.5**	34.8	47.1	63.8	86.1	**116**	155	208	278	370
35	**1.42**	**2**	**2.81**	**3.95**	**5.52**	**7.69**	**10.7**	**14.8**	**20.4**	**28.1**	**38.6**	**52.8**	**72.1**	**98.1**	**133**	**180**	**244**	**328**	**441**
36	**1.43**	2.04	2.9	4.1	**5.79**	8.15	11.4	16	22.3	**30.9**	42.8	59.1	81.4	112	**153**	209	285	387	524
37	**1.45**	2.08	2.99	4.27	**6.08**	8.64	12.2	17.2	24.3	**34**	47.5	66.2	92	127	**176**	243	333	457	624
38	**1.46**	2.12	3.07	4.44	**6.39**	9.15	13.1	18.6	26.4	**37.4**	52.8	74.2	104	145	**203**	281	390	539	743
39	**1.47**	2.16	3.17	4.62	**6.7**	9.7	14	20.1	28.8	**41.1**	58.6	83.1	118	166	**233**	326	456	636	884
40	**1.49**	**2.21**	**3.26**	**4.8**	**7.04**	**10.3**	**15**	**21.7**	**31.4**	**45.3**	**65**	**93.1**	**133**	**189**	**268**	**379**	**534**	**750**	**1052**

FIGURE 4.1 Table of growth factors for compound returns.

the end of the year, you would have made $10 on the $100. This is equivalent to 10% return on investment. It's represented by the simple equation:

$$\frac{110 - 100}{100}$$

which equals 0.10 or 10%.

This definition applies to one year only. It's not a compound rate that applies to more than one year. If you plugged in 673 from 20 years of growth, the calculation using this equation would show 5.73 or 573%. That's not the way returns are calculated. The actual returns are on a one-year basis. (Banks and some other institutions often quote rates on a daily or quarterly basis as well as an annualized basis, but we will use only the annual definition.)

In this book, we use the preceding equation to calculate the actual return for every year since 1926 to modern times for groups of securities like large company stocks, corporate long-term bonds, and Treasury bills. There are firms that maintain an annual index for groups of securities like these. We used Global Financial Data at www.globalfindata.com as our source. After calculating the actual returns, we make an inflation adjustment (we'll discuss that later) by using each year's actual inflation. These histories of inflation-adjusted returns are the data that we use in *The Real World* computer program (which you can find at my web site: www.analyzenow.com) to make most of the projections used in this book as well as the information to support the tables used in our preretirement and postretirement plans.

The returns in this book are total returns, that is, they assume that all dividends and interest are reinvested. That's what a mutual fund reports as well. But when you look at a history of stock market prices, it may understate the growth because it simply shows the price of the stock and does not assume the dividend is reinvested. Stock dividends are generally so small in modern terms that this may seem like a small technical difference, but we want to do it the correct way. That means that we have to get our data from a source that shows total returns. You can find these in references at your library or on the Internet, but you'll have to look for that word *total*.

Before discussing the inflation adjustment, let's just look at some basic data for a single year, because you will see some valuable information about how well you are doing with your investments, and whether you should change your investment approach and/or the inputs into your retirement plans in Chapter 5 or 6.

Are Your Investments Good Choices or Dogs?

Do you know your return for last year? The chances are that you don't have the foggiest idea how your investments performed in the past. Yet that knowledge is the only way to determine whether you could use some better investments and to ensure that your retirement plan has any validity. A group of older ladies in an investment club got very famous when they wrote a book about their fantastic investment performance titled *The Beardstown Ladies' Common-Sense Investment Guide: How We Beat the Stock Market—And How You Can Too.* They astonished the world in numerous radio and TV interviews and even published an audiocassette. Their performance was much better than professional stock pickers. Unfortunately, it turned out that they didn't know how their investments actually performed. An accountant looked at their investment performance and found that their actual return was 9.1%, not the 23.4% the book reported. The book now comes with an insert explaining that they made an error—and the book doesn't sell very well now since they actually underperformed the market. Most of the increase of their investments came from the new money they were adding each year, not from the growth of their securities.

I've found that most people think their returns are better than they actually are. I've seen people fire their financial managers after they found out how they were really doing by using the simple calculations that follow. First, we'll show you the equation used to make the calculation. Then we'll show you an easy way to use a table to determine how well you did for those of you who are averse to using your grade school math.

It can be confusing to determine your actual return when you are making deposits and/or taking withdrawals during the year, as the Beardstown ladies found out the hard way. Like them, if you made some very large deposits, your year-end balance might be influenced more by the deposits than by the growth of the investments. Of course, the reverse is true if you were taking out money. In a moment we'll show you how to determine your return with a simple table, but those of you who are interested in using an equation to calculate the return for your own investments last year might like to use the one that follows. Unlike the previous simple equation for returns, this gives an approximate return when you have deposits and withdrawals. It would have saved the Beardstown ladies a lot of embarrassment. Here it is:

$$\frac{\text{Year-End Balance} - \text{Start of Year Balance} - \text{Deposits} + \text{Withdrawals}}{\text{Start of Year Balance} + (0.5 \times \text{Deposits}) - (0.5 \times \text{Withdrawals})}$$

To illustrate the equation with numbers, if we had a mutual fund that started the year at $100,000 and ended the year at $110,000 after deposits totaling $3,000 and withdrawals totaling $7,000, the return on investment would be:

$$\frac{110,000 - 100,000 - 3,000 + 7,000}{100,000 + (0.5 \times 3,000) - (0.5 \times 7,000)}$$

which equals 14,000 / 98,000 = 0.143 (rounded) or 14.3%.

This is the return for one year. The main limitation on the equation is that it does not work for periods more than one year. You have to make a new calculation for each year. Because you are now in the real world, each year will have a different return. Some years you will get negative numbers when the stock market goes to pot.

There is a curious thing about this equation. That result is always a before-tax return even if the only withdrawal you made was to pay taxes. I've seen this point misrepresented several times in newspapers and magazine articles that used an equation similar to this. The reason it is always a before-tax return is that the equation doesn't know or care how you used the withdrawal. For example, if the $7,000 was for someone's new car, the return would be 14.3%. If the $7,000 was used to pay income taxes, it's still a 14.3% return. The same number can't be a before-tax return at the same time it is an after-tax return.

The equation works for a single security, or a group of securities, or for all of your investments taken together so that you can get a composite. It works for taxable investments, tax-exempt investments, and deferred tax investments. I now generally make a calculation for all of my investments together just to see if I'm better or worse than the assumptions I've used for my forecasts. I expect it to be better than my assumptions when I know the stock market has done well, and vice versa. If you've turned your investments over to someone else to manage, you might want to do two analyses: one for stocks and one for fixed income investments. If your stocks are way behind the S&P 500 index for the year, start looking for someone else to do the investing for you. If the return on your fixed income investments is more than 1% below one of the intermediate-term bond indexes you can find in almost any financial magazine, you ought to find out why.

If you are averse to using equations you can estimate your own before-tax return for last year using Figures 4.2 and 4.3. To see how this works, let's use the same example demonstrated by the equation: the year-end balance was $110,000 and the starting balance was $100,000, and you deposited $3,000 and withdrew $7,000 for tax and other uses.

Your annual deposits and withdrawals are easy to calculate. In fact, most bank, broker, and mutual fund reports tabulate the values for you. You can make the calculation from the information in the reports they send you. An employer savings plan would certainly report withdrawals (because they are taxable) but might not give you deposit information. However, you know the percentages of your wages and your employer's contribution to the plan, so it's easy for you to calculate.

About the only time you might have to do some more calculations is if you have bonds or stocks where the interest or dividends come in the form of a check directly to you instead of an automatic deposit. If you do not reinvest any part of those interest or dividends, you must count the part you did not reinvest as withdrawals. The same thing is true if you own rental property. If you do not reinvest the rent in property tax, loan payments, or maintenance costs, and

Calculate Your Own Return

Row	Item	Value
1	Year-end balance	110,000
2	Starting balance	100,000
3	Ending balance divided by starting balance (Row 1 divided by Row 2)	1.10
4	Deposits	3,000
5	Withdrawals	7,000
6	Net deposits (Row 4 minus Row 5)	− 4,000
7	Net deposits divided by starting balance (Row 6 divided by Row 2)	− 0.04
8	Return from Figure 4.3 using inputs from Row 3 and Row 7	14%

FIGURE 4.2 Find out if your own return for last year met your expectations.

spend the money for your personal expenses or income taxes, the amount used for personal expenses and income taxes would also be considered a withdrawal. This is because the equation assumes you will always reinvest your returns. If you don't, they are withdrawals by definition.

Now enter your numbers in Figure 4.2 as we have done. In this example, withdrawals are larger than deposits, so Row 6 is a negative number. That means that Row 7 is also a negative number.

Now use the values from Row 3 and Row 7 to find the nearest row and column respectively in Figure 4.3. In the example, at the intersection of 1.10 and −0.04 we find 14%. That's the return for the year. You can do this in just a few minutes, and it's well worth the effort to do at least once, as you'll see shortly. After doing it once, it's likely you'll do it again next year.

Because year-end investment balances reflect any investment costs that were deducted along the way, you've already accounted for their costs. However, the return may not include the costs of your investment manager unless she took her cut from your investments. However, if you got out your checkbook and paid her from your wages, Social Security, or pension, you'll need to make an

Are Your Returns As High As They Should Be?

Row 3 from Figure 4.2	Net Deposits Divided by Initial Balance (Row 7 from Figure 4.2)															
	-0.10	-0.08	-0.06	-0.04	-0.02	0.00	0.02	0.04	0.06	0.08	0.10	0.12	0.14	0.16	0.18	0.20
0.70	-19%	-21%	-23%	-25%	-28%	-30%	-32%	-35%	-37%	-40%	-42%	-45%	-47%	-50%	-53%	-56%
0.73	-16%	-18%	-20%	-22%	-24%	-27%	-29%	-31%	-34%	-36%	-39%	-41%	-44%	-46%	-49%	-52%
0.77	-13%	-15%	-17%	-19%	-21%	-23%	-26%	-28%	-30%	-33%	-35%	-38%	-40%	-43%	-45%	-48%
0.80	-10%	-12%	-14%	-16%	-18%	-20%	-22%	-24%	-27%	-29%	-32%	-34%	-37%	-39%	-42%	-44%
0.83	-6%	-8%	-10%	-12%	-15%	-17%	-19%	-21%	-23%	-26%	-28%	-30%	-33%	-36%	-38%	-41%
0.87	-3%	-5%	-7%	-9%	-11%	-13%	-15%	-18%	-20%	-22%	-25%	-27%	-29%	-32%	-34%	-37%
0.90	0%	-2%	-4%	-6%	-8%	-10%	-12%	-14%	-16%	-19%	-21%	-23%	-26%	-28%	-31%	-33%
0.93	3%	1%	-1%	-3%	-5%	-7%	-9%	-11%	-13%	-15%	-18%	-20%	-22%	-25%	-27%	-30%
0.97	6%	4%	3%	1%	-1%	-3%	-5%	-7%	-10%	-12%	-14%	-16%	-19%	-21%	-23%	-26%
1.00	10%	8%	6%	4%	2%	0%	-2%	-4%	-6%	-8%	-11%	-13%	-15%	-17%	-20%	-22%
1.03	13%	11%	9%	7%	5%	3%	1%	-1%	-3%	-5%	-7%	-9%	-11%	-14%	-16%	-19%
1.07	16%	14%	12%	10%	9%	7%	5%	3%	1%	-1%	-4%	-6%	-8%	-10%	-12%	-15%
1.10	19%	17%	16%	14%	12%	10%	8%	6%	4%	2%	0%	-2%	-4%	-7%	-9%	-11%
1.13	22%	21%	19%	17%	15%	13%	11%	10%	8%	6%	4%	1%	-1%	-3%	-5%	-7%
1.17	25%	24%	22%	20%	18%	17%	15%	13%	11%	9%	7%	5%	3%	1%	-1%	-4%
1.20	29%	27%	25%	24%	22%	20%	18%	16%	14%	13%	11%	9%	6%	4%	2%	0%
1.23	32%	30%	28%	27%	25%	23%	22%	20%	18%	16%	14%	12%	10%	8%	6%	4%
1.27	35%	33%	32%	30%	28%	27%	25%	23%	21%	19%	18%	16%	14%	12%	10%	7%
1.30	38%	37%	35%	33%	32%	30%	28%	27%	25%	23%	21%	19%	17%	15%	13%	11%
1.33	41%	40%	38%	37%	35%	33%	32%	30%	28%	26%	25%	23%	21%	19%	17%	15%
1.37	44%	43%	41%	40%	38%	37%	35%	33%	32%	30%	28%	26%	24%	22%	21%	19%
1.40	48%	46%	45%	43%	42%	40%	38%	37%	35%	33%	32%	30%	28%	26%	24%	22%

FIGURE 4.3 Find your return for the year.

adjustment. For example, if you were paying an investment manager a 1% fee from your wages, reduce the return in Figure 4.3 by 1%.

Using Returns to Give Your Investments a Tune-up

Remember, return is a measure of power. This makes your return a great way to determine if you need a tune-up, or a new financial manager—or earned bragging rights if you beat the market. Of course, you could separate your investments in separate classes of stocks and fixed income investments, do an analysis on each, compare the results with an index for that class, and see where you are underperforming the market. But there is an easier way.

Do the calculation for all of your investments together and compare the return with that of a balanced mutual fund that has roughly the same distribution of stocks and fixed income investments as you do. Almost all of the large mutual fund companies offer balanced funds. Their web sites will describe the funds and show the returns from last year, or you can phone them and ask, or you can get your public librarian to help you locate the information. If your performance is more than 1% lower than the fund, you should consider the benefit of some different investments. If you have a financial manager, you should make at least a one-time check that the manager's investment choices aren't far behind the market. If they are, get a new manager. In fact, if you are paying someone to manage your money, the least you should do is make this kind of a check once a year. If you are paying someone to do some work for you, you need some kind of review to see that you are getting your money's worth. That's what this does.

There's one other thing you can do with your own actual return for last year. That's to determine whether your actual returns can support the financial plans for your future as determined in Chapter 5 for preretirement plans or Chapter 6 for postretirement plans, or plans you make using some commercial source, or plans developed by a professional. As a practical matter, all of these plans are based on some assumptions about future returns, but actual annual returns will often be either much higher or much lower.

You hope that the real world actual returns will average out to a larger number than your plan's assumption, rather than a smaller one. In the meantime, you have no choice but to compare your actual return to the assumption in the plan. If your actual return for the year is higher, just relax. Don't try to adjust the return in your plan upward. There will be down years that follow, almost as surely as night follows day. If your actual return is lower than assumed in the plan, you should show some concern. Try to determine if the reason was a significant market drop by comparing what happened with some balanced fund, or whether your investment choices just weren't that good. If it's the latter, read Chapter 3 again to see if you want to make some changes. On the other hand, it's impossible to always have the best investment choices for any given year. So the best course might be to see what happens at the end of this next year. If your actual return is lower than the assumptions in your plan for two years in a row, seek some professional help or at least some consolation.

To compare your actual results with those in the plans in Chapter 5 or 6, you will have to adjust your return for inflation.

Accounting for Inflation: Real Returns

Now that you know how to calculate your actual returns, you are ready to move on to the next critical step. The returns you just calculated were not adjusted for inflation. What is more important than the actual return on investment is the *real* return. This is an inflation-adjusted return that factors in that a dollar is worth less at the end of the year than it was at the beginning of the year. Think back to the very first example we looked at: $100 growing at 10% to $110 at the end of the year. That $110 is not worth what $110 would buy at the beginning of the year. With 10% inflation, it would be worth only $100 so the real return would be zero. There are years when the actual returns are low and inflation is high, so the real return can be negative. That's bad news, but it's a fact of life.

Often people approximate the real return by subtracting inflation from the actual return. However, the more precise equation is

$$\frac{\text{Actual return \% } - \text{ Inflation}}{100\% + \text{Inflation}}$$

For example, if the actual return was 10% and inflation was 4%, the real return would be

$$\frac{10\% - 4\%}{100\% + 4\%}$$

which is 6% / 104% = 0.058 (rounded) or 5.8%. This is the number you want to compare with the returns on which your Chapter 5 or 6 plans are based.

So, how do you find out the inflation rate for last year? The easiest way to do this is to call your local public library and ask if they can give you the Consumer Price Index–Urban. If you are already on Social Security, you can calculate inflation yourself because your payments increase by the amount of inflation each year. Just divide this year's Social Security by last year's and you'll get a number that will look something like this: 1.035. Then subtract 1.000 and get 0.035. Then multiply by 100 to get a percent: 3.5%.

Some of you may wonder why we use real returns, that is, inflation-adjusted returns, in our planning. We do it to see a projection based on the current value of our money, not some highly inflated dollars in the future. Some planning programs don't do this, but to prevent you from being misled, they should correct your results with an inflation adjustment in the end. In that case, you'll get the same results using our real returns, assuming the last minute inflation adjustment uses exactly the same period of history for the inflation adjustment and for the returns. To illustrate this, suppose you had an investment of $100 that grew at 10% a year for 20 years. Figure 4.1 shows that would grow to $6.73 \times \$100$, or $673. Now suppose there was 4% inflation over that same 20 years. You could go back to Figure 2.6 to find the factor to convert $673 into today's dollar values: $0.456 \times \$673 = \$307$. Or you could convert the actual return of 10% into a real return based on 4% inflation of 5.8% as we worked with before. A financial calculator would show that $100 compounds at 5.8% to $307. You get the same answer either way. You won't get the same answer if you approximate the real return by just subtracting inflation from the actual return. In this example, the approximate real return is 6.0%. Using 6.0%, Figure 4.1 shows that the $100 would compound to 3.21 times $100 over 20 years, or $321, which would be somewhat optimistic.

We chose to use real returns in our methods because it eliminates the problem of ensuring that the inflation correction was for the same period as were the returns. When a program asks you to enter your own return and inflation as two separate entries, it's unlikely that they will be for the same time period. Often, I see programs citing a return based on 30 to 40 years of history while they recommend an inflation rate based on more than 70 years of history. That's really misrepresenting historical security performance.

Using Real Returns in Your Retirement Planning

Virtually all retirement planning articles, books, and even computer programs gloss over the choice of a return on investment for your analysis. Unfortunately, that single item has more to do with your projection than practically any other piece of information. Typically, a reference will give you a place to insert your own assumption about your return, but they'll often suggest that you use 8% before retirement, 7% after retirement, and 3% inflation. These would give you approximately a 5% real return before retirement and 4% after.

Some computer programs attempt to shed more light. For example, there are retirement planning programs that will suggest specific returns depending on your allocations. There are more sophisticated computer programs that attempt to give you some statistical visibility so that you'll introduce some conservatism. For example, they'll say that if you want 70% confidence, use a return of so much. Virtually none of these programs reflects your costs of owning these securities nor the fact that equivalent returns are lower for retirees because of reverse dollar cost averaging. And often the inflation assumption is inconsistent.

In all of the work I've done so far, I've come to the conclusion that some very simple computations will give returns that you can use confidently in a plan for the future—if future returns follow similar patterns to those in the past. Now that's a big *if*, so I believe that postretirement analysis should be conservative for that reason alone. That's especially true if the last few years had extraordinary returns that sent markets to really uncomfortable highs.

Preretirement Returns

When you develop your preretirement plan in Chapter 5, you will need to base that plan on a real return up to the point you retire and another real return after you retire. There are several reasons why you need separate returns for each period. First of all, you can take more investment risk before retirement so your allocation can have more stock than after retirement. But there is another important difference. You need more than a 50/50 chance that your plan will succeed after you retire. You can be more optimistic before retiring because, if things don't come out just right, you can always work longer and save more. But those aren't options after you retire.

Our preretirement planning procedure requires that you determine returns for each period consistent with the allocations for each period. However, since all historical return information is based only on compound growth (think preretirement), not on continual withdrawals (think postretirement), we will show you how to modify the postretirement return accordingly.

You can either use Figure 4.4 to calculate the real returns that represent your particular allocation of investments, or you can use the more general representation in Figure 4.5 that, unless you have unusual investments, may save you

Calculate the Real Return for Your Plan

1	2	3	4	5
Security	**Investment Value**	**% of your Investments**	**Representative Real Returns**	**Real Return (col. 3 x col. 4)**
Stocks	$50,000	50%	6.7%	3. 35%
Growth stocks			9.0%	0%
Other equities				
Bonds	$40,000	40%	2.4%	0.96%
Other fixed income investments				
Money markets, T-bills, short-term CDs, etc.	$10,000	10%	0.8%	0.08%
Totals	$100,000	100%		4.39% 4.4% rounded
		Estimated costs (for funds, brokers, etc.)		1.5%
		Net real return (total real return minus estimated costs)		2.9%

FIGURE 4.4 Use this table to calculate a net real return on your investments.

Amount of Stock Largely Determines Real Returns

Stock as % of Investments	Portfolio Description				Long-Term Real Return Excluding Costs
	Large Co. Stock	Growth Co. Stock	Long-Term Corp. Bonds	Treasury Bills	
90%	50%	40%	0.0%	10%	7.0%
80%	50%	30%	10.0%	10%	6.4%
70%	50%	20%	20.0%	10%	5.7%
60%	50%	10%	30.0%	10%	5.1%
50%	50%	0%	40.0%	10%	4.4%
40%	40%		50.0%	10%	4.0%
30%	30%		60.0%	10%	3.5%
20%	20%		70.0%	10%	3.1%
10%	10%		80.0%	10%	2.7%
0%	0%		90.0%	10%	2.3%

FIGURE 4.5 By calculating the percentage of stock in your portfolio, you may find a representative real return listed that you can use for retirement planning. Remember to subtract investment costs before using the real return in your plan.

some work. There is no way to make a perfect prediction of the future even with Figure 4.4 because there are so many bumps, twists, and turns ahead that the future can't be exactly like the past. We use the retirement autopilot method to help make the corrections, but extremely bad real return estimates will make it harder for the autopilot to steer you back on course.

We'll start with Figure 4.4, because that is what we used to get the numbers in Figure 4.5 anyway, and it's a great tool to include special investments or values of your own choosing. In column 1 of Figure 4.4, we list some securities that are useful to represent the allocations of almost anyone's investments. Actually, Figure 4.4 is very easy to use if you performed an allocation analysis using Figure 3.7. The first entry is "Stocks." You can use this to represent all of your stocks, or if you think it makes more sense, you can break stocks down into some other categories. Many people have funds for small cap stocks and/or growth stocks, so we've made a place for those in the next entry, "Growth stocks." Then you can add a row or more for whatever special equity entries you want, as long as you have some basis for estimating a long-term real return for them. "Bonds" could be used to represent all of your fixed income investments, or, again, you could use an extra row or two to represent particular fixed income investments where you can estimate their long-term real returns. "Money markets" is the last entry, which could also represent other short-term fixed income investments such as lower-interest CDs or a credit union savings account.

In column 2, list the total value of each type of security. Add them up in the last row. In column 3, show the investments in each category as a percent of the total investments. For example, $50,000 stock is 50% of $100,000 total investments. Of course, all of the individual percentages in column 3 should add up to 100%.

Column 4 is important because it lists the historical data for long-term real returns for each type of security. We have entered the long-term real returns from 1926 through 1994. We did not include the past few years because they may prove to be optimistic in light of what Alan Greenspan calls their "irrational exuberance." Furthermore, leaving them out may prove to add a touch of conservatism, which I've found is often the best thing when your plans require looking far ahead. We used the S&P 500 index to represent stocks, the corporate long-term bond index to represent bonds, and the short-term Treasury bill index to represent money markets. The growth stock real return is a little arbitrary since we chose a small stock value to represent this category. If you add your own special entries, you will have to add your estimate of their long-term real return in column 4.

Remember, you are trying to estimate a real return that will represent the future. Since it's unlikely you'll be able to do that with any precision, it's important that you don't enter real returns that are too optimistic, that is, too high. I know there are people who think that the financial world is now on a new paradigm of high growth forever, and that the government will prevent both market meltdowns and high inflation. I don't. But it's your plan.

To determine your real return in column 5, simply multiply the value in column 3 by the values in column 4 in each row. Then add up the values to get your total real return. Keep in mind, though, that this return is based on security indexes alone. It does not account for the costs of buying, owning, and selling securities, so it's likely to overstate the return you'll actually get on your investments. At the present time, these costs average about 1.3% for mutual funds, but you can look in the prospectus of a fund and find its costs. If you pay a money manager the typical 1% or higher, you would have to add that. If you buy stocks and bonds from a broker, add up the broker's charges for a year and divide by the investment value at the beginning of the year. Full service brokers often charge 2% for both buying and selling, so if you bought and sold a security in the same year, it would cost you 4%. Using a discount broker or trading on the Internet is usually much less expensive, but you may not receive as much information and the reports might not look as good. Subtract the total of the costs as a percent of your investments as in the example and get the real return you will use in your retirement plan. Alternately, if you subtract your costs for individual funds or investments from each of the returns in column 4, you'll get a more accurate result than using an estimated cost adjustment in column 5.

Unless you want to use some special investment categories in Figure 4.4, you may find it easier just to look at Figure 4.5 and find a real return based on indexes for the most common kind of securities. The returns on a group of investments are largely determined by the percentage of stock in the portfolio. Over the long term, a portfolio with a large stock percentage is going to have a higher return than a portfolio with a small stock percentage. Figure 4.5 illustrates this point. Each portfolio consists of the securities listed. If your allocation is similar to any of these models, you are likely to get good results using the real return shown in the last column. Just don't forget to subtract an estimate of your costs as a percent of your investments before using the real return from the figure in your plan.

Theory versus Reality in Preretirement Planning

All retirement plans are based on some kind of theory. Almost all plans use a constant real return that, in turn, produces a perfectly smooth theoretical forecast of the future. There are no ups and downs as in real life. We're now going to show how theory and reality compare so that you understand the basis for the retirement autopilot method.

Let's look at some very long term examples in Figure 4.6 to illustrate the difficulty of making a long-term projection without redoing the analysis each year. Figure 4.6 shows the investment balances (adjusted for inflation) for a person who saved $5,000 a year (also inflation adjusted) starting at age 30 and ending at age 70. We chose a portfolio like the 70% stock portfolio in Figure 4.5 and made a theoretical projection using the same type of calculations as in a commercial or professional planning program. The theoretical projection used a 5.7% real return from Figure 4.5 and gave, of course, a perfectly smooth prediction.

Then we made a number of runs using *The Real World* program with the same asset allocation and annual deposits where we changed the starting year of the scenario each time. We chose the years 1939 and 1949 as starting years for each of the scenarios in Figure 4.6 to illustrate some points. This may seem like ancient history, but we have to go back to get 40 years' worth of data. In the long run, the 1949 case concluded where the theory said it would. Even the 1939 case came close. But, ouch! Look what happened in between. The 1949 scenario produced returns that were often far short of the theory, so retirement at an early age would have been out of the question. On the other hand, the 1939 case looked fantastic until just before age 65 when investment balances really plummeted. At age 55, the 1939 scenario provides about three times the balance as the 1949 scenario. That's why one generation might have it easy and the next not.

There are some important lessons here besides the fact that you can get very

Theory versus Reality for Preretirement Savings

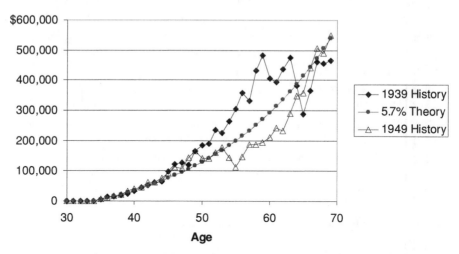

FIGURE 4.6 Theoretical and historical inflation-adjusted investment balances for someone saving $5,000 a year in a portfolio with 70% stock.

lucky or very unlucky. The first lesson is that you are not going to be able to pick an exact return to predict the future, but there is some tolerance for a mistake in preretirement planning. For example, you could work a couple more years and get back on target. Another lesson is that you should really make a new plan each year to bring you back to your target more quickly. Still one more lesson is that it wouldn't hurt to use a slightly more conservative (smaller) real return in your planning. The effect would be a plan that would tell you to save a little more each year, which would give you some protection against the possibility of 1949-like scenario consequences.

Theory versus Reality in Postretirement Planning

As in the preretirement case, theory and reality are quite different. Only the difference is much larger in postretirement planning. To illustrate this, we're going to look at a theoretical prediction and then a couple of doses of reality. All start with a person retiring early at age 55 so that we can see some rather long histories. The theoretical equations are built into financial calculators and commercial computer retirement planning programs. To determine the amount of money you can spend annually, you enter your investment balance, the number of years you want your investments to last, and your real return assumption. (As a fine point, these calculations also require that you designate whether withdrawals will be made at the beginning or end of the year. By calculating the withdrawals both ways and taking an average, you get a very good approximation for withdrawals being spread uniformly through the year instead of being bunched up either at the beginning or end of the year.) The reality cases come from *The Real World* program.

We're going to use a case of a 55-year-old starting retirement with $1 million and attempt to make the maximum withdrawals that the theoretical model says should last 30 years. In the case of a retiree, we'll use a more conservative allocation than for the preretirement case we just reviewed. Here the allocation consists of 50% stocks, 40% bonds and 10% T-bills. Figure 4.5 shows a return of 4.4% for that mix, so we plug that into a financial calculator or retirement planning program and find that we can withdraw $59,400 annually and end up with a zero balance in 30 years. The $59,400 is increased each year to compensate for inflation. We'll use that inflation-adjusted $59,400 withdrawal in all of the projections in Figure 4.7, both theoretical and real.

Figure 4.7 should produce no surprises. The theoretical case once again is a nice smooth curve that is more or less in the middle of the historical cases, one of which starts in 1953 and the other in 1963. These particular starting years are not extremes. There are about as many starting years that look better than the 1953 case as there are years that look worse than the 1963 starting case. The 1963 history is just an example of a scenario that turns out worse than the theory expected. This is what I call the *dark side.* The money runs out at age 73 after only 18 years instead of the 30 years it was supposed to last. The 1953 scenario represents cases that came out better. It's the *bright side.* In that luckier scenario, the money would last until the retiree was 88 years old. I don't believe that a serious retiree would want to count on the future being on the bright

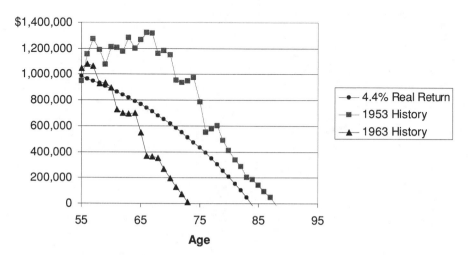

Theory versus Rea ity for a Retiree

FIGURE 4.7 Theoretical and historical inflation-adjusted investment balances for a retiree withdrawing $59,400 a year.

side. A retiree must have some insurance for the dark side, particularly when the 1953 case is not unique. Although almost half of the possible starting years were below the theoretical line based on 4.4% real return, almost one-quarter of the possible starting cases looked about as bad as or worse than the 1953 historical case. I don't think a retiree would want to take a significant chance that the investments would run out 10 or more years early.

The way to add more conservatism to the theoretical analysis is to assume a lower return. After trying a large number of different possibilities, I've concluded that retirees will do well to divide any estimated real return by 2 to get results that will be conservative for a major part, but not all, of dark side results. In fact, let's see how that fares in Figure 4.8 using one-half the real returns for the theoretical case: 2.2% instead of 4.4%. When we make our calculations using a 2.2% real return, the maximum annual withdrawal would be $45,400 instead of $59,400. That's a big difference, but it's what is required to represent the dark side. There are still roughly about 20% of the starting years where results can be worse than the theory, but the retirement autopilot method will be able to pull the retiree out of a crash dive and stretch the money farther than shown in Figure 4.8. It will mean reduced withdrawals late in life, but that's the real life consequence for a streak of years with bad returns.

Using the Web or a Commercial Computer Program? Be Careful!

A popular retirement planning method is to get on the Internet, find a web site with a simple retirement planning program, enter a few numbers, and, *bang*, out comes an answer. The problem is that most of these simple programs are set

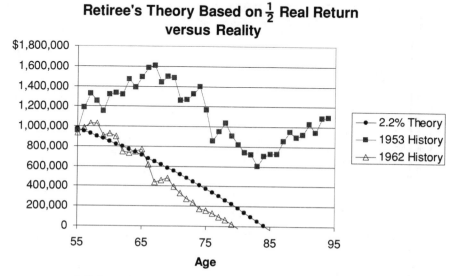

FIGURE 4.8 Inflation-adjusted investment balances for a retiree withdrawing $45,400 each year. The theory here uses one-half the real return of Figure 4.7.

up so that a return is already entered as a default value that, in my view, is an optimistic look at past results. Even those with a step up in complexity that are based on mixed portfolios of your choice most often suggest returns for the mix that are optimistic by historical standards and don't provide plans with any capability of coping with the results that may be less than average. The same thing is true of inflation. Often the default value doesn't even correspond to the historical period from which stock and bond returns come. That combination can be deadly. There are still some sites that don't account for taxes when they should, and practically no sites remind you to enter the costs of investment services.

Conservatism is important to a retiree. I have been surprised by how many people want to see the dark side of a retirement analysis. That's a projection of what will happen if you find yourself in the bottom half of future performance. Remember that most of the time, default returns are based roughly on a 50% chance that you will be above the projection and a 50% chance that you will be below the projection. Unfortunately, when costs and inflation are underestimated, you are already being forced into the bottom 50%. Then when you consider that these are withdrawal scenarios, not the savings scenarios on which return histories are based, there is much less than a 50% chance that your actual investment performance will meet your plan's objectives. But even without those glaring errors, there is so much variation in returns that a person should probably say, "I want an 80% (or whatever) chance of making sure I have enough money by historical standards in withdrawal scenarios."

Of course, no one can predict what future returns on investment will be, but with all of the supposed sophistication in the financial analysis area, you'd think that the programs would realistically report the kind of historical returns that would be useful for financial projections. Instead, we see simple market index results without any reductions for costs, statistical conservatism, or the fact that returns are lower when you are withdrawing money than when you are accumulating it. Use of these kinds of returns in a retirement projection can be downright misleading!

There are now several web sites that are doing some simulations to look at the dark side. Financial Engines made some of the early attempts, followed by T. Rowe Price and some others. Though not perfect (and nothing ever will be), they are showing retirees that they cannot spend as much money in retirement if they want more than a 50% chance that their money will hold out. It's interesting to read the material on the chat sites that comment about these matters. Virtually all of the comments are from retirees who have trouble accepting that they are probably spending too much money now. They don't know how to do the more complex analysis themselves, so they refer to other results from major financial firms, software vendors, or web sites that give them the answers they want to hear.

To represent how a particular portfolio might have performed in either a preretirement or postretirement scenario historically, it is better to use different types of returns. Postretirement returns should be more conservative, not only to give you a better than 50% chance of your money lasting, but also because withdrawal scenarios, where you are regularly taking money out of your accounts rather than making deposits into them, react badly to irregular returns and inflation.

To illustrate the problems with the majority of the simplistic programs on the Web as well as many commercial software programs, let's look at a sample result and then compare that with a couple of real-world cases. Our example will be for a person with $200,000 investments at age 45 who retires at age 65 after saving $10,000 each year as adjusted for inflation. This means the then-year dollars of savings will go up each year by the amount of inflation. State and federal income taxes average 16%. The retirement resources are all invested in a relatively conservative portfolio: 50% in large company stocks with 1.5% costs, 40% in long-term corporate bonds with 1% costs, and 10% in money markets with 0.3% costs. These are all in deferred tax accounts, and the portfolio is rebalanced continuously to keep the allocations constant.

Typically, the web site would recommend doing your calculations with a 7% return (or sometimes even higher) and 3% inflation for this allocation. It would show investments building to over $700,000, running out of money at age 85, and a spending level of about $52,000 before tax or $43,700 after tax. The web program then produces an incredibly smooth investment profile as shown in Figure 4.9. Of course the investments run out exactly as predicted.

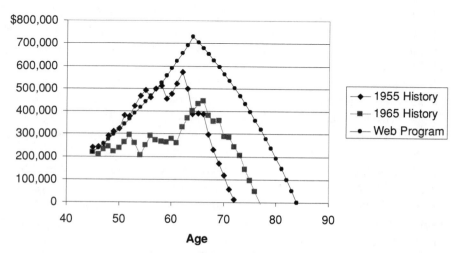

Simple Web Programs Don't Reflect Reality

FIGURE 4.9 Historical and theoretical inflation-adjusted investment balances for a 45-year-old retiring at age 65.

Figure 4.9 also shows some real-world histories for the same set of investments but this time we are accounting for costs and using the actual historical returns and inflation for each of the years in the scenarios. One of these starts in 1955 and the other in 1965. There are always some people who look very carefully at charts, so we should explain that the investment balances are for the end of the year shown; that's why the first year has a balance greater than the starting amount of $200,000 and the last year is the end of age 84, that is, the 85th birthday. There is nothing special about these two particular years. The are just representative of many of the possible scenarios. When we did historical simulations for each year starting in 1926 and going forward, only those that started in 1932 and 1933 did better than the web program results.

It's not hard to see how optimistic the typical default values are for most retirement programs. If you insist on employing them, at least use a conservative return for the retirement phase to allow for investment costs and reverse dollar cost averaging. It's the primary reason why we believe you should use about one-half of the real return you would otherwise calculate for postretirement planning.

Reverse Dollar Cost Averaging

Perhaps you have heard of *dollar cost averaging*. Financial analysts know that if you regularly save a fixed dollar amount every month, you often accumulate larger investment balances in a market where the prices are varying. The theory is that when the market has fallen, your dollars buy more shares, while when the market is high, you buy fewer shares for the same monthly amount. What no one talks about is the poor retirees who are not saving a fixed amount each month; they are withdrawing a fixed amount instead. The net result is that they most often deplete their balances early because they are cashing in a large number of shares when the market is low and only a few shares when it is high. This is exactly the opposite to what any investor would like to do.

The easiest way to demonstrate this is with a simulation. A very simple demonstration of reverse dollar cost averaging was shown in Chapter 1, Figure 1.4, where we had one loss year followed by a big gain year. We'll use a little more realism this time and show both how dollar cost averaging helps the saver before retirement and how it hurts the retiree after retirement even though both have exactly the same market conditions.

To demonstrate the simulation, we need to illustrate a case with returns that go up and down. Figure 4.10 shows a highly idealized case with varying returns as well as one that has constant returns of 7%. Constant returns represent the dream world of most planners. When you look at the varying returns, you'll note that the peaks are much greater than the valleys. That's because it takes a much bigger positive return to offset a negative return and still end up with 7% compound return at the end of 10 years. That's what we want, though, to make

Constant and Varying Returns

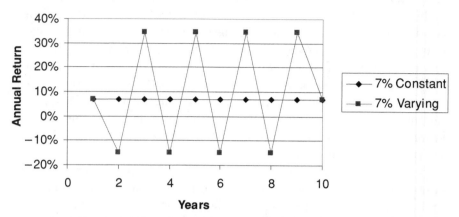

FIGURE 4.10 Constant and varying return scenarios, each of which compounds to 7% at the end of 10 years.

a fair comparison: both cases ending up with 7% compound return. The standard computation for returns reported by mutual funds assumes an initial deposit with no other deposits except dividends until the end of the period, so it is here: The same amount deposited in either the varying return or constant return investment grows to the same value at the end of 10 years so that they both have a 7% compound return.

Returns influence the stock market price per share. With a 7% constant return, the price per share will steadily increase, as shown in Figure 4.11. But

Stock Market Prices Change

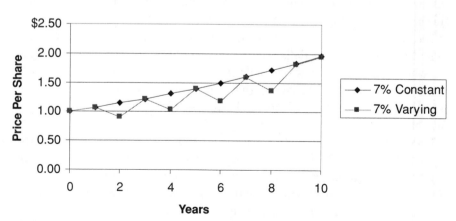

FIGURE 4.11 See how the stock price changes when returns vary compared with steady returns.

the figure also shows what would happen to the price per share in the varying return conditions of Figure 4.10. Note that in the years where the return drops, the price per share also drops. That's exactly what happens in the stock market. Price and return are inseparably linked. Of course, the real market isn't this idealized and has some emotion mixed in.

Let's now take a look at how dollar cost averaging helps savers who put in a constant amount per month. We're going to make this very simple by assuming that the saver put in $1,000 each year. In Figure 4.12, we see that the case based on varying returns provides a larger balance than the one with constant returns. In fact, the ending balance has a compound rate of over 9% instead of 7%. This is the benefit of dollar cost averaging.

But there's a balance in all things. While the regular saver benefits from varying returns, more often than not the person who is taking money out of the stock market on a regular basis gets hurt. Let's look at that in Figure 4.13. In this case we start with a beginning investment balance of $7,000 and withdraw $1,000 each year. In the constant return case the investment lasts the retiree for the full 10 years. This is the planner's dream. In the real world of varying stock prices, the retiree is broke after 8½ years. That's because it's so hard for a retiree to recover from taking out too much when the market is down even though the annual returns over a long time compound to the same return as the planner's dream.

To be able to take out $1,000 each year for 10 years, the retiree would have needed an initial balance of $7,794 with varying returns. That translates to a 4.8% return, much less that the planner's dream of a constant 7% return. This is a painful fact. Yet it's not recognized in any planning analysis I've seen, except

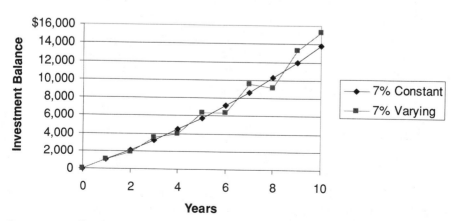

FIGURE 4.12 Varying returns usually help savers achieve larger investment balances over time.

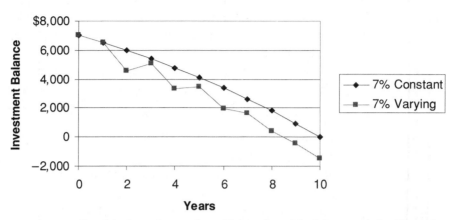

Reverse Dollar Cost Averaging Hurts Retirees

FIGURE 4.13 People who make regular withdrawals get hurt in a market with varying prices.

as an inherent thing that occurs for those few programs that actually work through real-world scenarios.

A Logical Explanation of Reverse Dollar Cost Averaging

For those who don't like to follow math demonstrations, here is a logical explanation for the reverse dollar cost averaging principle. For every buyer of stock, there must be a seller. Each trade had a unique price agreed to between the buyer and seller. That price determines the return of the stock. Now if a regular buyer of stock gets a higher than average return using dollar cost averaging, then the person on the other side of the transaction, who is selling the stock on a regular basis, must be getting a lower than average return. That's because the return of all traders must average that determined from the history of stock prices. If that were not so, everyone would be doing better than average. This is a zero sum game. For every winner, there must be a loser. The loser is the retiree who is regularly withdrawing money.

Be Wary of Compound Growth Projections!

Retired people often attend retirement seminars conducted by financial planners, brokers, insurance agents, financial firms, mutual fund companies, asset managers, tax experts, accountants, publishers, and estate lawyers. Over the years, I've probably attended a hundred of these to assess the ideas and knowledge of the speakers. Some of these people I've heard several times because it's more fun to watch them than to attend a movie. Although these sessions are all meant for retirees, not all are about retirement planning even though they may be advertised that way. They are all about selling something.

The pitch often begins by noting the remarkable performance of the stock market, often using relatively recent information heavily biased with the huge returns of recent years. I'll not use any of the most flagrant examples, but I'll go back to some notes I made in a seminar in the mid-1990s for a theme I've heard over and over again. The speaker started by noting that the average return for the S&P 500 from 1926 until then was 12.2%. (Before 1957, the index had 90 stocks.) That seemed a little high to me, so after the seminar I went to the library to check it out. It's true that the average was 12.2%, but that number was the sum of all of the returns divided by the number of years.

That's not a fair average to measure stock performance. You have to use a compound return to get the true performance, just as we did in Figure 4.1 where we take the ratio of the ending price to the beginning price and look on the table in the row with the number of years involved. Compounding takes more of a beating than an *average* when the market goes down. In this case, the compound return was really 10.2%, not 12.2%.

What about costs? Well, to the speaker's credit, it turned out he was recommending low-cost funds with only about 0.5% costs, while many planners actually sell funds with high front-end loads and high costs that include a commission back to the planner. But, the firm he was with charged a fee of 1% (as we found out later in a question from the audience concerning how he got paid). Anyway, that's a total of 1.5% cost each year. Subtract that from the 10.2%, and we're down to 8.7%. I imagine that most of his audience was in the 28% tax bracket, and the returns he was quoting didn't include taxes, which would reduce the return to 6.3%. So now the true return is starting to look more like 6.3%, not 12.2%.

After telling us about the 12.2% return, the speaker took out his financial calculator, and using numbers he already knew by heart, calculated that $1,000 would grow to almost $10,000 in 20 years, and for those who might live another 20 years, would grow to almost $100,000 at the end of the 40th year. Wow! The audience gasped. Then he pointed out that was just from the first $1,000. Those results could be repeated every year with every new deposit of another $1,000. These people were going to get rich.

Well, maybe in the theoretical world. What would the more realistic 6.3% return produce in 20 years, or in 40 years? The answer is that $1,000 would compound to $3,300 in 20 years and $11,500 in 40. All of a sudden, we don't have such a good pitch any more. Who wants an investment that will grow to those miserly levels?

Still, reality has not set in. Over those same period of years from 1926 through 1994, I found that inflation was 3.1%. Using the same equation to adjust for inflation that we saw earlier, the real return here is (6.3% − 3.1%) / 103.1% / 3.1%, which just coincidentally equals the inflation rate. Inflation took away almost half of the actual return. How does $1,000 compound at 3.1% over those same periods of time? The answer is that the investment will really be worth about $1,800 in 20 years and $3,400 in 40 years. But didn't the salesman say almost $100,000? He was high only by about by 2,800%! In real life, we don't get rich that quick.

Compounding is a powerful thing. The trick is to save the money for a long time and keep the government and too many financial services from taking a big dip. If you put $1,000 away for a grandchild in a tax-managed S&P index fund with a 10.2% return and only 0.2% costs, the before-tax return would be 10%. If you don't move the money from fund to fund, the chances are good that you could avoid most taxes until your death. After 65 years, that $1,000 would grow to $490,000. When you die, all of the prior capital gains growth is forgiven for tax purposes, but let's assume that you gifted the stock, so your grandchild would have to pay capital gains taxes. If the grandchild doesn't cash the stock in all in the same year, she might get by with a 10% capital gains or even lower. That still leaves $441,000, which really sounds like a lot until you consider inflation. Inflation of 3.1% would reduce its value to a modest $61,000. Even so, you have still provided some significant retirement money for your grandchild.

Paul Merriman, a great public speaker and founder of the Merriman funds, tells the hypothetical story of a Roman who, 2,000 years ago, invested one penny in a savings account at 3% interest. That would compound to $470,000,000,000,000,000,000,000,000 over those 2,000 years, which is more money than there is in the whole world today. Of course, with just 3% inflation, over 2,000 years, it would be worth just one penny today.

The message in all of these lessons is clear. Returns that don't account for inflation are *terribly* misleading. Returns without cost considerations are almost dishonest. Returns that don't allow for taxes, either along the way or in the end, deny reality.

Let's face it, someone selling a financial product is likely to show the results in the most favorable light possible. Most people don't believe that there is more than one way to look at financial results, so they assume that what they see is gospel. There are often many ways to present financial information, and these are all studied carefully by marketing organizations and management before a public release. A seminar speaker has thought about many alternative ways to get people interested. Look for the lessons you have learned here. You'll see rosy investment scenarios with a whole new perspective.

CHAPTER 5

Preretirement Planning

Three things are necessary for the salvation of man: to know what he ought to believe; to know what he ought to desire; and to know what he ought to do.*

In this chapter we're going to show you how to complete a winning retirement plan for those who have not yet retired. (If you are already retired, you can skip right over this and go to Chapter 6, unless you are like many retired people who feel that their adult children need some pointers that you'd like to pass on.) You already have developed a good foundation for your plan. You understand that you need to be prepared for some adversity ahead because you will have financial surprises including such things as the stock market occasionally going to pot, inflation not always being low, and tax rates possibly increasing.

However, to help protect yourself from these things, you have, by following the logic in Chapter 3, included the first three elements of a plan: You have (1) chosen an allocation of securities that fits your needs, risk tolerance, and cash requirements, (2) selected the best vehicles for your own tax considerations, and (3) outfitted these vehicles with investments that you feel you can manage. These give you a solid departure point.

The final steps in your plan are in this chapter. Ultimately, you want to know when you can afford to retire and how much to save each year, not just to meet your retirement goals, but for other things along the way as well. We're not only

*Thomas Aquinas, *Two Precepts of Charity,* about 1250.

going to show you how to come up with quantitative answers, but offer you a planning system that can cope with the inevitable changes ahead. To get to this end point, you are going to have to pass through some "gates." My wife and I are inveterate skiers. When skiers race, they must wind their way through gates before they get to the finish line. If they miss a gate, they are disqualified and lose, no matter what their speed. I'm going to use that same analogy here to show you the gates through which you must pass to develop your own winning retirement plan.

Gate 1. The first step is to get a rough idea of your future retirement income by considering both your current retirement investments and the amount you are saving annually. We'll show you how to do this using what I call the quick and dirty method. After you've done this analysis, it's possible that you may decide that, at least for now, you are saving enough. However, from experience, I've learned that most people find they have to do more. Also, when you get within nine years of retirement, you cannot afford to be cavalier about your retirement plan, so quick and dirty is just too rough for a serious plan. At that point you'll need to head for the next gate, and you should start doing an analysis once a year.

Gate 2. If you are getting close to retirement, or if you are disappointed in the forecast from quick and dirty, you are ready to go for the next gate. This requires that you determine how much you will need on an annual basis in retirement as well as a rough guesstimate of infrequent expenses such as a new automobile. We are going to show you some different ways to analyze your retirement needs with progressively greater degrees of accuracy. The closer you get to retirement, the better your information needs to be. As you approach retirement, it often happens that you must face a great reconciliation. That's where you must decide whether you want to increase your preretirement savings or find out how to live on a much smaller budget.

Gate 3. The third step is understanding how retirement age affects retirement resources that do not come from savings. Of course, those items are Social Security, a pension if you are eligible, and possibly an annuity. Retiring at a later age helps improve Social Security benefits, especially for a surviving spouse, and there can be an even greater benefit to delaying retirement for those who get a pension. We'll explain some of those mechanics so that you can include them in your estimates.

Gate 4. The fourth step is doing a detailed analysis using the retirement autopilot to calculate how much you should save on an annual basis. As you might expect, it depends on some things you have already established for your retirement plan, namely, the allocation and selection of investments. This will employ a new level of technology in retirement planning, one that will help you deal with a rough-and-tumble stock market performance as you near retirement.

Gate 5. One more refinement is necessary to complete your plan. That's to nail down your future retirement date. We'll show you how to do that as well as evaluate an early retirement offer, in case you are precipitously faced with that decision as so often happens when companies downsize or enter into a merger.

This will complete your preretirement plan. Now you have your asset allocation, the best vehicles for your tax considerations, investments that you feel competent to manage, a reconciliation between the amount you must save now and what you can spend in retirement, and a likely retirement age. That gives you the knowledge you need to implement a winning retirement plan.

Gate 1. Quick and Dirty

The first thing that it's good to do is to see if your current savings approach is roughly headed in the right direction. This is easy to do with a quick and dirty analysis. I call it *quick and dirty* because (1) it's really a fast way to make a retirement projection, but (2) it reduces your ability to customize the data in order to gain simplicity. However, if you are satisfied with the result, and you are more than about nine years from retirement, you can stop after completing the quick and dirty analysis and not go any further until next year. When you are less than nine years from retirement, you should use the more comprehensive retirement autopilot method. I've provided tables that will let you use quick and dirty up to within three years of retirement for those who are still very uncertain about their future plans but would like a ballpark estimate anyway.

Quick and dirty isn't a custom-tailored plan, as the autopilot method is, but that doesn't mean it is a lightweight method. If your circumstances are close to one of the particular "canned" allocation scenarios it uses, you can get very accurate results with it. These canned scenarios represent three different kinds of investors: aggressive, moderate, and conservative. Behind the results for each kind of investor is a model portfolio that is divided into two parts: one for the buildup of investments during the preretirement years and another more conservative part for the retirement years, which assumes that you will reduce your stock allocation after you retire. (We'll describe these scenarios when you get to the step in the method where you must select one.) The returns for each scenario are based on historical statistical results that model a 50% chance of accumulating enough savings before you retire and roughly an 80% chance that, once you do retire, your investments would last 25 years. These percentages mean that you would have succeeded in 50 or 80% of all possible scenarios from 1926 to 1995. The reason for using only a 50% preretirement probability is that you always have the opportunity of working a little longer or saving a little more before you actually retire. The reason for using a higher postretirement probability is that once you retire, your ability to add to your savings is very limited, so you want high confidence that you are not going to run out of money long before you die.

Before you begin your quick and dirty analysis, you are going to need to gather some information, including the total of your retirement investments, the amount you are saving each year, a Social Security Personal Earnings and Benefit Estimate Statement (PEBES), and a pension estimate from your employer if you are eligible for a pension. If you have earned any Social Security retirement benefits, you should be getting a PEBES every year automatically from the Social Security Administration, but if you've lost yours, just call 1-800-772-1213 for another copy. Once you've gathered your information, you are ready to begin your analysis. We will guide you through the steps using some sample data. See Figure 5.1.

Step 1. Enter the current balance of any investments you expect to use for retirement. If you know part of your existing investments will be used for something other than retirement, such as children's college costs, subtract the current cost of those items from the current value of your total investments to approximate the investments dedicated to retirement. For example, if your current investment balance was $500,000 but you thought you might use $80,000 for children's college expenses, then you would enter $420,000, as in the example in Figure 5.1.

Step 2. Multiply your gross wages (paycheck before deductions) times the number of pay periods in a year. If you are currently receiving any of the following, count them as wages: alimony, child support, government support payments, annuity, or a pension. Do not count interest, dividends, or rent as wages. If your gross wages each month were $5,000, you would enter 12 × $5,000, or $60,000 as in our example.

Step 3. Divide Step 1 by Step 2.

Step 4. Savings here means your annual additions to investments. Savings, by our definition, includes *only* savings that come from wages and employer matching funds. If you were saving $400 per month and your employer was contributing $200 per month, you would multiply $600 × 12 months for $7,200. Savings do not include any savings that you might be making from interest, dividends, or rent payments. If you are using any part of interest, dividends, or rent payments for your current support, subtract that part from the savings you took from wages. If the amount you are spending from interest, dividends, and rents exceeds the amount you are saving from wages, stop here and get professional help with your plan. You are using the wrong color ink for an income analysis.

Step 5. Divide your annual savings by your annual wages and multiply by

100 to convert to a percentage. In the example, that's $100 \times \$7,000 / \$60,000$, or 12%.

Step 6. Our tables require that you use a number of years until retirement that is any one of the following: 3, 6, 9, 12, 15, 20, 25, or 30. (This is one of the reasons this method is not as good as the retirement autopilot method. However, if one of those numbers matches your intentions, it accurately projects the

Use Quick and Dirty to
Estimate Your Retirement Income

Step	Item	Example
1	Retirement investments.	$420,000
2	Current annual wages.	$60,000
3	Investments divided by wages. (Step 1 divided by Step 2.)	7
4	<u>Annual</u> savings. (Don't include returns from investments.)	$7,200
5	Annual savings as % of annual wages. (100 times Step 4 divided by Step 2.)	12%
6	Years until retire.	9
7	Aggressive, moderate, or conservative investor.	Moderate
8	Value from following figures closest to inputs above, e.g., use Fig. 5.4 for 9 years. Under Moderate, get 0.52 using Steps 3 & 5 inputs above. (See text.)	0.52
9	Step 2 times Step 8.	$31,200
10	Annual Social Security & COLA pension.	$12,000
11	Annual fixed pension times current age as %.	$10,000 x 56% = $5,600
12	Estimated retirement income. (Step 9 plus Step 10 plus Step 11.)	$48,800

FIGURE 5.1 Follow these quick and dirty steps to estimate your before-tax income in retirement.

future of our model portfolios.) Pick the number from this list that is closest to the number of years you are from retirement.

Step 7. Decide whether you are an aggressive, moderate, or conservative investor. This choice establishes the model investment portfolios. The details behind these assumptions are in Figure 5.10, but basically, an aggressive investor would be someone who has an allocation with about 75% stock before retirement and 60% during retirement. (We always assume you will adjust your allocation after you retire to a more conservative mix.) A moderate investor is someone who has an allocation with about 50% stock before retirement and 40% during retirement. And a conservative investor would have an allocation of about 25% before retirement and 20% during retirement. We'll assume that the person doing this analysis decides that 50% stock is close to his current allocation, so we enter "Moderate." These canned portfolios are rather crude by comparison to the more customized ones used in the retirement autopilot method, but they are a lot better than many of the quickie programs you'll find on the Internet or in magazine articles on retirement planning.

Step 8. Now you will have to refer to one of the tables on the following pages (see Figures 5.2 through 5.9), depending on the number of years you selected in Step 6. In this case, Figure 5.4 represents the 9 years we entered in our example. Choose the section for aggressive, moderate, or conservative investors that you entered in Step 7. Pick the row for the nearest value to Step 3 (that's 7 in the example) and look in the column with the nearest savings rate to Step 5 (12% in the example). For our sample moderate investor, the result is 0.52.

Step 9. Multiply Step 2 times Step 8. That's $60,000 × 0.52 in our example, or $31,200. This is the annual before-tax retirement income from your investments. Behind this analysis is the growth of your investments until retirement, and then a subsequent constant inflation-adjusted annual withdrawal ($31,200 in this case) that will use up your investments after 25 years of retirement.

Step 10. Look in your Social Security PEBES for the amount that best matches the age you might retire. You will have three choices on that form: age 62, full retirement age, and age 70. (The full retirement age for Social Security is gradually creeping up from age 65 to age 67.) The report will show a monthly amount. If you are married, add 50% more, or add your spouse's payments to yours if that will give a larger amount. Then multiply by 12 to get your annual value, or $12,000 in the example. The simplifications used here to estimate your spouse's future Social Security benefits are not as fined-tuned as in the retirement autopilot method, but they will do just fine with nine or more years until retirement.

If you will get a COLA pension, just add it to the Social Security amount. If you get a COLA pension with a cap of 2 or 3% maximum growth per year, put one-half of it with Social Security and the other half with fixed pensions below.

Step 11. Calculate your annual fixed pension (if any). Most employers give their employees an annual estimate of this benefit for retirement. If not, ask for an estimate. Let's say the annual amount was $10,000. Now multiply that value times your age expressed as a percentage. In the example, we have a 56-year-old person. Therefore, we multiply the $10,000 by 56% and get $5,600. The reason for doing this is that a fixed pension is worth only a fraction of a COLA pension (remember Figure 1.1).

Step 12. Add Steps 9, 10, and 11. This is your estimated before-tax income in retirement. If you subtract income tax from that number based on your retirement net tax rate, the remainder is approximately how much you can spend in that first year of retirement, and its value will be worth approximately the same dollar value as it is today.

In the historical simulations we ran using these sample data, your $48,800 per year retirement income would have lasted for 25 years in roughly 80% of all possible retirement scenarios from 1926 on. After that, you would have only a pension and Social Security because you would have used up your investments. If you use the more detailed autopilot method, we won't ever let you use up your investments, but the annual amounts you can spend will gradually decline to lower values each year.

Let's look at this example a little more. Suppose you estimated that your net tax rate (remember Chapter 2) would be 10%. Then you would have $48,800 less $4,880 tax or $43,920 for retirement expenses. You can compare that with your current take-home pay, which probably excludes most of your taxes, savings, Social Security deductions, and so on. In the example, if $43,920 is greater than your current annual take-home pay, you are probably going to be able to enjoy the same kind of lifestyle that you have now or perhaps even better. In that case, you might not need to go further in your analysis.

However, that seldom happens. As a practical matter, most people who reach their 50s find that they are far short of their needed retirement savings and don't have a pension to help. They end up with three choices: (1) Retire at an older age and/or take a part-time job. (2) Try to save more money each year and invest it better. (3) Think about how they can reduce their need for income when they are retired. Quick and dirty will help you evaluate the second of these choices (see Figure 5.10), but the retirement autopilot method will help you evaluate all of your options.

3 Years Until Retirement
Investment Factors

AGGRESSIVE

Investments Divided by Wages	Annual Savings as % of Wages							
	3%	6%	9%	12%	15%	18%	21%	24%
1	0.06	0.07	0.07	0.08	0.08	0.09	0.09	0.10
2	0.12	0.13	0.13	0.14	0.14	0.15	0.15	0.16
4	0.24	0.25	0.25	0.26	0.26	0.27	0.27	0.28
6	0.36	0.37	0.37	0.38	0.38	0.38	0.39	0.39
8	0.48	0.48	0.49	0.49	0.50	0.50	0.51	0.51
10	0.60	0.60	0.61	0.61	0.62	0.62	0.63	0.63
12	0.72	0.72	0.73	0.73	0.74	0.74	0.75	0.75
16	0.95	0.96	0.96	0.97	0.97	0.98	0.98	0.99
20	1.19	1.20	1.20	1.21	1.21	1.21	1.22	1.22

MODERATE

Investments Divided by Wages	Annual Savings as % of Wages							
	3%	6%	9%	12%	15%	18%	21%	24%
1	0.06	0.06	0.07	0.07	0.08	0.08	0.08	0.09
2	0.11	0.12	0.12	0.12	0.13	0.13	0.14	0.14
4	0.22	0.22	0.23	0.23	0.24	0.24	0.24	0.25
6	0.32	0.33	0.33	0.34	0.34	0.35	0.35	0.36
8	0.43	0.44	0.44	0.44	0.45	0.45	0.46	0.46
10	0.54	0.54	0.55	0.55	0.56	0.56	0.57	0.57
12	0.64	0.65	0.65	0.66	0.66	0.67	0.67	0.68
16	0.86	0.86	0.87	0.87	0.88	0.88	0.89	0.89
20	1.07	1.08	1.08	1.09	1.09	1.09	1.10	1.10

CONSERVATIVE

Investments Divided by Wages	Annual Savings as % of Wages							
	3%	6%	9%	12%	15%	18%	21%	24%
1	0.05	0.06	0.06	0.07	0.07	0.07	0.08	0.08
2	0.10	0.11	0.11	0.11	0.12	0.12	0.13	0.13
4	0.20	0.20	0.21	0.21	0.21	0.22	0.22	0.23
6	0.29	0.30	0.30	0.31	0.31	0.32	0.32	0.32
8	0.39	0.40	0.40	0.40	0.41	0.41	0.42	0.42
10	0.49	0.49	0.50	0.50	0.51	0.51	0.51	0.52
12	0.59	0.59	0.59	0.60	0.60	0.61	0.61	0.62
16	0.78	0.78	0.79	0.79	0.80	0.80	0.80	0.81
20	0.97	0.98	0.98	0.99	0.99	0.99	1.00	1.00

FIGURE 5.2 Find your investment factor if you are 3 years from retirement.

6 Years Until Retirement
Investment Factors

Investments
Divided by
Wages

AGGRESSIVE
Annual Savings as % of Wages

Wages	3%	6%	9%	12%	15%	18%	21%	24%
1	0.08	0.09	0.10	0.11	0.12	0.13	0.14	0.15
2	0.15	0.16	0.17	0.18	0.19	0.20	0.21	0.22
4	0.29	0.30	0.31	0.32	0.33	0.34	0.35	0.36
6	0.42	0.43	0.44	0.45	0.46	0.47	0.49	0.50
7	0.49	0.50	0.51	0.52	0.53	0.54	0.55	0.56
8	0.56	0.57	0.58	0.59	0.60	0.61	0.62	0.63
10	0.70	0.71	0.72	0.73	0.74	0.75	0.76	0.77
12	0.83	0.84	0.86	0.87	0.88	0.89	0.90	0.91
14	0.97	0.98	0.99	1.00	1.01	1.02	1.03	1.04

Investments
Divided by
Wages

MODERATE
Annual Savings as % of Wages

Wages	3%	6%	9%	12%	15%	18%	21%	24%
1	0.07	0.08	0.09	0.10	0.11	0.12	0.13	0.13
2	0.13	0.14	0.15	0.16	0.17	0.17	0.18	0.19
4	0.25	0.25	0.26	0.27	0.28	0.29	0.30	0.31
6	0.36	0.37	0.38	0.39	0.40	0.41	0.42	0.43
8	0.48	0.49	0.50	0.51	0.52	0.53	0.54	0.55
10	0.60	0.61	0.62	0.63	0.64	0.65	0.66	0.67
12	0.72	0.73	0.74	0.75	0.76	0.76	0.77	0.78
15	0.89	0.90	0.91	0.92	0.93	0.94	0.95	0.96
18	1.07	1.08	1.09	1.10	1.11	1.12	1.13	1.14

Investments
Divided by
Wages

CONSERVATIVE
Annual Savings as % of Wages

Wages	3%	6%	9%	12%	15%	18%	21%	24%
1	0.06	0.07	0.08	0.09	0.09	0.10	0.11	0.12
2	0.11	0.12	0.13	0.14	0.15	0.16	0.16	0.17
4	0.22	0.22	0.23	0.24	0.25	0.26	0.27	0.28
6	0.32	0.33	0.34	0.34	0.35	0.36	0.37	0.38
8	0.42	0.43	0.44	0.45	0.46	0.47	0.47	0.48
10	0.53	0.53	0.54	0.55	0.56	0.57	0.58	0.59
12	0.63	0.64	0.65	0.66	0.66	0.67	0.68	0.69
16	0.84	0.85	0.85	0.86	0.87	0.88	0.89	0.90
20	1.04	1.05	1.06	1.07	1.08	1.09	1.10	1.10

FIGURE 5.3 Find your investment factor if you are 6 years from retirement.

9 Years Until Retirement
Investment Factors

Investments Divided by Wages

AGGRESSIVE
Annual Savings as % of Wages

	3%	6%	9%	12%	15%	18%	21%	24%
1	0.10	0.11	0.13	0.15	0.16	0.18	0.20	0.22
2	0.18	0.19	0.21	0.23	0.24	0.26	0.28	0.29
3	0.26	0.27	0.29	0.31	0.32	0.34	0.36	0.37
4	0.33	0.35	0.37	0.39	0.40	0.42	0.44	0.45
5	0.41	0.43	0.45	0.47	0.48	0.50	0.52	0.53
6	0.49	0.51	0.53	0.54	0.56	0.58	0.60	0.61
8	0.65	0.67	0.69	0.70	0.72	0.74	0.75	0.77
10	0.81	0.83	0.85	0.86	0.88	0.90	0.91	0.93
12	0.97	0.99	1.00	1.02	1.04	1.06	1.07	1.09

Investments Divided by Wages

MODERATE
Annual Savings as % of Wages

	3%	6%	9%	12%	15%	18%	21%	24%
1	0.08	0.10	0.11	0.13	0.14	0.15	0.17	0.18
2	0.15	0.16	0.18	0.19	0.21	0.22	0.24	0.25
3	0.21	0.23	0.24	0.26	0.27	0.29	0.30	0.32
5	0.34	0.36	0.37	0.39	0.40	0.42	0.43	0.45
7	0.47	0.49	0.50	0.52	0.53	0.55	0.56	0.58
9	0.60	0.62	0.63	0.65	0.66	0.68	0.69	0.71
11	0.73	0.75	0.76	0.78	0.79	0.81	0.82	0.84
13	0.86	0.88	0.89	0.91	0.92	0.94	0.95	0.97
15	0.99	1.01	1.02	1.04	1.05	1.07	1.08	1.10

Investments Divided by Wages

CONSERVATIVE
Annual Savings as % of Wages

	3%	6%	9%	12%	15%	18%	21%	24%
1	0.07	0.08	0.10	0.11	0.12	0.14	0.15	0.16
3	0.18	0.19	0.21	0.22	0.23	0.25	0.26	0.27
5	0.29	0.30	0.32	0.33	0.34	0.36	0.37	0.38
7	0.40	0.41	0.43	0.44	0.45	0.47	0.48	0.49
9	0.51	0.52	0.54	0.55	0.56	0.58	0.59	0.60
11	0.62	0.63	0.65	0.66	0.67	0.69	0.70	0.71
13	0.73	0.74	0.76	0.77	0.78	0.80	0.81	0.83
15	0.84	0.86	0.87	0.88	0.90	0.91	0.92	0.94
17	0.95	0.97	0.98	0.99	1.01	1.02	1.03	1.05

FIGURE 5.4 Find your investment factor if you are 9 years from retirement.

12 Years Until Retirement
Investment Factors

Investments Divided by Wages	AGGRESSIVE Annual Savings as % of Wages							
	3%	6%	9%	12%	15%	18%	21%	24%
0	0.02	0.05	0.07	0.10	0.12	0.15	0.17	0.20
1	0.12	0.14	0.17	0.19	0.21	0.24	0.26	0.29
2	0.21	0.23	0.26	0.28	0.31	0.33	0.36	0.38
3	0.30	0.32	0.35	0.37	0.40	0.42	0.45	0.47
4	0.39	0.42	0.44	0.47	0.49	0.51	0.54	0.56
5	0.48	0.51	0.53	0.56	0.58	0.61	0.63	0.66
7	0.67	0.69	0.72	0.74	0.77	0.79	0.82	0.84
8	0.76	0.78	0.81	0.83	0.86	0.88	0.91	0.93
9	0.85	0.88	0.90	0.93	0.95	0.97	1.00	1.02

Investments Divided by Wages	MODERATE Annual Savings as % of Wages							
	3%	6%	9%	12%	15%	18%	21%	24%
0	0.02	0.04	0.06	0.08	0.11	0.13	0.15	0.17
1	0.09	0.11	0.14	0.16	0.18	0.20	0.22	0.24
2	0.17	0.19	0.21	0.23	0.25	0.27	0.29	0.31
4	0.31	0.33	0.35	0.37	0.39	0.41	0.44	0.46
6	0.45	0.47	0.50	0.52	0.54	0.56	0.58	0.60
8	0.60	0.62	0.64	0.66	0.68	0.70	0.72	0.74
10	0.74	0.76	0.78	0.80	0.83	0.85	0.87	0.89
12	0.89	0.91	0.93	0.95	0.97	0.99	1.01	1.03
15	1.10	1.12	1.14	1.17	1.19	1.21	1.23	1.25

Investments Divided by Wages	CONSERVATIVE Annual Savings as % of Wages							
	3%	6%	9%	12%	15%	18%	21%	24%
0	0.02	0.04	0.06	0.07	0.09	0.11	0.13	0.15
1	0.08	0.10	0.11	0.13	0.15	0.17	0.19	0.21
2	0.14	0.15	0.17	0.19	0.21	0.23	0.25	0.27
4	0.25	0.27	0.29	0.31	0.33	0.35	0.37	0.38
6	0.37	0.39	0.41	0.43	0.45	0.46	0.48	0.50
8	0.49	0.51	0.53	0.55	0.56	0.58	0.60	0.62
12	0.73	0.74	0.76	0.78	0.80	0.82	0.84	0.86
16	0.96	0.98	1.00	1.02	1.04	1.05	1.07	1.09
20	1.20	1.22	1.23	1.25	1.27	1.29	1.31	1.33

FIGURE 5.5 Find your investment factor if you are 12 years from retirement.

15 Years Until Retirement
Investment Factors

Investments
Divided by
Wages

AGGRESSIVE
Annual Savings as % of Wages

	3%	6%	9%	12%	15%	18%	21%	24%
0	0.03	0.07	0.10	0.13	0.17	0.20	0.23	0.27
1	0.14	0.17	0.21	0.24	0.27	0.31	0.34	0.37
2	0.25	0.28	0.31	0.35	0.38	0.41	0.45	0.48
3	0.35	0.39	0.42	0.45	0.49	0.52	0.55	0.58
4	0.46	0.49	0.53	0.56	0.59	0.62	0.66	0.69
5	0.57	0.60	0.63	0.67	0.70	0.73	0.76	0.80
6	0.67	0.71	0.74	0.77	0.80	0.84	0.87	0.90
7	0.78	0.81	0.84	0.88	0.91	0.94	0.98	1.01
8	0.89	0.92	0.95	0.98	1.02	1.05	1.08	1.12

Investments
Divided by
Wages

MODERATE
Annual Savings as % of Wages

	3%	6%	9%	12%	15%	18%	21%	24%
0	0.03	0.06	0.08	0.11	0.14	0.17	0.19	0.22
1	0.11	0.14	0.16	0.19	0.22	0.25	0.27	0.30
2	0.19	0.21	0.24	0.27	0.30	0.33	0.35	0.38
3	0.27	0.29	0.32	0.35	0.38	0.41	0.43	0.46
5	0.43	0.45	0.48	0.51	0.54	0.56	0.59	0.62
7	0.59	0.61	0.64	0.67	0.70	0.72	0.75	0.78
9	0.74	0.77	0.80	0.83	0.86	0.88	0.91	0.94
11	0.90	0.93	0.96	0.99	1.02	1.04	1.07	1.10
13	1.06	1.09	1.12	1.15	1.17	1.20	1.23	1.26

Investments
Divided by
Wages

CONSERVATIVE
Annual Savings as % of Wages

	3%	6%	9%	12%	15%	18%	21%	24%
0	0.02	0.05	0.07	0.10	0.12	0.14	0.17	0.19
1	0.09	0.11	0.13	0.16	0.18	0.21	0.23	0.25
2	0.15	0.17	0.20	0.22	0.25	0.27	0.29	0.32
4	0.28	0.30	0.32	0.35	0.37	0.40	0.42	0.44
6	0.40	0.43	0.45	0.47	0.50	0.52	0.54	0.57
9	0.59	0.61	0.64	0.66	0.69	0.71	0.73	0.76
12	0.78	0.80	0.83	0.85	0.87	0.90	0.92	0.95
15	0.97	0.99	1.02	1.04	1.06	1.09	1.11	1.14
18	1.16	1.18	1.20	1.23	1.25	1.28	1.30	1.32

FIGURE 5.6 Find your investment factor if you are 15 years from retirement.

20 Years Until Retirement
Investment Factors

Investments
Divided by
Wages

AGGRESSIVE
Annual Savings as % of Wages

	3%	6%	9%	12%	15%	18%	21%	24%
0	0.05	0.10	0.15	0.20	0.25	0.30	0.36	0.41
0.5	0.12	0.17	0.22	0.27	0.32	0.37	0.42	0.47
1	0.19	0.24	0.29	0.34	0.39	0.44	0.49	0.54
1.5	0.25	0.31	0.36	0.41	0.46	0.51	0.56	0.61
2	0.32	0.37	0.42	0.48	0.53	0.58	0.63	0.68
3	0.46	0.51	0.56	0.61	0.66	0.71	0.76	0.81
4	0.59	0.65	0.70	0.75	0.80	0.85	0.90	0.95
5	0.73	0.78	0.83	0.88	0.93	0.98	1.04	1.09
6	0.87	0.92	0.97	1.02	1.07	1.12	1.17	1.22

Investments
Divided by
Wages

MODERATE
Annual Savings as % of Wages

	3%	6%	9%	12%	15%	18%	21%	24%
0	0.04	0.08	0.12	0.16	0.20	0.24	0.28	0.32
1	0.13	0.18	0.22	0.26	0.30	0.34	0.38	0.42
2	0.23	0.27	0.31	0.35	0.39	0.43	0.47	0.51
3	0.32	0.36	0.40	0.44	0.49	0.53	0.57	0.61
4	0.42	0.46	0.50	0.54	0.58	0.62	0.66	0.70
5	0.51	0.55	0.59	0.63	0.67	0.71	0.75	0.80
6	0.61	0.65	0.69	0.73	0.77	0.81	0.85	0.89
8	0.79	0.83	0.88	0.92	0.96	1.00	1.04	1.08
10	0.98	1.02	1.06	1.10	1.14	1.19	1.23	1.27

Investments
Divided by
Wages

CONSERVATIVE
Annual Savings as % of Wages

	3%	6%	9%	12%	15%	18%	21%	24%
0	0.03	0.07	0.10	0.14	0.17	0.20	0.24	0.27
1	0.10	0.14	0.17	0.21	0.24	0.27	0.31	0.34
2	0.17	0.21	0.24	0.28	0.31	0.34	0.38	0.41
3	0.24	0.28	0.31	0.35	0.38	0.41	0.45	0.48
5	0.38	0.42	0.45	0.49	0.52	0.55	0.59	0.62
7	0.52	0.56	0.59	0.63	0.66	0.69	0.73	0.76
9	0.67	0.70	0.73	0.77	0.80	0.83	0.87	0.90
12	0.88	0.91	0.94	0.98	1.01	1.04	1.08	1.11
16	1.16	1.19	1.22	1.26	1.29	1.33	1.36	1.39

FIGURE 5.7 Find your investment factor if you are 20 years from retirement.

25 Years Until Retirement
Investment Factors

Investments Divided by Wages	AGGRESSIVE Annual Savings as % of Wages							
	3%	6%	9%	12%	15%	18%	21%	24%
0	0.07	0.15	0.22	0.29	0.37	0.44	0.51	0.59
0.5	0.16	0.23	0.31	0.38	0.45	0.53	0.60	0.67
1	0.25	0.32	0.39	0.47	0.54	0.61	0.69	0.76
1.5	0.33	0.41	0.48	0.55	0.63	0.70	0.77	0.85
2	0.42	0.49	0.57	0.64	0.71	0.79	0.86	0.93
2.5	0.51	0.58	0.65	0.73	0.80	0.87	0.95	1.02
3	0.59	0.67	0.74	0.81	0.89	0.96	1.03	1.11
3.5	0.68	0.75	0.83	0.90	0.97	1.05	1.12	1.19
4	0.77	0.84	0.91	0.99	1.06	1.13	1.21	1.28

Investments Divided by Wages	MODERATE Annual Savings as % of Wages							
	3%	6%	9%	12%	15%	18%	21%	24%
0	0.06	0.11	0.17	0.22	0.28	0.33	0.39	0.45
1	0.17	0.22	0.28	0.33	0.39	0.45	0.50	0.56
2	0.28	0.33	0.39	0.45	0.50	0.56	0.61	0.67
3	0.39	0.45	0.50	0.56	0.61	0.67	0.72	0.78
4	0.50	0.56	0.61	0.67	0.72	0.78	0.83	0.89
5	0.61	0.67	0.72	0.78	0.83	0.89	0.95	1.00
6	0.72	0.78	0.83	0.89	0.95	1.00	1.06	1.11
8	0.95	1.00	1.06	1.11	1.17	1.22	1.28	1.34
10	1.17	1.22	1.28	1.34	1.39	1.45	1.50	1.56

Investments Divided by Wages	CONSERVATIVE Annual Savings as % of Wages							
	3%	6%	9%	12%	15%	18%	21%	24%
0	0.04	0.09	0.13	0.18	0.22	0.27	0.31	0.36
1	0.12	0.17	0.21	0.26	0.30	0.35	0.39	0.44
2	0.20	0.25	0.29	0.34	0.38	0.43	0.47	0.51
3	0.28	0.32	0.37	0.41	0.46	0.50	0.55	0.59
4	0.36	0.40	0.45	0.49	0.54	0.58	0.63	0.67
6	0.51	0.56	0.60	0.65	0.69	0.74	0.78	0.83
9	0.75	0.79	0.84	0.88	0.93	0.97	1.02	1.06
12	0.98	1.03	1.07	1.12	1.16	1.21	1.25	1.30
15	1.22	1.26	1.31	1.35	1.40	1.44	1.49	1.53

FIGURE 5.8 Find your investment factor if you are 25 years from retirement.

30 Years Until Retirement
Investment Factors

Investments Divided by Wages

AGGRESSIVE
Annual Savings as % of Wages

	3%	6%	9%	12%	15%	18%	21%	24%
1	0.32	0.43	0.53	0.63	0.73	0.83	0.94	1.04
2	0.54	0.65	0.75	0.85	0.95	1.06	1.16	1.26
3	0.77	0.87	0.97	1.07	1.17	1.28	1.38	1.48
6	1.43	1.53	1.63	1.74	1.84	1.94	2.04	2.14
9	2.09	2.20	2.30	2.40	2.50	2.60	2.71	2.81
12	2.76	2.86	2.96	3.06	3.17	3.27	3.37	3.47
15	3.42	3.52	3.63	3.73	3.83	3.93	4.04	4.14
16	3.64	3.75	3.85	3.95	4.05	4.15	4.26	4.36
3	0.77	0.87	0.97	1.07	1.17	1.28	1.38	1.48

Investments Divided by Wages

MODERATE
Annual Savings as % of Wages

	3%	6%	9%	12%	15%	18%	21%	24%
0	0.07	0.15	0.22	0.29	0.37	0.44	0.51	0.59
1	0.21	0.28	0.35	0.43	0.50	0.57	0.65	0.72
2	0.34	0.41	0.48	0.56	0.63	0.70	0.78	0.85
3	0.47	0.54	0.62	0.69	0.76	0.84	0.91	0.98
4	0.60	0.67	0.75	0.82	0.89	0.97	1.04	1.11
5	0.73	0.81	0.88	0.95	1.03	1.10	1.17	1.25
6	0.86	0.94	1.01	1.08	1.16	1.23	1.30	1.38
7	0.99	1.07	1.14	1.22	1.29	1.36	1.44	1.51
8	1.13	1.20	1.27	1.35	1.42	1.49	1.57	1.64

Investments Divided by Wages

CONSERVATIVE
Annual Savings as % of Wages

	3%	6%	9%	12%	15%	18%	21%	24%
0	0.06	0.11	0.17	0.23	0.29	0.34	0.40	0.46
1	0.14	0.20	0.26	0.32	0.37	0.43	0.49	0.54
2	0.23	0.29	0.35	0.40	0.46	0.52	0.57	0.63
3	0.32	0.38	0.43	0.49	0.55	0.60	0.66	0.72
4	0.41	0.46	0.52	0.58	0.63	0.69	0.75	0.81
6	0.58	0.64	0.69	0.75	0.81	0.87	0.92	0.98
9	0.84	0.90	0.96	1.01	1.07	1.13	1.18	1.24
12	1.10	1.16	1.22	1.27	1.33	1.39	1.45	1.50
15	1.37	1.42	1.48	1.54	1.59	1.65	1.71	1.76

FIGURE 5.9 Find your investment factor if you are 30 years from retirement.

Quick and Dirty Allocations and Returns

	Aggressive	Moderate	Conservative
Preretirement Allocations and Returns after 1% Costs			
Large company stocks	50%	50%	25%
Growth stocks	25%		
Long-term corp. bonds	15%	40%	65%
Treasury bills	10%	10%	10%
Total allocation	100%	100%	100%
Long-term real return	5.0%	3.4%	2.2%
Postretirement Allocations and Returns after 1% Costs			
Large company stocks	50%	40%	20%
Growth stocks	10%		
Long-term corp. bonds	30%	50%	70%
Treasury bills	10%	10%	10%
Total allocation	100%	100%	100%
Long-term real return	4.0%	3.0%	2.0%
$1/2$ real return	2.0%	1.5%	1.0%

FIGURE 5.10 Details of the assumptions used in the quick and dirty method for investment allocations and associated returns for three different portfolios: aggressive, moderate, and conservative.

Gate 2. Assess Your Future Needs

In order to determine how much you must save before retirement, you must first estimate how much you will need to spend each year in retirement. If your retirement expenses are going to be large, your savings will also have to be large. The worst thing would be to retire and find you had completely underestimated your financial requirements. We are going to ask you to divide your retirement needs into two categories. The first is an estimate of annual expenses that are likely to occur every year. The second is for expenses that will occur infrequently. Infrequent expenses might be new automobiles, a vacation home, or provisions for some expensive work on your home.

As a practical matter, your estimate of how much you need in retirement changes every succeeding year. Your ideas about what constitutes a reasonable lifestyle change. Inflation nudges the values incrementally upward each year. And as you get older, you start to compromise your retirement financial goals with financial realities. This means that you must reevaluate your needs every time you make a new retirement plan. Subsequent estimates will take less time if you save your information from one year to the next.

You do have to start somewhere, however. And the earlier you start with reasonable levels of sacrifice to save more, the closer your ideals will come to your ultimate financial capabilities. The first thing to do to get there is to estimate your annual normal living expenses in retirement. We're going to show you four alternatives: the textbook 70% method, my 100% alternative, a top-down method, and a bottom-up analysis. As you'll see, these vary quite a bit in terms of complexity and accuracy.

The 70% Approximation

There are many texts and computer programs that recommend that you start by assuming that you can live quite comfortably in retirement on 70% of your current gross wages. (You can get a figure for gross wages from your paycheck stub or tax return.) Unfortunately, this 70% estimate is really a crude measure that can lead to very misleading results.

There are several reasons that analysts use the 70% figure. One is that your current wages provide for things that are not needed in retirement, things such as the deductions for Social Security, Medicare, savings plans, union dues, and so on. It also assumes your tax rate will be lower in retirement. But the main factor is that statistics show that retirees spend less than working folks. This latter point, I believe, is misleading. The fact is that the majority of retired people just can't afford to spend what they'd like to. The reality of their retirement is far from their dream. You come from a different planet if you think that the majority of retirees spend only a small amount of money because that's all they want to spend. Tell that to some of the elderly people my wife and I visit who have drug bills exceeding $1,000 a month and often forego their prescriptions to be able to pay for food. Tell that to elderly people who have to work nights at the local convenience store or as a Santa Claus in order to earn money for gifts for grandchildren or an airplane ticket to visit them. These people are spending what they can afford to spend, not what they want to spend.

I live in an affluent community. I doubt if there are many people here who spend less now than when they were working. I know that most spend considerably more. Not only do they have more activities and more time to travel, but also many of them are paying for things that were perks while they were working. We also have some associates who spent far too much when they first retired. It wasn't very many years before they discovered the reality that their savings were not being replenished by high returns. Those fixed pensions that once seemed adequate are now diminished by inflation. The inevitable happens. They forsake the social groups they no longer can afford and soon thereafter sell their home to find more economical quarters. Better planning can help you avoid these pitfalls. It's part of a winning retirement plan.

The 100% Alternative

If you are more than five years from retirement, are saving very little, and are not supporting a large family of teenagers, I think you should consider the 100% alternative for estimating your retirement spending. This means that you'll need the same equivalent gross income after retirement as your current gross income from wages. Remember that the 70% method assumes you won't need the 7.65% for Social Security and Medicare deductions or the 15% (or whatever) deduction for your 401(k) or similar plan. It assumes that your taxes will be lower because of lower income and a lower tax rate on Social Security payments. Finally, the 70% method most often means you'll spend less in retirement than when working. On the other hand, a real winning retirement plan would give you more for retirement expenses than your current expenses. It would give you more money for recreation and some provision for those expenses brought on just because you get older in retirement—items such as uninsured medical/dental/eye expenses and large prescription drug bills. Plus, it's easy to estimate. Of course, it doesn't give you the level of confidence of the two more detailed methods that follow.

The Top-Down Analysis

We'll show you how to do a top-down analysis next. It requires more thinking than the 70% mantra or the 100% alternative, but the budget will be tailored to your real situation. You can account for changes you think might be important in comparing your retirement with your current situation. This type of analysis is easy when you are close to retirement but becomes more difficult the younger you are. See Figure 5.11.

Step 1 is simply the amount you have left on your paycheck after all of the deductions for income tax, FICA (Social Security), Medicare, employer's savings plan, and so on. Multiply that by the number of pay periods in the year to get an annual amount.

Step 2 is the amount of your take-home pay that you are saving yourself, that is, the amount that is not being deducted from your wages for your employer's savings plan.

Step 3 is your current annual budget for expenses other than income tax or

A Top-Down Analysis Is a Better Way to
Estimate Retirement Needs

Step

1	Annual take-home pay (Gross wages less all deductions)	37,400
2	Amount from take-home pay that is used for annual savings not in employer's plan	2,000
3	Current annual expenses, or, if unknown, Step 1 minus Step 2	35,400
4	Expenses peculiar to children that won't be needed in retirement	5,000
5	Other things not needed in retirement	1,000
6	Step 4 plus Step 5	6,000
7	Basic retirement expenses (Step 3 minus Step 6)	29,400
8	Other expenses desired during retirement	5,000
9	Total retirement expenses (Step 7 plus Step 8)	34,400
10	Last year's federal and state income tax from tax return	10,000
11	Last year's taxable income from tax return	60,000
12	Step 10 divided by Step 11 or your own estimate of tax rate in retirement	0.17 (rounded)
13	1.00 minus Step 12	0.83
14	Approximate gross income needed to support retirement expenses (Step 9 divided by Step 13)	41,445

FIGURE 5.11 Use a top-down analysis to reach a more accurate estimate of your retirement needs than the percentage methods.

savings. If you don't have such a budget, subtract Step 2 from Step 1 to get an estimate.

Step 4 requires some thought unless you have reached the point where your children are no longer at home. Then it's easy because the number is probably zero. If not, just try to estimate the big things like tuition, college support, a child's automobile expenses, extra clothes, allowances, a fraction of your annual food bills, or any large uninsured medical costs that you recall. Or, if you are one of those people who keep really detailed records of expenses, you can divide many of your expenses by the number of people in your family and assume each child requires that share. You'll never get a perfect number for this, and you should keep in mind that many retirees discover they still give adult children gifts or subsidize their living for a while.

Step 5 gives you a chance to account for other costs that might go away after you retire. Perhaps you'll need less expensive clothes, one less automobile, no life insurance premiums, and so forth.

Step 8 also requires a little thought. You might put in an allowance for greater use of your automobile, or support of a recreational vehicle, or an allowance for more vacation expenses, or support of a hobby. I find that retirees are buying more high-tech stuff than they had imagined they would—things like new computers, digital cameras, dish TVs, or Internet services. Also you might want to add provisions for uninsured medical, dental, eye care, and drug costs. And you might foresee additional costs for maintenance services that you may not be able to do yourself anymore. All of this is highly subjective, but you cannot afford to say that these costs won't exist. Believe me, many of them will. At the same time, there is no way you can get a really accurate forecast, so you'll just have to pencil in some rough estimates.

The rest of the steps are purely mechanical. They add an approximate income tax to your expenses so that your results are the equivalent of the gross income you would need to support the expenses you expect in retirement. This should give you a result that is pretty much consistent with your present lifestyle.

The Bottom-Up Analysis

A bottom-up analysis is harder than a top-down analysis, because you must list all of your current expenditures and, for each item, estimate whether you will need more or less in retirement. It requires you to have a fairly accurate record of your current expenses. If you can do this without forgetting some major expense, you will get the most accurate results of all of the various methods. People who are nearing retirement and are starting to determine whether they can afford to live on their retirement resources almost always use this method. You can use a form like the one in Figure 5.12 to make a meaningful breakdown of all of your expenses. Do not try to make an adjustment for future inflation— we will allow for that later.

The problem with a bottom-up analysis is that it's easy to forget or leave out items and then find yourself trying to reconcile your expenses with your lowball budget. For a number of years I was chairman of a company subsidiary in the construction business. All of our work was fixed price. Therefore, anything that we left out of our estimate had to come from the company's pocket and not the customer's. Often the most valuable people in our company were the estimators who could enumerate the vast majority of costs. But even these experts often left out things. I find most retirees feel they left out a lot of things too when they first estimated their retirement budgets. If you really expect to end your home

Bottom-Up Analysis of Retirement Needs

Row	Item (Annual Amounts)	Current Expenses	Expenses in Retirement
1	Rent and debt payments		
2	Utilities & maintenance		
3	Total auto expenses		
4	Food		
5	Uninsured medical		
6	Insurance		
7	Real estate taxes		
8	Entertainment		
9	Vacation		
10	Gifts & charities		
11	Clothing		
12	Other		
13	Total annual expenses		Example: 35,000
14	Estimated tax rate in retirement or last year's income taxes divided by taxable income		0.17
15	1.00 minus Step 14		0.83
16	Estimated gross income required (Row 13 divided by Row 15)		42,169

FIGURE 5.12 The bottom-up analysis gives the best projection of retirement needs—if you don't forget anything.

mortgage payments sometime early in retirement, and are really sure that you will never again buy a house with a mortgage, you could leave out your mortgage payments in the first entry of Figure 5.12, for example. But don't forget that you will have to continue to pay the property taxes and insurance that may now be escrowed for you as part of your mortgage payment. These are the things it is all too easy to leave out of your calculations.

When we do a bottom-up analysis, we are trying to represent the annual expenses you will have, on the average, in about the first 10 years of your retirement. It's pretty hard to do either a top-down or a bottom-up analysis when you are relatively young and can't really comprehend the financial consequences of additional physical help as you get older. When you reach your 60s, however, either you'll be touched personally by physical problems or you'll see the difficulties your older associates are having. The time comes when you can no longer do many of the household chores and have to contract for the help. That may be followed by the need to pay someone to come in to help with personal care, and that may be followed by the need to live in an assisted care facility. Finally, a nursing home may be in your future. Each level requires additional financial support from your own savings, your children's savings, an insurance policy, or welfare. You won't be able to estimate very many of these expenses before retirement, but try to imagine whether you have enough financial flexibility to pay some substantial expenses when you are older by giving up other items you've budgeted for earlier in your retirement—for instance, your travel budget might have to go down as your need for assistance goes up. Having provided the major support for elderly parents and in-laws, I know the things we prefer not to think about don't come cheap.

So do a bottom-up analysis very conscientiously! I say this not to discourage the analysis, because it is a good thing to do before committing to retirement. Just don't be casual about it. Ignoring some items will come back to bite you. Hard!

Infrequent Expenses

One final category to consider when you are estimating your retirement needs is infrequent expenses. Infrequent expenses are very large value items that are paid either over time or with a withdrawal from investments. If the payments are made over time, a loan is required. The payments you make on the loan should be recorded as part of your normal expenses in all of the previous methods. Any expenses that are paid from investments are not counted as part of those normal expenses. These could include a down payment for a vacation home or if you bought an automobile with cash from an investment account. In the planning methods that follow, we will ask you to estimate any infrequent expenses you may foresee in the future.

Gate 3. Estimating Your Social Security, Pension, and Annuity Income

To do your retirement planning properly, you must have the right data to use for your inputs. That means that you must understand what values to use when you are entering your income from Social Security and pensions, and from any annuities you might have. The answers are not always on the projections you get from the government or your employer, and they can vary according to your circumstances. When and how you choose to take your benefits can also have a big impact; there's much to consider.

The Benefits of Social Security

Social Security is the most valuable retirement resource that many people have. No employer, other than the government itself, offers lifetime benefits that increase every year with inflation and that are backed by the power to levy taxes for their support. Because of its inflation protection alone, Social Security is more than one-third better than a fixed pension that makes the same payments years down the line as it does when you first retire. Social Security also gives you a tax advantage. Much of the income from Social Security is tax exempt for lower-income recipients, and even higher-income people enjoy a modest tax exemption. Pensions have no such tax advantage.

Consider also that Social Security is obtained cheaply, especially for lower-income workers, who get larger Social Security payments relative to the amount they were taxed. Unless you are self-employed, you get 100% matching contributions by your employer no matter how much you contribute. That's better than almost all employers, who generally match only a part of the 401(k) savings of their employees. And with Social Security, a nonworking spouse collects benefits as well and has only to decide when to start collecting. With pensions, not only is there no spousal benefit, but to receive payments for the surviving spouse, the employee must elect to take lower pension payments.

Social Security is not subject to stock or bond market fluctuations (at least at present). You don't have to watch its value on a ticker tape or get an expert opinion on when to sell. If you wanted to buy an investment that gave the same benefits, it would probably cost more than most people could possibly afford. Its value is approximately the product of the annual payments you receive times your life expectancy. Even with only modest inflation, the next generation will see many married couples effectively become millionaires just from Social Security. It's far more than most people will save for retirement on their own.

Finally, Social Security has a very attractive survivor benefit at no extra cost. A surviving widow, for example, gets the same benefit as her deceased husband. You would pay dearly for this alternative with a pension. And, Social Security has added benefits if you become disabled.

ESTIMATING SOCIAL SECURITY PAYMENTS

You can get a detailed estimate of your future benefits from the Social Security Administration. Social Security automatically mails a statement to all individuals over age 25 who are not currently receiving benefits. Addresses are obtained through IRS tax records. The estimate is based on certain assumptions about your future wages. It will not answer *all* of your questions, however. For additional information from the Social Security Administration, call 1-800-772-1213. (The phone is really busy Mondays and the first week of the month.)

The estimates you get of your Social Security payments will be in today's values, which is exactly what you should use for the planning analysis we will do in this chapter. The estimates will be based on what the Social Security Administration calls your *full retirement age* (FRA), which will be between ages 65 and 67 depending on when you were born. This is what old-timers like myself used to call the *normal* retirement age because, until more recent affluence made early retirement more practical, people normally retired when they got their full Social Security benefit. I still refer to the size of the payment that you will get at full retirement age as the normal benefit. For most of past history, the full retirement age was 65. However, in order to keep the Social Security program solvent, Congress changed the rules so that people who collect Social Security in the future will have to wait up to another two years to receive their full Social Security payments. Your own report will state what that age will be for your case. Starting Social Security before or after your full retirement age will change the benefit. If you take the benefits early, your payments will be less than normal. If you take the benefits late, the payments will be more than normal. Theoretically, people will receive about the same total amount of money until death whether they start early with less or start late with more.

There is substantial disagreement about whether early retirees should start taking Social Security at age 62 or wait till their full retirement age of 65 to 67. The majority of financial people say you should take benefits early because you might not live as long as the average person, so you should get your money while you can. I have a different view. I say most of the time it's better to wait until your full retirement age. Why? Because of the severe financial problems most people have if they do live past the average life expectancy. Sure, if both you and your spouse retired because you were in really poor health, take Social Security early. Otherwise, it is probably better to scrimp a little at first for the increased benefits later.

Another significant disadvantage to early retirement is that an early retiree may not have health insurance from age 62 to age 65. Medicare will continue to be effective at age 65 regardless of an individual's FRA. Also, new legislation passed in 2000 removed all work restrictions for recipients age 65 and over.

If there's any significant chance that you or your spouse might be long-lived, take your Social Security later. If you want to retire early, but need Social Security payments early to make that possible, you should seriously consider working longer. Taking Social Security payments early because you "need" the money early tells me that you are retiring too young. A few extra years of work and saving would give you a more rewarding retirement, at least financially.

SOCIAL SECURITY SPOUSAL BENEFITS

Each year you work and pay taxes into Social Security, you get "credits." If your spouse has earned his or her own credits for Social Security payments on his or her own work record, you should add your spouse's estimated Social Security payments to your own when you are doing your analysis. Even if your spouse has no credits, when your spouse is the normal retirement age, she or he is entitled to 50% of the working spouse's FRA payments unless your spouse retires early. When your spouse begins Social Security payments, she or he will be paid whichever benefit amount is higher. The two benefits are not combined, and your election to take checks early is a permanent reduction.

Because retiring earlier or later than the full retirement age reduces or increases your benefits, you will need to adjust your figures for that. If you plan to retire at or before age 62, you should use the age 62 payments for Social Security as inputs to our analysis. We'll show you how to adjust the numbers to account for the fact that you will not have any payments until you are age 62. You can estimate the Social Security payments for retiring over age 62 with a piece of graph paper by making a chart like the one in Figure 5.13, or you can get specific information for any age you want by contacting the Social Security Administration. You will find three data points on your Social Security report: payments for age 62, payments at your full retirement age, and payments at age 70. Plot those three points and draw straight lines between them. It's easy.

Figure 5.13 shows the effect that retirement age has on Social Security payments. It shows how the monthly payments depend on both your retirement age and the year you were born. The chart is based on three cases, each of which assumes a payment of $1,000 a month at the full retirement age, or $12,000 a year. The full retirement age is 65 for those born before 1938. It is age 66 for those born between 1943 and 1954. It continues to increase month by month until it reaches age 67 for those born in 1960 and after. Your benefits go down if

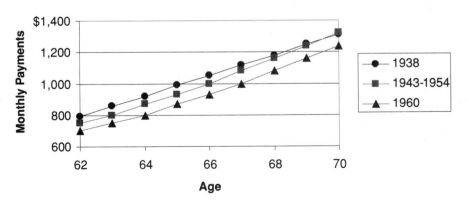

FIGURE 5.13 You can make a chart to determine your Social Security benefits at retirement ages other than the standard 62, full retirement age, and age 70.

you retire early and go up if you retire later than your full retirement age. This makes a big difference.

EARLY SOCIAL SECURITY PAYMENTS FOR A NONWORKING SPOUSE REALLY HURT!

When a couple are different ages, Social Security benefits can get complicated. It's tempting for a nonworking spouse who is younger than the working spouse to take the spousal benefits early, so they can both start drawing their retirement money at the same time. This is unfortunate. Figure 5.14 shows the effect of early payments for a nonworking spouse if a working spouse has a FRA benefit of $1,000 a month. Unless the nonworking spouse waits until her or his FRA, there is a severe penalty. Even more dramatic is that there is no increase in benefit for delaying payments beyond the nonworking spouse's FRA. While the minimum payment is 37.5% of the working spouse's FRA benefit, the maximum is only 50% of the working spouse's FRA benefit.

IF BOTH SPOUSES TAKE EARLY SOCIAL SECURITY PAYMENTS

Another scenario is when both spouses choose to take their Social Security payments early. It can be especially painful if your spouse has been a nonworking spouse and does not have significant Social Security credits of her or his own. Let's use an example of a person born before 1938 who would get $12,000 full retirement age benefit at age 65 and let's suppose that person is the husband. If the wife is younger than the husband and also retires at age 65, she would be entitled to 50% of the husband's full retirement age benefit, or $6,000 in this case. The two together would receive $18,000 a year.

But now suppose that the husband retires at age 62 and therefore gets $9,600. If the wife elects to wait until she is 65 before taking her spousal bene-

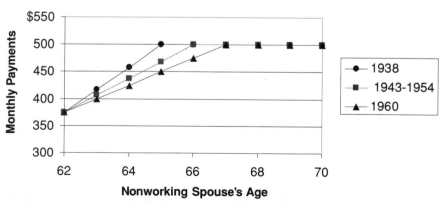

FIGURE 5.14 Early benefits for a nonworking spouse are painfully smaller.

fit, she'll get 50% of $12,000, or $6,000, so that the two of them together will get $15,600. The situation is aggravated if the wife also takes early retirement at age 62. Then she is entitled to only 37.5% of the $12,000 full retirement age benefit of the working spouse, or $4,500 per year, so the two of them together will get only $14,100. This is 78% of what the two of them could get if they waited until they were age 65. These numbers are all for a couple who were both born before 1938. It gets worse for a couple born after 1959. That's because the government increased the full retirement age for people born in later years. It's one of the reasons why people will be working longer in the future.

LATE SOCIAL SECURITY PAYMENTS

Figure 5.13 shows that working longer than your full retirement age increases your benefits. If your wages also increase during this time, and you are age 65 or above, the full retirement age payments may also increase. Therefore, you will benefit both from the higher factor for late retirement and the increase in your theoretical earnings value. Although the working spouse will get most of the gain in this scenario, the nonworking spouse will get some gain from the increase in the working spouse's payments. One thing to keep in mind, however, is that the maximum benefit for a nonworking spouse is tied to between 37.5 and 50% of the full retirement age payments of the working spouse, not the working spouse's actual payments. The nonworking spouse would *not* get 37.5 to 50% of the age 70 value of the working spouse, for example, even if the working spouse continued to work till age 70.

The increased benefit from working must be weighed against the couple's tax rate and resultant increased tax liability, especially if one spouse has early Social Security payments. Often the tax liability offsets any dollar increase to the Social Security benefit. The continued wages, tax liability, and Social Security benefit amount must all be weighed together to determine if any financial benefit will result from continued employment.

LOOK AHEAD BEFORE MAKING A SOCIAL SECURITY COMMITMENT

When you do your preretirement planning, you are going to have to input a value for payments that will correspond to the age you elect to start Social Security payments. When you are far from retirement, you might just assume that you and your spouse will elect to take payments at your full retirement ages. That makes the computation easy, and I believe that most people will ultimately do that anyway. However, when you are getting close to retirement, you will probably want to see if you can afford to take early retirement. Then, to make a good decision, you are going to have to make different plans for each age of retirement. Even if it looks like you would be able to afford taking early retirement as well as early payment of Social Security benefits, give the latter a second thought. We have set up the planning method so that you can easily separate your retirement date from the date you take the Social Security election. So you could retire early from work, but wait a couple of years before beginning to take Social Security. I favor the latter approach because of my own personal experiences, which will illustrate some of the problems you should be considering carefully before making any retirement choices.

Each month, my wife and I visit four elderly women who live alone in inexpensive housing and are trying to survive on Social Security. Sometimes they get a little help from their children. These are very nice ladies who deserve better, but their financial condition today has been determined by circumstances and irrevocable decisions made long ago. You could face this same situation in your old age.

Typical of people in this condition, they are either widows or were divorced many years ago. Every penny counts dearly. Their Social Security checks are a fraction of those received by people who were able to make the maximum contributions while working. The ladies we visit are still physically capable of caring for themselves, but they have friends who need assisted care and are even more stressed financially, especially as Medicare continues to reduce allowable services such as bathing assistance or blood testing.

These ladies are part of a large group of people who are seriously affected when the price of prescription drugs increases far faster than the inflation rate that is used to calculate their Social Security increases. When a doctor prescribes a new medicine, many elderly people have to consider what they are going to give up in exchange because their savings were exhausted long ago.

The other day I read another of those articles that suggests that a person will be better off financially if they start taking Social Security payments at age 62 rather than 65 or later. Typically, these articles look for the "break-even" age that you would have to outlive in order to justify taking Social Security later than 62. At the break-even age, the total amount you would get from Social Security is the same if you started drawing your benefits at age 62 as it would be if you started drawing your benefits at your normal retirement age of 65 to 67. This means that the break-even age is around age 81. If you live longer, you win by waiting—if all that counts is the total amount of money you'll get from the government.

This is a great theory for those who expect to die young, but it has little to do with the real world of elderly people. Once you have waited to start taking Social Security at the later date you have significantly more to spend. Many of the elderly, not even close to the break-even age, now desperately need the 20% or more Social Security they could have had if they had waited until a later age to start taking their benefits. On top of that, in the real world, many women live well past the break-even age. And, with the evolution of modern medicine and better health care, men are living longer too. My own father didn't start taking Social Security until he was 70. Like many people, he lived far longer than any table predicted, so that was the right decision. Compared to the four ladies we visit and the vast majority of elderly people, his Social Security payments made him relatively well off.

There are a number of people in our community who "took advantage" of early retirement programs offered by their employers during downsizing periods when business conditions were bad. Those who retired under age 62 were especially hard hit in retrospect, even though they got a bump in retirement benefits in exchange for retiring early. Without Social Security payments, they had to draw down their savings at a terrifying rate. Their former employers made out well, but the early retirees didn't. Most of these retirees found that they really didn't have the resources to retire and many are now back at work, but they are in jobs that provide small or no retirement benefits. Because they are working, and under age 65, their Social Security payments are reduced as well. (There is no reduction to Social Security payments if the worker is age 65 or older.) They would have been much better off spending a few more years working under the cover of a pension and/or company savings plan.

So keep in mind that, like the four ladies we visit, you may someday be very dependent on every penny that comes from Social Security. Further, either you, your spouse, or both, may well live past the break-even age that justified taking Social Security at age 62. When you do, you'll pay the piper! If you can't afford to delay Social Security to your full retirement age, perhaps you should reconsider whether you should be entering retirement early. When you are doing your detailed preretirement planning and are thinking about retiring early, do another analysis to take a look at what will happen if you delay Social Security till your full retirement age even if you retire from work earlier. I think you will find it well worth the effort.

DOUBTS ABOUT SOCIAL SECURITY VIABILITY?

If you aren't confident that the Social Security system will still be viable when you reach retirement age, there is a way that you can reflect your doubts about future Social Security payments in your plans. In the extreme, you could leave it out, but it is highly unlikely that Social Security will disappear completely. If you believe that you will receive less than the government now estimates for you, then you could enter only a fraction of the government's value in your analysis. More likely, Social Security will no longer increase as fast as inflation in general, or as fast as your personal inflation rate, which may be higher, or Social Security might be fully taxed in the future. If you think those things are likely, then put part of your future Social Security payments under Social Security and the rest under the fixed pension category. I base my own personal retirement plans on Social Security growth at only two-thirds of my personal inflation rate, so I put two-thirds of my Social Security under the COLA income or Social Security categories and the other one-third under the fixed pension category. It's crude, but it's at least a gesture toward my view of the future of Social Security.

Pensions

Employers are getting away from pension plans and converting to savings plans instead. As a practical matter, most people don't stay with an employer long enough to get much of a pension now anyway. So if your employer does not offer a pension plan, or the pension you earned from a previous employer is negligible, you can skip this part. However, many people will count heavily on such plans. In the good old days, the combination of Social Security and a pension was supposed to support you till death. The combination of higher inflation and extended life expectancies has knocked that theory to pieces.

Nevertheless, if your employer offers a pension plan, it is most likely going to be based on one of two concepts: Either the pension will have a cost of living adjustment that will increase annual payments to offset inflation, or, more commonly, the pension will be fixed in value so that you get the same annual payments each year of retirement. When you are retired, you can spend all of the after-tax income from a COLA pension, but if you spend all of your after-tax fixed pension each year, your real purchasing power will decline as inflation increases. Few people really recognize the dreadful power of accumulated inflation.

COST-OF-LIVING-ADJUSTED PENSIONS

Many government jobs and a few industries with very strong unions offer pensions that are very attractive in comparison with industry norms because they have annual cost of living adjustments (COLAs). Often these pensions have a cap on the maximum inflation protection they will give, perhaps 2 or 3% per year. COLA pensions are sweet deals even with a cap!

If you are going to get a COLA pension, its value will be given to you in today's dollars. When you actually start getting the pension, the amount will be more—depending on the amount of inflation that has occurred in the meantime. Social Security is a kind of COLA pension. You'll later see that we generally analyze Social Security separately though because some special rules apply if you retire before age 62. You should not try to make an inflation adjustment to a COLA pension. We'll do that for you.

If you are already getting a COLA pension, say from a retired military job, then use this year's annual amount as a COLA pension entry in the planning analysis. If you expect to get a COLA pension in the future when you retire, enter your employer's estimate in the planning analysis. Your employer may forecast some growth because you will earn greater benefits from future work between now and when you retire, but the employer will not increase the estimate based on any inflation growth. You should get exactly what you need for the planning analysis: your future COLA pension expressed in today's dollar values.

But what if your COLA pension has a cap so that it is limited to only 2 or 3% inflation a year even if the actual inflation rate is higher? Well, you do something like I do with my Social Security planning. You input part of your COLA pension under the COLA entry of the planning analysis and the other part under the fixed pension entry. If I were doing the analysis with a 2% cap, I would put one-half of the COLA pension in one place and the other half in the other.

With a 3% cap, I'd put three-fourths of the COLA pension as a COLA pension entry and one-fourth as a fixed pension entry. Again, this is rather crude, but it's a gesture in the right direction. You'll never be able to get a perfect answer to this in the real world of changing inflation conditions.

FIXED PENSIONS IN OUR PROJECTIONS

Fixed pensions are pensions where the amount you receive each year after retirement does *not* have a COLA. If you are going to get a fixed pension, its value may be given to you in today's dollars, or it may be based on some assumption about your wage growth. My old employer would do the latter, but you had to read the fine print to discover how much escalation they used.

It is not easy to determine what value of your fixed pension you should use in a retirement planning analysis. Most retirement planning references either make this a complete mystery by ignoring the subject or otherwise lead you astray with poor instructions. We'll lead you through the steps when we get to the planning calculations, but it turns out that to use our tables, you must have today's values of your future pension. To be precise, we're actually looking for today's value for your first year's pension payment.

Your employer generally will make an estimate of your *future* value at retirement based on the anticipated length of service and, perhaps, some wage growth. You can convert that to today's dollars with the help of Figure 2.6. For example, if you had 10 years until you retire, and you expect inflation might average 3%, you would multiply your employer's forecast of, say, $10,000 by 0.744 to get $7,440 to use as today's value for our analysis. Technically, you should use an inflation rate adjusted for wage growth assumptions. The adjusted inflation rate would equal your inflation assumption plus your wage growth assumption minus your employer's wage growth assumption. Realistically, you don't know what either inflation or wage growth will be, so the practical solution is to use an inflation rate equal to your employer's wage growth assumption. If in doubt, just use 3% for an adjusted inflation rate. You do not have to be ultraconservative for calculations involving the period before you actually retire.

PENSION VALUES DEPEND ON LENGTH OF SERVICE

Since pension values depend on how long you have worked for your employer, you should know how to modify it for changes in the length of service. Typically, pensions are calculated with a formula like this:

$$(\text{Perhaps } 1.5\%) \times (\text{Years of service}) \times (\text{Ending wage measure})$$

Each employer will have his own percentage credit in this formula and there can be different ways to measure years of service and ending wage. For example, many employers use the average of the highest five years of pay to calculate the ending wage. Sometimes, the pension will be reduced by one-half of your expected Social Security because the employer feels he should get some credit for all of the years he matched your Social Security taxes with tax payments from the company. If you can get the formula, you can estimate your own pension benefit, but to get a rough estimate of the effect from retiring earlier or later than your employer quote, just multiply the quote times the following fraction:

$$\frac{\text{Your assumed years of service}}{\text{Employer's assumed years of service}}$$

That won't be exact, but it will give you something to work with until you can get your employer to be more specific for the situation that interests you.

IF YOU ARE ALREADY GETTING FIXED PAYMENTS BEFORE YOU RETIRE

Perhaps you are entitled to a fixed pension from a previous employer. It doesn't matter whether you are already receiving the payments or whether you will get them in the future. You are still going to have to calculate today's value of those payments in the first year of your (final) retirement. To get today's value, use Figure 2.6 in exactly the same manner as we did in the preceding example for a fixed pension. (The reason for this is that your current payments will be worth much less by the time you actually reach retirement.) For example, if you were already getting fixed payments of $10,000 a year, and you had five years until retirement, then Figure 2.6 shows us that 3% inflation would reduce the purchasing power to $0.863 \times \$10,000 = \$8,630$ in your first year of retirement. Use $8,630 in our analysis.

DISCOUNTING YOUR FUTURE PENSION

If there is some possibility that the source of your pension could get into serious financial trouble, then you should reduce its value in the analysis. If this is only a small possibility, it is worth discounting your pension by some small amount, perhaps 1% above the inflation rate, to allow for it. Of course, if you should leave your current employer for another job, your pension would be a lot less. If this is a possibility, you should make your estimate of your future pension based on the circumstances between now and your eventual retirement.

Annuities

A pension is a kind of annuity. It is an annuity that makes payments for the rest of your life, and sometimes for a surviving spouse, as well. Technically, an annuity is a contract between you and a financial institution to whom you or your employer pay a large amount of money up front so that you can get your payments for life or otherwise a certain number of years (known in the trade as *term-certain*). Your employer may offer you a choice of a lump sum on retirement or an annuity. Unless the amount is trifling, it is worth your while to pay to get an expert opinion to determine which alternative is best for you. Often the returns on an annuity are so low that you would be better off to take the lump sum, but the lifetime payments may have other attractive features in your particular case. If the annuity option is considered severance pay, you will have Social Security and Medicare deductions taken out until you die, so you should also consider that negative feature.

If you are a number of years away from retirement, the best thing to do is to assume you will get the lump sum and include it with your investments in your preretirement planning analysis. That's because, until you annuitize, it is an investment anyway. But when you get near retirement, and before the time comes to seek advice from a professional planner or accountant, you may derive great benefit by making two postretirement plans. The one would be based on adding the lump sum to your investments. The other would be based on getting annual payments. Then see which one gives you the greatest retirement budget. Virtually all of these annuities offer only fixed payments, so you would analyze that alternative just as if you had a fixed pension. In some cases, you may be offered an annuity that has payments that grow every year, probably at an amount less than inflation. In that remote case, put part of the annual annuity payments under the COLA entry and the other part under the fixed pension entry.

Which Survivor Option Should I Use for Planning?

The value of your pension and annuity will depend on the survivor option you choose for your spouse. Your employer benefit report may not show these options, in which case you want to talk to someone who understands the options you will be offered when you do retire. You and your spouse may have the choice of continuing with your full pension, 75% of your pension, 50% of your pension, or, under some conditions, no payments to the surviving spouse at all after you die. Of course, your pension payments will be a lot less if your pension has to last for your spouse's life, as well. The highest payments will be if you have no survivor benefits. For our preretirement planning analysis, just choose the value of pension that corresponds with the survivor option you think you will select. If you don't know anything about this subject, choose a middle ground by doing your planning with the pension that corresponds to 50% payments for the surviving spouse.

Incidentally, at some point before you retire, you most likely will find that an insurance company is offering a free seminar on the subject of pension planning. There is significant controversy about whether it is better to select an option with or without pension payments for the surviving spouse. Your employer will not let you select an alternative with no survivor payments unless your spouse also signs a statement. The insurance agent will urge your spouse to accept this alternative and buy a life insurance policy to protect the surviving spouse. There is no perfect answer to this dilemma. I'd be cautious and keep in mind that insurance products are usually expensive.

Gate 4. Planning with the Retirement Autopilot

The next thing you must do is determine how much you should be saving to meet your retirement goals. These goals should cover both the annual expenses you anticipate in retirement and any major purchases after you retire. These could be things like a vacation home, a sailboat, a lifetime dream cruise, or whatever. You will find, of course, that the amount you want to spend in retirement largely determines the amount that you need to save each year before retirement. Other things that increase the amount you need to save are major purchases or expenses (e.g., college for children) that will draw down your investments before retirement. You can try out various combinations on the preretirement worksheet in Figure 5.15.

The first thing to do is make a copy of Figure 5.15. Work from a copy because you will want to do this analysis again, both in succeeding years and because you may want to experiment with different amounts of retirement expenses as well as different retirement years, security allocations, and the like. It's easy to do this if you draw some more blank columns on the right-hand side of the copy and use one of the blank columns for each scenario. If you have a computer spreadsheet program, you can copy Figure 5.15, as well as Figure 5.16, and then let the computer do the math for you.

We'll offer some help for each step along the way, but most of the entries are self-explanatory. The main thing to keep in mind is that all entries should be before-tax values, not after-tax values, and everything should be in today's dollar values. We don't want you to try and guess what something might cost in the future. We already account for that by using historical economic and financial data in the tables where you will find values that correspond to your own customized inputs.

Some of you would like to know the theory behind the preretirement plans. You may recognize that because all of the work is done on a before-tax basis, the method will give excellent results for deferred tax investments, but you may question the accuracy when taxable investments are involved. In fact, the method as designed gives results that are almost as accurate as a method that separates taxable and deferred tax investments. That's because of two things. The first is that most people actually pay the taxes on their investment returns from their wages while working. This means that their investments are actually growing at a before-tax rate of return. The second is a correction for those instances where people pay some of their taxes from investment withdrawals. These withdrawals are a negative saving in our method, so even in this instance, the investments are growing at a before-tax rate of return.

Using the Preretirement Worksheet

Figure 5.15 is easy to complete if you choose one of the standard retirement ages: 62, your Social Security full retirement age, or age 70. Much of the complexity that follows is to cover cases for other ages.

Preretirement Worksheet

Step	Description	Example
1	Annual Social Security and COLA pension for you and spouse. See Step 1 instructions in text.	18,000
2	Annual fixed pension or annuity. Today's $ value equals employer's estimate times Fig. 2.6 factor. See Step 2 instructions.	13,200
3	Calendar year you will retire _____. Enter your age (or younger spouse if couple) in that year.	55
4	Factor from Fig. 5.16 using Step 3 and your chosen inflation estimate.	0.48
5	Step 2 times Step 4.	6,336
6	Current annual before-tax cash flow from investment real estate.	2,000
7	Estimated annual retirement expenses (including income tax & debt payments) in today's $.	40,000
8	Step 1 plus Step 5 plus Step 6.	26,336
9	Step 7 minus Step 8.	13,664
10	Real return before retire. See Fig. 4.4 or Fig. 4.5. Example: 70% stock and 1% costs.	5.7% - 1% = 4.7%
11	$\frac{1}{2}$ x real return after retire. See Fig. 4.4 or Fig. 4.5. Example: $\frac{1}{2}$ x (4.0% at 40% stock less 1% cost).	$\frac{1}{2}$ x (4.0% - 1%) = 1.5%
12	Factor from Fig. 5.17 using values closest to Steps 3 & 11.	26.9
13	Step 9 times Step 12.	367,562
14	Major purchases during retirement, e.g., condo. See text for tax adjustment.	60,000

(Figure 5.15 continued on next page.)

Step 1. You should automatically be getting a report from the Social Security Administration every year. If you can't find it, call 1-800-772-1213 and ask for an Earnings and Benefit Estimate Statement. If you plan on retiring before age 62, reduce the age 62 value in your Social Security report by 3.6% for each year retirement will be under 62. For example, if you plan on retiring at age 55, that's seven years earlier than 62, so 7 × 3.6% = 25.2% reduction. (This does not mean you will actually be getting a lower payment before age 62. It's just a way

15	Step 13 plus Step 14.	427,562
16	Current balance of all investments less equity used to produce cash flow in Step 6.	150,000
17	Large expenses before retirement, e.g., kid's college expenses. See text for tax adjustment.	100,000
18	Step 16 minus Step 17. If negative, show minus sign.	50,000
19	Number of years until you retire.	20
20	Factor from Fig. 5.18 for values closest to Step 10 and Step 19.	2.65
21	Step 18 times Step 20. (Show a minus sign if Step 18 is negative.)	132,500
22	Step 15 minus Step 21. (If negative, congratulations!)	295,062
23	Factor from Fig. 5.19 using values closest to Step 10 and Step 19.	33.9
24	Step 22 divided by Step 23. (Enter 0 if negative.)	8,704
25	The amount of Step 6 that you are reinvesting.	1,000
26	Savings from wages this year equals Step 24 minus Step 25.	7,704
27	Current gross annual wages excluding employer matching contributions to savings.	60,000
28	Estimated savings as percentage of wages: 100 times (Step 26 divided by Step 27).	12.8%

FIGURE 5.15 Use this preretirement worksheet to determine how much you need to save in order to support your future retirement expenses along with any preretirement purchases you will fund with investments.

of fooling the analysis to give the correct result for delayed payments.) If you will get a cost-of-living-adjusted pension, make the same kind of correction if necessary and add it to your Social Security. See the section earlier in this chapter to find out how to adjust your Social Security for you and your spouse for retiring at ages over 62. Be sure to use annual values, not the monthly ones in your report.

Step 2. This is simply your employer's estimate of your future annual pension if (1) you can start fixed pension payments in the year you retire and (2) if your employer did not assume any wage increases when calculating the expected value of your pension. If either of these things is not true, or you are

Fixed Pension Factors

Age of Younger Spouse	Life Expectancy Years	Fixed Pension Factors for Different Inflation Rates		
		3%	5%	7%
55	34.4	0.63	0.48	0.37
56	33.4	0.63	0.48	0.38
57	32.5	0.64	0.49	0.39
58	31.5	0.65	0.50	0.39
59	30.6	0.66	0.51	0.40
60	29.7	0.66	0.52	0.41
61	28.7	0.67	0.53	0.42
62	27.8	0.68	0.54	0.43
63	26.9	0.69	0.55	0.44
64	25.9	0.69	0.56	0.45
65	25.0	0.70	0.57	0.46
66	24.1	0.71	0.58	0.47
67	23.2	0.72	0.59	0.48
68	22.3	0.73	0.60	0.50
69	21.5	0.73	0.61	0.51
70	20.6	0.74	0.62	0.52
71	19.8	0.75	0.63	0.53
72	18.8	0.76	0.64	0.54
73	18.1	0.77	0.65	0.55
74	17.3	0.77	0.66	0.57
75	16.5	0.78	0.67	0.58
76	15.7	0.79	0.68	0.59
77	15.0	0.80	0.69	0.61
78	14.2	0.81	0.70	0.62
79	13.5	0.81	0.72	0.63

FIGURE 5.16 Select a future inflation value. Then find the fixed pension factor in the row corresponding to your retirement age (if single) or the age of the younger spouse (if married).

uncertain, the simplest thing to do is to multiply your employer's estimate times a factor from Figure 2.6 using the 3% column and the number of years until you will collect the payments. For example, with 20 years until retirement and an estimated fixed pension of $23,800, you would calculate an adjusted pension of 0.554 (from Figure 2.6) times $23,800 which would be $13,200.

If you have the time and inclination to be more precise, you'll have to adjust for one or both of these conditions. Adjustment 1: If you will retire before you are eligible to take payments, make the same kind of adjustment as for Social Security. This means you'll have to reduce the annual pension by 3.6% for each year between your retirement date and the year of the first payment in order to fool the equations. Adjustment 2: If your employer assumed some wage growth in calculating the expected value of your pension, you should first calculate an adjusted inflation rate equal to your assumed inflation plus your employer's wage growth percentage assumption minus your own estimate of wage growth percentage. With this adjusted inflation rate and the number of years between now and the year of the first payment, get a factor from Figure 2.6. Then multiply your annual pension estimate, accounting for adjustment 1 if necessary, times the factor from Figure 2.6. Whereas these two adjustments will improve the accuracy of your projections if your wages will increase at the same rate as inflation, the future is likely to be different than your assumptions. Recognize that projecting the ultimate value of a fixed pension is quite speculative until you are within a few years of retiring.

Step 3. Enter the year you plan to retire in the center column. If you are single, enter the age you will be in the year you plan to retire in the last column. If you are married, enter the age of whichever spouse is younger in the year you want to retire.

Step 4. Go to Figure 5.16. Select a column corresponding to an inflation rate you think will apply to your retirement years. It is better to select a conservative (higher) inflation rate, than a lower one, because it is impossible to guess what may happen. As contrasted with the preretirement adjustments in Step 2, this postretirement adjustment cannot afford any optimism. Most economists would probably say that an estimate of 5% inflation is fairly conservative, while an estimate of 3% may not be. Inflation has been much higher than 5% at times in the United States and even higher in many foreign countries. Once you've decided on a percentage, go down the column for the inflation rate you choose until you get to the age you entered in Step 3. Enter that factor in Figure 5.15. (*Alert:* In Step 2, we explained how you use Figure 2.6 to adjust your future pension to get today's dollar values. Step 4 is not a substitute for that. It is an addition to that adjustment.)

Step 6. Only make an entry here (before-tax annual rent minus costs, interest, and property taxes, not depreciation) if you expect to own this investment real estate through most of your retirement. If you make an entry here, don't include your equity in this real estate in Step 16. Although it will not be as accurate, if you prefer you can enter zero here and include all investment real estate equity in Step 16.

Step 7. We want your estimate of your expenses after you retire, expressed in today's dollars. Expenses include normal annual retirement living expenses, income tax, and annual debt payments, including any payments for a home mortgage that you will be making for at least five years of retirement. You can use a rough estimate of between 70 and 100% of your current annual wages for your expense estimate or a more detailed analysis from Figure 5.11 or 5.12 (see gate 2 earlier in this chapter for details).

Step 10. Here we are looking for your estimate of the real return (approximately the actual return minus inflation) for your investments before you retire. You can do a detailed calculation in Figure 4.4, or you can select a value from Figure 4.5, since real returns are largely dependent on the amount of stock or stock funds in your investment allocation. In the example, we assumed that the pre-retirement allocation was 70% stocks, so Figure 4.5 gave a real return of 5.7%. Also in the example, we assumed a smarter than average investor that had less than average costs of 1% of assets. Therefore, the net real return in the example is 4.7%. If you are uncertain about your investment costs, you might use 0.5% if you are using all index funds, or 2% if you are paying someone to manage your investments, or 1% in all other situations, as we have in this example. If more than one-third of your investments are real estate equity, use Figure 4.4 to determine your real return.

Step 11. This entry is used to give you a conservative real return for post-retirement. The instructions on Figure 5.15 show that you use only one-half of the real return that you think your particular allocation might yield. This helps to account for reverse dollar cost averaging and produces results that would correspond to roughly 80% confidence, if future investment return statistics are similar to those in the past. In the example, Figure 4.5 shows 4% real return with 40% stocks. Subtracting 1% for costs, the net return is 3%. Dividing the 3% real return by 2 gives 1.5% real return. If more than one-third of your investments are real estate equity, use Figure 4.4 to determine your return.

Step 12. Go to Figure 5.17 and get the factor in the column nearest to the value in Step 11 and the row for Step 3.

Step 14. Here you enter retirement expenses that are not included in your normal annual expenses in Step 7. Include large purchases like autos or a vacation home in today's values. Total the estimated value at today's prices. Then, divide by (1.00 minus your income tax rate expressed as a decimal). Example for $51,000 expenses and 15% income tax rate: $51,000 / (1.00 − 0.15) = $51,000 / 0.85 = $60,000.

Step 16. Investments are the total current balance of all of your investment accounts including employer savings plans, stocks, CDs, mutual funds, bank accounts, and so on. Include any investment real estate equity (market price minus debt) that was not used as a source for cash in Step 6. It is better not to include your home equity for preretirement plans. (See Chapter 3.)

Step 17. This is an entry for large preretirement expenses that you know will come from your existing investments and not be paid from your wages. You must make an adjustment for income tax using the equation from Step 14 even though you may pay for these items with investments that have no tax due when you make a withdrawal. This is a quirk of the method that allows us to do an analysis without separately accounting for taxable and deferred tax investments. (A practical note:

Postretirement Savings Factors

Age of Younger Spouse	Savings Factors for Various Real Returns								
	4.0%	3.0%	2.5%	2.0%	1.5%	1.0%	0.5%	0.0%	-1.0%
55	18.9	21.6	23.2	24.9	26.9	29.1	31.6	34.4	41.1
56	18.6	21.2	22.7	24.4	26.3	28.4	30.8	33.4	39.7
57	18.4	20.9	22.3	24.0	25.8	27.8	30.0	32.5	38.4
58	18.1	20.5	21.9	23.4	25.1	27.0	29.2	31.5	37.1
59	17.8	20.1	21.5	22.9	24.6	26.4	28.4	30.6	35.8
60	17.5	19.8	21.0	22.5	24.0	25.7	27.6	29.7	34.6
61	17.2	19.3	20.6	21.9	23.4	25.0	26.7	28.7	33.3
62	16.9	19.0	20.1	21.4	22.8	24.3	26.0	27.8	32.1
63	16.6	18.6	19.7	20.9	22.2	23.6	25.2	26.9	30.9
64	16.3	18.1	19.1	20.3	21.5	22.8	24.3	25.9	29.6
65	15.9	17.7	18.7	19.7	20.9	22.1	23.5	25.0	28.4
66	15.6	17.2	18.2	19.2	20.3	21.4	22.7	24.1	27.3
67	15.2	16.8	17.7	18.6	19.6	20.7	21.9	23.2	26.1
68	14.9	16.3	17.1	18.0	19.0	20.0	21.1	22.3	25.0
69	14.5	15.9	16.7	17.5	18.4	19.4	20.4	21.5	24.0
70	14.1	15.4	16.1	16.9	17.7	18.6	19.6	20.6	22.9
71	13.8	15.0	15.7	16.4	17.1	18.0	18.9	19.8	21.9
72	13.3	14.4	15.0	15.7	16.4	17.1	17.9	18.8	20.7
73	13.0	14.0	14.6	15.2	15.9	16.6	17.3	18.1	19.9
74	12.6	13.5	14.1	14.6	15.3	15.9	16.6	17.3	18.9
75	12.1	13.1	13.6	14.1	14.6	15.2	15.8	16.5	17.9
76	11.7	12.6	13.0	13.5	14.0	14.5	15.1	15.7	17.0
77	11.3	12.1	12.5	13.0	13.4	13.9	14.5	15.0	16.2
78	10.9	11.6	12.0	12.4	12.8	13.2	13.7	14.2	15.3
79	10.5	11.1	11.5	11.8	12.2	12.6	13.1	13.5	14.5

FIGURE 5.17 Select a real return for postretirement investments. Then find the savings factor in the row corresponding to your retirement age (if single) or the age of the younger spouse (if married).

If you will be under age 59½ when incurring the expenses in Step 17, the funds can't come from a 401(k). You should not put all of your savings in deferred tax plans. Instead, you should make sure that your savings in other investments will be sufficient to support these expenses to avoid an early withdrawal tax penalty.)

Step 18. If Step 17 is larger than Step 16, you will get a negative number here. Make sure that you enter the minus sign in this case. This indicates you not only haven't saved much for retirement, but also are going to use most of your current annual savings for large expenses before you retire. The alternative is to buy these large items using a loan and make the loan payments out of your current wages. In that case, these large purchases would not be in Step 17. Of course, that will reduce the amount you can save each year. You'll have to make that choice yourself. Better yet: See if you can get by without the large purchases at all.

Step 20. Go to Figure 5.18 and find the factor in the column for Step 10 and the row for Step 19.

Step 22. If you have a negative number in Step 21, remember your high school math: minus a minus is a plus. So if Step 15 is $400,000 and Step 21 is,

Preretirement Current Savings Factors

Years till Retire	Savings Factors for Various Real Returns								
	8.0%	7.0%	6.0%	5.0%	4.0%	3.0%	2.0%	1.0%	0.0%
0	1.00	1.00	1.00	1.00	1.00	1.00	1.00	1.00	1.00
2	1.17	1.14	1.12	1.10	1.08	1.06	1.04	1.02	1.00
4	1.36	1.31	1.26	1.22	1.17	1.13	1.08	1.04	1.00
6	1.59	1.50	1.42	1.34	1.27	1.19	1.13	1.06	1.00
8	1.85	1.72	1.59	1.48	1.37	1.27	1.17	1.08	1.00
10	2.16	1.97	1.79	1.63	1.48	1.34	1.22	1.10	1.00
12	2.52	2.25	2.01	1.80	1.60	1.43	1.27	1.13	1.00
14	2.94	2.58	2.26	1.98	1.73	1.51	1.32	1.15	1.00
16	3.43	2.95	2.54	2.18	1.87	1.60	1.37	1.17	1.00
18	4.00	3.38	2.85	2.41	2.03	1.70	1.43	1.20	1.00
20	4.66	3.87	3.21	2.65	2.19	1.81	1.49	1.22	1.00
22	5.44	4.43	3.60	2.93	2.37	1.92	1.55	1.24	1.00
24	6.34	5.07	4.05	3.23	2.56	2.03	1.61	1.27	1.00
26	7.40	5.81	4.55	3.56	2.77	2.16	1.67	1.30	1.00
28	8.63	6.65	5.11	3.92	3.00	2.29	1.74	1.32	1.00
30	10.1	7.61	5.74	4.32	3.24	2.43	1.81	1.35	1.00
32	11.7	8.72	6.45	4.76	3.51	2.58	1.88	1.37	1.00
34	13.7	9.98	7.25	5.25	3.79	2.73	1.96	1.40	1.00
36	16.0	11.4	8.15	5.79	4.10	2.90	2.04	1.43	1.00
38	18.6	13.1	9.15	6.39	4.44	3.07	2.12	1.46	1.00
40	21.7	15.0	10.3	7.04	4.80	3.26	2.21	1.49	1.00
42	25.3	17.1	11.6	7.76	5.19	3.46	2.30	1.52	1.00
44	29.6	19.6	13.0	8.56	5.62	3.67	2.39	1.55	1.00
46	34.5	22.5	14.6	9.43	6.07	3.90	2.49	1.58	1.00
48	40.2	25.7	16.4	10.4	6.57	4.13	2.59	1.61	1.00
50	46.9	29.5	18.4	11.5	7.11	4.38	2.69	1.64	1.00

FIGURE 5.18 Select a real return for preretirement investments. Then find the investment savings factor for the number of years until you retire.

say, −$100,000, then Step 15 minus Step 21 is $400,000 + $100,000, or $500,000. If Step 22 results in a negative number, you can stop here because you probably already have enough savings. Still, remember to do another calculation next year, especially if there is a drop in the securities markets.

Step 23. Go to Figure 5.19 and find the factor that is in the column closest to Step 10 and the row closest to Step 19.

Preretirement Annual Savings Factors

Years till Retire	Savings Factors for Various Real Returns								
	8.0%	7.0%	6.0%	5.0%	4.0%	3.0%	2.0%	1.0%	0.0%
1	1.04	1.04	1.03	1.03	1.02	1.02	1.01	1.01	1.00
2	2.16	2.14	2.12	2.10	2.08	2.06	2.04	2.02	2.00
4	4.69	4.60	4.51	4.42	4.33	4.25	4.16	4.08	4.00
6	7.63	7.40	7.18	6.97	6.77	6.57	6.37	6.18	6.00
8	11.1	10.6	10.2	9.79	9.40	9.03	8.67	8.33	8.00
10	15.1	14.3	13.6	12.9	12.2	11.6	11.1	10.5	10.0
12	19.7	18.5	17.4	16.3	15.3	14.4	13.5	12.7	12.0
14	25.2	23.3	21.6	20.1	18.7	17.3	16.1	15.0	14.0
16	31.5	28.9	26.4	24.2	22.3	20.5	18.8	17.3	16.0
18	38.9	35.2	31.8	28.8	26.2	23.8	21.6	19.7	18.0
20	47.6	42.4	37.9	33.9	30.4	27.3	24.5	22.1	20.0
22	57.7	50.7	44.7	39.5	34.9	31.0	27.6	24.6	22.0
24	69.4	60.2	52.3	45.6	39.9	34.9	30.7	27.1	24.0
26	83.2	71.1	60.9	52.4	45.2	39.1	34.0	29.7	26.0
28	99.2	83.5	70.6	59.9	51.0	43.6	37.4	32.3	28.0
30	118	97.8	81.4	68.1	57.2	48.3	41.0	35.0	30.0
32	140	114	93.6	77.2	64.0	53.3	44.7	37.7	32.0
34	165	133	107	87.2	71.3	58.6	48.5	40.5	34.0
36	195	154	123	98.2	79.2	64.2	52.5	43.3	36.0
38	229	179	140	110	87.7	70.2	56.7	46.2	38.0
40	269	207	159	124	96.9	76.5	61.0	49.1	40.0
42	316	239	181	139	107	83.3	65.5	52.1	42.0
44	371	275	206	155	118	90.4	70.2	55.2	44.0
46	435	317	233	173	129	97.9	75.1	58.3	46.0
48	510	366	264	193	142	106	80.1	61.5	48.0
50	597	421	299	215	156	114	85.4	64.8	50.0

FIGURE 5.19 Select a real return for preretirement investments. Then find the annual savings factor for the number of years until you retire.

Step 24. This is the total amount you must save each year to support the expenses you listed in Steps 7, 14, and 17.

Step 25. This step refers to only that part of your real estate cash flow from Step 6 that is being reinvested. Step 6 was the before-tax annual cash from your investment real estate. You may be using some of that cash to support your current living expenses. If so, subtract the amount going into current living expenses from Step 6. You'll get the amount that is being reinvested either in some securities or in some more real estate or to pay down principal on real estate loans. Another way to get the amount of Step 6 that you are reinvesting is to see how much of that cash flow you are investing in securities, or for purchasing more investment real estate, or for making payments to principal on investment real estate loans.

Step 26. This is the bottom line. It is the estimated amount you must save from your wages and employer contributions to your savings plan each year. In subsequent years, you will have to increase the amount approximately by the amount of inflation, but much depends on your investment performance relative to your assumed returns in Step 10.

If you are like most people who do an analysis like this the first time, this amount is considerably larger than your current capability to save. This is a good time to reassess whether you can afford all of those expenses as well as whether you can afford to retire as early as you assumed. On your copy of this worksheet, enter another column and try again until you reach a balance between the most you can save each year and the expenses you can afford in Steps 7, 14, and 17.

If you are making withdrawals from your investments to pay income tax on investment income, these are negative savings. The reason is that we are using before-tax returns, which implies that taxes on investment income are paid from wages. Therefore, you must increase the savings you calculate in Step 26 by the amount you take from investments to pay the taxes that investments incur.

Step 27. Enter your gross annual wages excluding any employer matching funds. Gross wages are wages before any deductions for taxes, savings plans, and the like.

Step 28. This is the percentage of Step 27 that you must save. That is split between you and your employer. In the example, suppose you calculated that your employer was making matching contributions to your savings plan of $2,400 this year. Subtract that from Step 26 to get $5,304, which would be your required savings contribution to meet your goal. That is 8.8% (rounded) of $60,000. Your employer's matching contribution is 4% of $60,000. Together they are 12.8%, which is just what is entered in Step 28. If the non tax-deferred part of Step 16 is less than Step 17, then most of Step 28 should go to non tax-deferred accounts.

Engaging the Autopilot

You have already done the hardest part of the autopilot analysis, but you can't do the remaining few steps until about a year from now. However, you've done the basics for your planning. You have determined an allocation, selected the best vehicles, picked investments you can manage, established a tentative retirement age, and determined how much you should save this year. Next year, these same steps will really be easy if you save this year's worksheet.

Next year you can engage the autopilot, which is still another step up in technology. You'll be using some feedback to help you stay on course. You do this with Figure 5.20.

Step 29. To fill in this step, just enter the results from Step 28 of Figure 5.15 from this year's analysis.

Step 30. Now enter the results from Step 28 of Figure 5.15 from last year's analysis.

Steps 31 through 34. These are simple mechanical steps that engage the retirement autopilot. By Step 34 you have a savings percentage for this year that has been adjusted to keep your retirement savings on track using the autopilot technology. Remember that the percentage in Step 34 is the sum of the percentage that your employer contributes to your savings plan plus your own savings. If your employer is contributing 4% of your gross wages to the savings plan, in the example, you would have to save 11.2% of your gross wages on your own. In a moment we'll show you an example of the large improvement in accuracy you achieve over time using the autopilot, but first, there are going to be times when you'll want to shut it off, that is, not use Figure 5.20. This is similar to what a pilot

Autopilot Adjustments

Step		Example
29	Results from Step 28 of this year's analysis.	12.8%
30	Results from Step 28 of last year's analysis.	16%
31	If Step 29 is less than Step 30, enter 75% of Step 30; otherwise, enter 0.	12%
32	If Step 29 is less than Step 30, enter 25% of Step 29; otherwise, enter 0.	3.2%
33	Add Step 32 to Step 31.	15.2%
34	If Step 29 is less than Step 30, enter Step 33 here; otherwise, enter Step 29.	15.2%

FIGURE 5.20 Apply the retirement autopilot to determine what percentage of your wages should be going into savings each year.

might do when he or she needs more control. For example, there may be reasons other than inflation or investment balance changes that explain why Step 28 is much different this year than last. Did something else change, such as adding a major expense or a significant change in your estimate of future returns? If you made large changes to items other than investment balances, you might want to ignore Step 34 altogether and just use Step 28 as your savings figure for this year.

On the other hand, if the result in either Step 28 or Step 34 is beyond your capability to save, you've got to go back to revise one or more of the other steps, such as the age you plan to retire (Step 3) or your desired retirement expenses (Steps 7 and 14). Or look at your large expenses before retirement (Step 17). When you make calls like these, you are adapting to whatever is new in the environment. Then the autopilot is no longer a simple system with a little bit of feedback; it's an adaptive autopilot that, in effect, changes the gain for the new situation.

The Preretirement Autopilot Benefits

So where's this autopilot we've been telling you about? You were probably looking for colored lights, dials, control knobs, and circuit cards. You've already seen it, and probably were distracted by those "If . . . ; otherwise, . . ." statements in steps 29 through 34 of Figure 5.20. You probably thought you were doing your income tax return again. What you were really doing is acting like a circuit card in the retirement autopilot.

Those autopilot steps did two things: (1) They provided feedback from last year's analysis, and (2) they said to be cautious if reducing last year's saving percentage. We'll talk separately about each of the points.

Most of the modern retirement planning methods provide some feedback. For example, you get feedback just by using an updated set of investment balances each year. That's not unimportant. The problem is that when you near retirement, it can drive your preretirement planning wild. One year it will say you have to save a lot, the next year it may say you don't have to save anything, and so on. It starts to cycle. The autopilot steps in and helps regain control.

The editor of this book doesn't like me to use engineering terms, but we're using an engineer's solution, so, if he'll close his eyes for a moment, I'll sneak in a paragraph for the engineers. When investment balances are large relative to annual savings, a relatively small difference in annual return can change the investment balances far more than can be corrected with an annual savings change. This puts the system out of control. So we add an outside loop with the autopilot. It provides damping to help bring back some stability. There will be times when the autopilot doesn't have enough strength to give the system the necessary stability. You'll know that, because even with the autopilot in Figure 5.20, you won't be able to save enough money to bring investment balances up to the level to meet your goal. Then you've got to add some intelligence and judgment. What you'll have to do is to change your goals, that is, the amount that you expect to spend in retirement.

Let's illustrate how the autopilot works. Figure 5.21 shows three different scenarios, all beginning in 1945 and culminating in retirement 20 years later in 1964. One scenario shows annual savings calculated using the shortcut method we saw in Chapter 1. It's oversimplified, but its principal problem is that it is just too optimistic about returns. In this example, its returns are 2% higher than the assumptions in the other two scenarios. The second set of computations is done using a typical commercial software program where we used the same estimated returns as with the autopilot. We want to show how the autopilot would differ in operation, not in assumptions. The third scenario is like the computer program except that we've added an autopilot.

What you should notice is that the shortcut method, because of its optimistic returns, always overreacts. As it nears retirement, one year it tells the user not to save anything, and the next year it tells the user to save a lot. The computer program with more realistic returns does better than the shortcut method, but it still cycles in a way that has to be frustrating to the user. The autopilot method slows down the motions and adds some shock absorption. But there are still going to be cases where the autopilot's feedback makes only a minor improvement.

Gate 5. Just before Retirement

When you get very close to retirement, the best thing to do is to go to Chapter 6 and calculate how much you could afford to spend if you were actually in retirement now. Use your current investment balances and your Social Security and pension estimates. Then, try to live for a year on that kind of a budget if it's less than the amount you currently spend. That's the acid test. You may

Autopilot Stops Oscillations

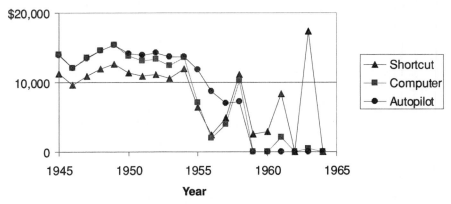

FIGURE 5.21 The autopilot gives practical annual savings profiles.

have some expenses while you are still working that you won't have after retirement, but remember that after retiring, there's a lot more time for leisure activities, and unless all that time is going to be spent in the woods under a tent or at the public library, there's more opportunity to spend money than while you were working. Although people often get more physically active after retiring, there's still a whole new set of health costs until Medicare insurance steps in at age 65, as well as another set of costs after that when you switch to a Medicare gap health insurance. People often forget that their medical, dental, hearing, and eye problems get worse as they get older. Even Medicare doesn't cover much of this, nor the majority of mounting prescription costs. So, if you can't actually live on a retirement budget now, it is very unlikely you will be able to do so later in life.

How Can I Improve My Retirement Benefits?

The three basic ways to improve retirement benefits are to

1. Work longer
2. Save more each year
3. Invest more aggressively and wisely

The best way to improve your retirement benefits is to work longer. The good news is that this can increase your savings, Social Security benefits, and pension values. The bad news is that you won't have as many years in retirement, but, then again, you can spend more each year because your savings won't have to last as long.

The next best thing you can do to improve your retirement benefits is usually to increase annual savings. When people really come face-to-face with how little they will get in retirement, they become highly motivated to save more. I've seen people increase annual savings to the point where they are saving one-half of their take-home pay. Most of us would have real trouble doing this, but when the reality of living off Social Security alone sets in, people really become interested in saving and investing.

Investing more aggressively to increase your retirement benefits may, or may not, be a good idea. That's why we say you should consider investing more aggressively and more wisely. If your savings are all in low-return fixed income accounts, you are not going to do as well in the long run as you would if part of your investments were in stocks or stock mutual funds.

To give you a quantitative feel for what these basic actions can do to improve retirement, we'll set up a very simple case for a 50-year-old couple who already have $100,000 in retirement investments, are saving $10,000 each year (adjusted for inflation), and want to take out $20,000 a year (adjusted for inflation) in retirement, which would begin at age 65. We'll look at three alternative investment plans.

1. Invest conservatively, which we'll define as keeping the amount of stock in your portfolio to a percent that is equal to 90 minus your current age, so, for example, at age 50 you would have 40% of your investments in stock. All stocks are large company stocks. Fifteen percent of the investments are in a money market and the rest are in long-term corporate bonds.

2. Invest moderately, by keeping the amount of stock in your portfolio to a percent of your investments that is equal to 105 minus your current age, so, for example, at age 50 you would have 55% of your investments in stocks. Twenty percent of the stock is in growth stocks and the rest is in large company stocks; 10% of the investments are in a money market and the rest is in long-term corporate bonds.

3. Invest aggressively, by keeping the amount of stock in your portfolio to a percent of your investments that is equal to 120 minus your current age, so, for example, at age 50 you would have 70% of your investments in stocks. Forty percent of the stock is in growth stocks and the rest is in large company stocks; 5% of the investments are in a money market and the rest is in long-term corporate bonds.

In all three cases we'll assume a 20% tax rate, 1.0% costs for stocks, 0.5% costs for bonds, and 0.3% costs for money markets. All returns are long-term returns calculated each year using Figure 4.4.

Next, we're going to look at some idealized computer results just to show you how the various approaches you take compare in importance.

Let's look first at what would happen if the annual savings numbers were different, since this is one of the first things most people consider. Figure 5.22 shows the growth of a moderate investment portfolio in the 15 years before retirement, after which $20,000 (inflation-adjusted) is withdrawn each year. The difference between three different annual savings levels varying from $7,500 to $12,500 is important. Figure 5.22 shows that, after retiring at age 65, the couple with the smallest annual savings would have run out of money at age 80, while the couple with the largest annual savings would have run out of money at age 88. So an extra $5,000 per year savings extended their investments by eight years.

Next, we'll look at what would happen to this same couple if they kept saving $10,000 per year but changed to different levels of investment aggressiveness. Figure 5.23 illustrates that the differences are significant and shows that the conservative couple would run out of money at about age 80 while the aggressive couple would have funds past age 90. So your asset allocations have more impact than the three different savings levels we chose to review earlier.

The third and usually last thing people consider is retiring later, but that is often the best choice. Here, we are only going to show what happens to investments, but the change in Social Security and pensions from additional years of

Investments Last Longer When You Save More

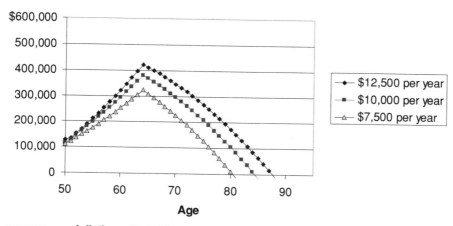

FIGURE 5.22 Inflation-adjusted investment balances for three different savings rates.

work will amplify these results. Figure 5.24 shows that retiring at 62 demolishes savings by about age 76 while retiring at age 68 provides funds till about age 92. Incidentally, it's better to stay on a job that has good retirement benefits than to try and seek some other work after retiring that may not offer any benefits at all.

There is real synergy if you look at various combinations of saving more, investing more aggressively, and working longer. Look at Figure 5.25. The bot-

It Can Pay to Invest Aggressively

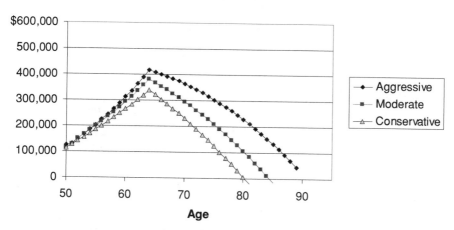

FIGURE 5.23 Inflation-adjusted investment balances for different investment portfolios.

Retiring Later Provides Major Benefits

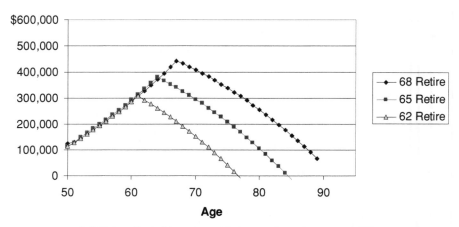

FIGURE 5.24 Inflation-adjusted investment balances for retirement at different ages.

tom case begins with a moderate portfolio and savings of $10,000 per year. By both saving more and being more aggressive, retirement funds could last up to around age 100. By doing all three things—saving more, investing more aggressively, and working longer—a completely different retirement lifestyle is possible. Annual spending could be $30,000 instead of $20,000.

It Pays to Save More, Invest Aggressively, and Work Longer

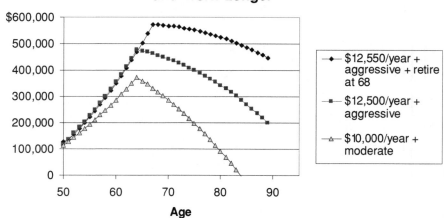

FIGURE 5.25 Investments last much longer by combining extra savings, being more aggressive, and retiring later.

Finally, to improve retirement benefits, don't forget these things:

- Stay away from high-fee or high-cost investments. If it costs 2% to manage your investments, and your average return is 8% before those costs are deducted, you have 6% return after the management costs.
- Put your fastest-growing investments in your employer's savings plan or IRA. If you have savings in addition to these, then put the more conservative part of your portfolio outside your employer's saving plan or IRA (unless you are interested in leaving substantial sums to your heirs).
- People in high tax brackets should consider investments with significant long-term capital gain potential outside of their deferred tax investments. This is another way to effectively defer taxes and has the added advantage of lower tax rates when redeemed or even no capital gains tax if given to a charity or left to heirs.
- Younger people should seriously consider the Roth IRA. Its tax-free growth will provide benefits to a long-term investor in the likely high-tax environment of the future—and you don't have to start making minimum withdrawals at 70½.

Fine-Tuning Your Retirement Date

Up to this point, we have been asking, "How much must I save to be able to spend a certain amount in retirement?" When you are very close to retirement, you can ask a different kind of question, namely, "How much can I afford to spend after I retire?" This changes the goal from a retirement spending objective to a retirement date selection.

We can use some of the same kind of tools as in Figure 5.15, but rearranged as in Figure 5.26, which starts with your inputs and ends with the amount you can spend for expenses and income taxes in retirement each year. We'll choose to use examples that will illustrate the synergy from combining all of the things you can do to increase retirement benefits: work longer, save more, and invest more aggressively. By looking at the bottom line, you'll see that the scenario for retirement at age 66 provides more than twice as many retirement benefits as retiring at age 58. This is not just because the people worked longer; it's also because the age 62 and 66 scenarios include increased annual savings and more aggressive investments. When you've finished trying out your own data in the worksheet, you'll have the information you need to make the decision whether you should have more money or more years in retirement.

The steps in Figure 5.26 are almost all self-explanatory. Here are the places where you might need some help.

Step 5. The longer you work, the larger your pension will be. The amount is dependent on the formula used by your employer, so the best thing to do is to ask your employer to give you a pension estimate for the retirement ages that

Retirement Income If Retire at Different Ages

Step		Retire at Age:		
		58	62	66
1	Your retirement age.	58	62	66
2	Years till retire.	4	8	12
3	Your Social Security * & COLA pension.	9,300	11,000	15,000
4	Spouse's Social Security * & COLA pension.	3,500	4,100	7,500
5	Fixed pension. (See Step 5 instructions.)	12,000	16,000	20,000
6	Fixed pension factor from Fig. 5.16 using Step 1.	0.50	0.54	0.58
7	Step 5 times Step 6.	6,000	8,640	11,600
8	% stock in investments before retirement and real return, e.g., Figure 4.5 less 1%.	30% / 2.5%	50% / 3.4%	70% / 4.7%
9	Factor from Figure 5.18 using values closest to Step 2 and real return in Step 8.	1.13	1.27	1.80
10	Current retirement investment balance times Step 9. (Example: current balance = $200,000.)	226,000	254,000	360,000

11	Factor from Figure 5.19 using values closest to Steps 2 and 8.	4.25	9.03	16.3
12	Annual new savings from wages.	5,000	7,500	10,000
13	Step 11 times Step 12.	21,250	67,725	163,000
14	Balance at beginning of retirement. (Step 10 plus Step 13.)	247,250	321,725	523,000
15	Major purchases during retirement, e.g., auto purchases. See text for tax adjustment.	40,000	40,000	40,000
16	Remaining balance for other expenses. (Step 14 minus Step 15.)	207,250	281,725	483,000
17	% stock in investments after retirement and $\frac{1}{2}$ real return, e.g., $\frac{1}{2}$ x (Figure 4.5 less 1%.)	30% / 1.25%	40% / 1.5%	50% / 1.7%
18	Factor from Figure 5.17 using values closest to Step 1 and real return in Step 17.	25.1	22.8	19.2
19	Retirement income from investments. (Step 16 divided by Step 18.)	8,257	12,356	25,156
20	Total retirement income in today's dollars. (Sum of Steps 3, 4, 7, and 19.)	27,057	36,096	59,256

* If retiring before age 62, reduce age 62 Social Security by 3.6% for each year retirement will be under 62 (e.g., at 58, 4 x 3.6% = 14.4% reduction).

FIGURE 5.26 Use this analysis to determine your retirement benefits at different retirement ages.

interest you. If this is difficult to get, then make a rough estimate using the following formula:

$$\frac{\text{Annual pension at X years of service multiplied by Y years of service}}{\text{X years of service}}$$

For example, if your employer says your pension is $20,000 per year after 20 years of service, and you want an estimate for 23 years of service, the equation would be:

$$\frac{\$20,000 \times 23}{20}$$

which would be $23,000 per year. After determining this value, you will have to make further adjustments just like you did using the instructions for Step 2 of Figure 5.15, because the same factors still apply.

Step 8. This is the real return on your preretirement investments. Since real return is largely determined by the percentage of stock in your portfolio, we used Figure 4.5 for guidance. In the age 58 retirement case, for example, a portfolio with 30% stock had a long-term real return of 3.5% as determined from indexes representing the various securities in the portfolio. In the example, we subtracted 1% from Figure 4.5's totals to represent investment costs. The resulting 2.5% is shown in Step 8. If you are not sure about your investment costs, use 0.5% if you are using all index funds, 2% if you are paying someone to manage your investments, or 1% in all other situations.

Step 10. This calculation requires your current balance of retirement investments. The sample data were calculated using a current balance of $200,000. If you know that you will be spending part of your retirement investments on some very large preretirement purchases, you should reduce the investment value by an adjusted cost for the purchases. To adjust the cost, divide by (1.00 minus your tax rate). For example, if you had something that cost $9,000 and a 10% net tax rate, the cost would be $9,000 / (1.00 − 0.10), which would be $10,000. After subtracting the adjusted cost from investments, multiply the remaining investments by the number from Step 9.

Step 15. Here you enter retirement expenses that are not to be included in your normal annual expenses. Include large purchases like autos, a vacation home, and so forth in today's values. Total the estimated value at today's prices. Then divide by (1.00 minus your income tax rate expressed as a decimal). Example for $18,000 expenses and 10% income tax rate: $36,000 / (1.00 − 0.10) = $36,000 / 0.90 = $40,000.

Step 17. This is the real return on your postretirement investments. You can use the same method as in Step 8 to determine its value. However, note that we use only one-half of the return in this analysis. The reason is that we need a return that accounts for reverse dollar cost averaging, and we want a high-confidence return for retirement work. In Chapter 4 we saw that by using one-half of the theoretical real return, we would succeed in about 80% of historical scenarios so that your money would last through retirement without serious penalties late in life.

Step 20. The resultant income in Step 20 is not the kind of income you would report on your tax return. Rather, it is a number that is the sum of the budget you can afford for retirement expenses plus the amount of income tax you would have to pay to get that much money from your investments. So if you had a net tax rate of 10%, in the age 58 example, you could budget $27,057 less $2,706 tax for a net budget for expenses of $24,351.

Your Figure 5.26 results are one of the most valuable benefits derived from this book if you are near retirement. I have seen countless people who would have given their eyeteeth if they had seen such an analysis before they finally decided to retire. Often you can make major improvements in your retirement lifestyle in those last few years before retirement.

Are You Faced with an Early Retirement Decision?

It's too bad, but one of the realities of modern times is that companies are continuing to *redefine* themselves. This is the language used by the top corporate executives to impress Wall Street and justify mergers, acquisitions, and downsizing. The reality is that, in many major companies, thousands of people will be offered some kind of incentive to depart voluntarily. You may find yourself in such a situation.

I have helped a number of employees with this kind of problem. They are really faced with three alternatives: (1) Accept the offer and retire now. (2) Reject the offer but stay with the firm in the hope that enough other people will leave instead. (3) Accept the offer and seek employment elsewhere. The best answer is highly dependent on your age at the time. Most 55 year olds will have real trouble with alternative (1).

This is one of the most important decisions you can make about retirement, and you are probably being forced to make up your mind quickly. Keep in mind that your employer is not going to make this offer to you unless it is to his or her advantage—and that definitely may not be to your advantage. Once you retire, you lose your existing job and its benefits. If you go to work someplace else, your new pension plan, if any, starts with a new set of years, which is far less effective than adding some years to your previous pension plan. You may have to face a vesting limit on your savings as well. And once you start getting Social Security, additional work may reduce the Social Security benefit or even wipe it out entirely.

You may be tempted by an early retirement package. It's designed to be just barely tempting, not generous. You can easily quantify the differences between the alternatives you have with an analysis such as in Figure 5.27. For example, suppose your employer offers you a package where he or she gives credit for another two years when calculating your pension and offers you a lump sum

Evaluating an Early Retirement Offer

Step	Description	Accept offer & retire now	Cases Reject offer but stay with same firm	Accept offer & work elsewhere
1	Your retirement age.	58	62	62
2	Years till retire.	0	4	4
3	Your Social Security * & COLA pension.	9,300	11,000	11,000
4	Spouse's Social Security * & COLA pension.	3,500	4,100	4,100
5	Fixed pension.	14,000	16,000	14,000
6	Fixed pension factor from Figure 5.16.	0.50	0.54	0.54
7	Step 5 times Step 6.	7,000	8,640	7,560
8	% stock in investments before retirement and real return, e.g., Figure 4.5 less 1% costs.	50% 3.4%	50% 3.4%	50% 3.4%
9	Factor from Figure 5.18 using Steps 2 & 8.	1.00	1.13	1.13
10	Add any lump sum offer to your current retirement investment balance. Then multiply that result times Step 9.	230k x 1.00 = 230,000	200k x 1.13 = 226,000	230k x 1.13 = 259,900

Step	Description			
11	Factor from Figure 5.19 using Steps 2 & 8.	NA	4.25	4.25
12	Annual new savings from wages.	0	7,500	0
13	Step 11 times Step 12.	0	31,875	0
14	Balance at beginning of retirement. (Step 10 plus Step 13.)	230,000	257,875	259,900
15	Major purchases during retirement, e.g., auto purchases. See text for tax adjustment.	40,000	40,000	40,000
16	Remaining balance for other expenses. (Step 14 minus Step 15.)	190,000	217,875	219,900
17	% stock in investments after retirement and $1/_2$ real return, e.g., $1/_2$ x (Figure 4.5 minus 1%).	50% 1.7%	50% 1.7%	50% 1.7%
18	Factor from Figure 5.17 using Steps 1 & 17.	25.1	22.8	22.8
19	Retirement income from investments. (Step 16 divided by Step 18.)	7,570	9,556	9,645
20	Total retirement income in today's dollars. (Sum of Steps 3, 4, 7, and 19.)	27,370	33,296	32,305

* If retiring before age 62, reduce age 62 Social Security by 3.6% for each year retirement will be under 62 (e.g., at 58, 4 x 3.6% = 14.4% reduction).

FIGURE 5.27 Compare your alternatives when faced with an early retirement offer.

that will be worth $30,000 after income tax. In the example for the last column in the table, we assume you will get a lesser job (as most commonly happens) without benefits or savings plan.

The steps in Figure 5.27 are identical to those in Figure 5.26, so the same instructions apply. However, there are two differences in its application. The first is that you must reflect the difference in the pension offers between the three alternatives in Step 5. The second is that the offer of a lump sum is added to Step 10.

If you examine the results in Figure 5.27, you will see that the early retirement offer is not as good as if you continued to work for an extra four years. In fact, each year you continue, you continue to reinforce the case against taking early retirement. In most early retirement offers I have evaluated, continued employment was a lot better than accepting an early retirement offer, especially for those people under age 62. However, in these situations, the employer usually at least hints at layoffs, which would be worse than not accepting the offer. This makes the choice a real gamble. What we've given you is a method where you can put some numbers to your own situation and make a more informed choice. Your own numbers, of course, will be quite different, as will the comparative results.

These are only some of the financial considerations. You also want to consider your health and other activities. Early retirement requires that you have some things to occupy yourself, perhaps another job, community or charitable services, or some projects that are really important to you. If not, you may have a problem that's worse than most people's financial problems from early retirement.

Mum's the Word!

In any event, don't be too hasty about telling people (including your employer) that you are considering retiring soon, even if the numbers seem to support your decision that this is the right thing to do. This decision is so important that you should go over your plan with an accountant or professional planner to get another view. Pay for a one-time consultation with at least one professional and consider getting a second opinion. Also give serious consideration to nonfinancial matters such as the use of your time and what you may be able to contribute to your family and community. After you've thought about these things in conjunction with the financial aspects, you may decide to change your mind about retiring soon!

CHAPTER 6

Spending in Retirement

Every man is rich or
poor according to the
degree in which he
can afford to enjoy
the necessities,
conveniences, and
amusements of
human life.*

Retirement is the time to start using your savings, and that is what this chapter is about. But you need to do it intelligently so that your funds will last the rest of your life, and so that you can help offset inflation's devastating cumulative effects over the 10, 20, 30, or even 40 years you may have ahead of you. This chapter is only for those who have already retired, although it can be helpful to those who are very close to retirement if they make a trial run to see how much they can afford to spend in retirement considering the resources they have already accumulated.

As I mentioned in Chapter 5, my wife and I are both avid skiers. Downhill skiers who race must pass through certain gates as they speed down the mountain. If they miss a gate, they can't win. So it is with retirement planning. You must pass through certain gates to get to a winning retirement plan. In fact, there are six gates. The first gate, appropriately enough, is to look ahead to see what is before you. That's exactly what the skier does as he waits at the starting gate for the signal to go.

Gate 1. To make the best use of the retirement autopilot, you should understand some of the fundamentals that make it such a powerful tool. By looking ahead and forecasting your future needs for money to make debt payments,

*Adam Smith, *The Wealth of Nations*, 1776.

purchase large value items occasionally, and pay taxes, we can reduce what otherwise could be intolerable budget ups and downs for normal living expenses.

Gate 2. To use the retirement autopilot method to best advantage, we are going to ask you to organize your inputs in a special way. In this process, you are going to have to visualize the future. For example, we want you to make an estimate, using today's prices, of large purchases you may want to make in the future. Then your final retirement plan will provide for the things you envision.

Gate 3. How much can you afford to spend each year for normal living expenses? That's the biggest question of all. It's possible that your initial answer is too low. Then you'll have to redo the plan until you strike a balance between the large future purchases in gate 2 and this year's affordable expenses. You may not be able to afford everything you want. Or you may have more than you need, in which case you can plan to give some away or leave an inheritance.

Gate 4. In the real world, investment values and inflation change every year thereby adding bumps and potholes in your retirement path. In gate 4 we'll show you a very simple autopilot adjustment to your affordable expenses that will smooth out the rough spots, just as the shocks on your car do on a bumpy road.

Gate 5. All of the planning in the world isn't any good if you can't control your finances so that you stay on track. A few simple steps can be powerful in ensuring that you fulfill the plan you established in the previous gates.

Gate 6. Here is the final gate. It asks you to look much further ahead and reminds you that you need to pay attention to insurance, IRA administration, and estate planning considerations. It won't provide you with all of the answers, but will offer some guidance.

Gate 1. Understanding the Fundamentals

The first thing you must know about planning is that you must look ahead. If you know something is coming far enough in advance, you can reduce its impact if it's something that requires money like a large future purchase. Conversely, you can take early advantage of something that will provide funds in the future, such as the sale of real estate or the benefits from making the last payment on a mortgage. Planning will make your financial life much better. Our first gate is to develop an understanding of how the planning process works by looking at the underlying fundamentals.

Retirement Resources

First, we'll start with the resources. These are the building blocks of your retirement plan, so we want to ensure that you enter the values in a special way that will make your planning much easier and more accurate. There are far too many retirement plans where the inputs are inconsistent with the planning method and, therefore, almost always, provide a plan that encourages spending too much too early, thereby leaving the retiree with too few resources late in life. These resources are

- Social Security, pensions, and annuities
- Investments, savings from part-time work in retirement, and reverse mortgages

Retirement Budgets

After carefully organizing our retirement resources, we're going to gradually use them up in a controlled manner so that the resources will last throughout our retirement life. These controls are in the forms of the following four budgets:

1. A budget for income tax
2. A budget for debt payments
3. A budget for large future purchases and possible emergencies
4. A budget for normal living expenses excluding the items separately budgeted previously

Unlike most budgeting methods, we're not going to simply subtract the first three budgets from our resources to get a budget for normal living expenses. That's not the basis of a good plan because normal livings expenses would have to go up and down when debt payments start and end. Similarly, normal living expenses would take a beating in the year of some large future purchase. Many retirement budgeting methods severely constrain and distort normal living expenses going from one year to another. As an example, we're not going to submit the retiree to the shock of a new automobile purchase all at once because we're going to anticipate its purchase in advance. That's what planning is all about.

In the retirement autopilot method, the normal living expenses will change little from year to year except for some upward increases to offset inflation. Therefore, we're going to give normal living expenses another name when they are the product of our planning process. We're going to call them *affordable expenses.*

In order to calculate affordable expenses, we ask that you organize income tax, debts, and reserves in a special way. They become inputs to your plan. The output of the plan is the fourth budget: annual affordable expenses. The affordable expenses will not change appreciably year to year because the planning method will distribute the effects from income taxes, loan payments, and large future purchases over your remaining life expectancy. You don't have to worry about how this is done because it is built into the equations that are behind the charts you will use for planning. We've already made the hard computations for you.

We said that affordable expenses increase a little each year to offset inflation. In actual practice, you will find that affordable expenses usually increase at a rate just a bit less than inflation until you are in your mid-80s, when you start to lose the battle to inflation. See Figure 6.1. Using our methods, you will, however, have some investments left on your last day, because the method accounts for the fact that you may outlive your *current* estimate of your life expectancy.

Figure 6.1 has two lines: The future dollar line represents the actual normal expenses in future dollar values, which have degraded purchasing capability. The other line represents the normal expenses in today's dollars, which allows us to relate to the values better. Today's dollars all have the same purchasing power in each year. Note how well the method holds purchasing power relatively constant until late in life. This may correspond to a reduced need for expenses later in life, perhaps because of less activity or the death of one's spouse. However, if you keep a reserve for other things that might be more costly late in life, you can afford those too. In fact, the particular case behind Figure 6.1 includes large debt payments for the first three years and the purchase of a motor home at age 69 that cost $100,000 when priced at age 65 but escalated to $112,551 when purchased at age 69. Note that you don't even see a wrinkle in the affordable expense lines. That's because we had a winning retirement plan. We looked ahead.

Some people like to think of affordable expense as an annual retirement paycheck that has 100% income tax withheld, as well as sufficient withholding to cover their debt payments and provisions for their estimate of reserve purchases that would not be part of their normal annual budget.

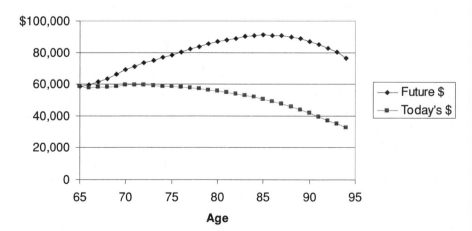

Affordable Expenses with 3% Inflation

FIGURE 6.1 This affordable expense budget shows how future dollars and today's dollar values diverge.

Your cash outlays will be greater than affordable expenses, because your cash outlays have to cover income taxes, debt payments, and the purchase of items included in reserves, as well as affordable expenses. Most people do not have to calculate their actual cash outlays if they divide their affordable expense budget by 12 for a monthly budget, or by 52 for a weekly budget, and keep their monthly or weekly spending within that level. Then they can get enough cash from their income and investments to pay for their expenses (limited to the affordable expense budget), taxes, debts, or large purchases as those individual needs arise.

The autopilot planning method stretches your funds out to the point where you will always have some balance unless you have a horrible market loss or purposefully withdraw the remaining money. We'll illustrate this with a theoretical example that has the same returns and inflation every year. That way you'll be able to see how smoothly the mechanization handles events that cause big perturbations in most other budgeting or forecasting systems. Look now at Figure 6.2. At age 65, the retiree began with $1 million that was split with one-half in an IRA deferred tax account and the other half in a taxable investment account. There were no draws on the IRA until age 70. Until then, all of the draws were on the taxable account. (Values shown in Figure 6.2 are end-of-year balances, so the first data point is at the end of age 65.)

You may wonder why there is a sudden drop in the taxable account. That's because the retiree bought a large recreational vehicle at age 69. Because the retiree had planned for it, there is virtually no year-to-year change in affordable expenses (Figure 6.1), which are meant to cover all of the normal expenses, not unusual large items.

History of Investment Balances

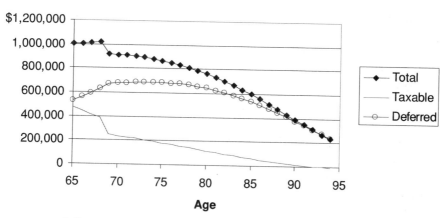

FIGURE 6.2 Inflation-adjusted investment balances for deferred tax and taxable accounts.

The Proof Is in the Pudding

Let's take a look at the example behind Figures 6.1 and 6.2. We are considering a 65-year-old couple who have three more $10,000 per year debt payments on a home. What would happen with most budgeting methods is that they would effectively get a raise of $10,000 in the fourth year when the mortgage payments end. That doesn't happen here, as we'll show.

We'd also like to illustrate a plan for some large future purchase. Most planning methods lead you to finance the purchase of large items because your budget can't take the strain of paying for these items outright. And if you pay for them from savings, the contribution to your future income decreases proportionately. There's a better way. With our method, you establish a reserve for that expensive item. The reserve doesn't have to be a separately identifiable investment. Then, before you actually purchase the item, you've already had a small reduction in your budget, and after the purchase, you'll have more in your budget than with other budgeting systems.

All of this is detailed in Figure 6.3. You can see the resources consisting of investments, Social Security, and a pension. Then there are the budgets for income taxes, major purchases, and debt payments. Finally, there is the budget for affordable expenses, which is shown in both future dollars and today's dollars. Affordable expenses are calculated using a method that we're going to describe later in the chapter. (However, since this simulation has constant returns and inflation, we did not employ any of the retirement autopilot smoothing features.) What you should note now is that there is very little change in today's dollar values each year. The entire history through age 94 is plotted in Figure 6.1.

The draw from investments plus Social Security plus pension equals all of the expenses each year. There are no draws from the IRA deferred tax account until age 70. Then the IRA draws are based on the recalculation method using IRS Publication 590 life expectancies. These draws are all deposited to the taxable account each year. All draws and deposits are made in the middle of the year, which gives the same approximate result as if the draws and deposits were divided by 12 and made monthly.

The point we are illustrating is shown dramatically with the major purchase of $112,551 at age 69 and the three remaining mortgage payments. Because our method is a total plan and looked forward to these events, the affordable expenses in Figure 6.1 stayed virtually the same each year. Thus, the normal living expenses, reflected in the affordable expense budget, don't incur major upheavals.

In real life, returns and inflation change each year, so there is some additional variation in affordable expenses. However, we smooth those effects with another feature of the retirement autopilot. That's the principal of feedback. We'll demonstrate its powerful effects later in the chapter.

Retirement Resources and Annual Budgets

Age of Younger Spouse	Def'd Tax Account* Year-End Balance	Def'd Tax Account* Required Draw	Taxable Account* Year-End Balance	Taxable Account* This Year Draw	Other Resources Social Security**	Other Resources Fixed Pension	Other Budgeted Items Income Taxes***	Other Budgeted Items Major Purchase	Other Budgeted Items Mortgage Payment****	Affordable Expense Future Dollars	Affordable Expense Today's Dollars**
	500,000		500,000								
65	530,000		473,793	54,570	12,000	10,000	7,800		10,000	58,770	58,770
66	561,800		445,791	54,786	12,360	10,000	7,618		10,000	59,528	57,794
67	595,508		414,665	56,188	12,731	10,000	7,422		10,000	61,497	57,966
68	631,238		390,468	47,648	13,113	10,000	7,199			63,562	58,168
69	669,113		246,823	162,207	13,506	10,000	7,040	112,551		66,122	58,749
70	675,804	32,481	237,306	56,099	13,911	10,000	10,680			69,330	59,805
71	681,197	34,132	227,301	57,669	14,329	10,000	10,905			71,093	59,539
72	684,748	36,234	216,705	59,762	14,758	10,000	11,195			73,326	59,621
73	686,866	37,831	205,735	61,106	15,201	10,000	11,405			74,902	59,128
74	687,184	39,703	194,356	62,735	15,657	10,000	11,656			76,737	58,812
75	685,518	41,648	182,605	64,378	16,127	10,000	11,915			78,590	58,478
76	681,676	43,664	170,524	66,030	16,611	10,000	12,185			80,456	58,123
77	675,768	45,445	158,238	67,306	17,109	10,000	12,418			81,997	57,511
78	667,297	47,589	145,725	68,956	17,622	10,000	12,706			83,873	57,113

* 6% actual returns in both accounts   ** 3% inflation   *** 15% net tax rate   **** 8% mortgage

FIGURE 6.3 Results from annual analysis using affordable expense calculations each year.

Gate 2. Organizing Your Inputs to the Plan

By completing the process in Chapter 3 for asset allocation, selection of the best vehicles from a tax standpoint, and then choosing investments you can manage, you have completed the first part of a successful retirement plan. In order to develop the remainder of the plan, we are going to ask you to assemble your information in a certain way. You can pull your retirement information together at any time of the year, but I usually do this myself right after I have completed my income tax return, because my mind is then on financial matters, and all my financial materials are readily at hand. You can either use the information as of the current date, or use values as they were at the beginning of the year. I do the latter for several reasons:

- It allows me to compare my investment performance with the market averages, which, by tax time, will show the performance for the full previous year.

- I have all of last year's investment balances, tax information, and updated Social Security payment values.

Before you begin, make a copy of Figures 6.4 and 6.6 because you will want to work from a new copy of these each year to enter updated values of your retirement resources and adjust them for the conditions you see ahead.

Organizing Resources with Lifetime Payments

We'll begin the process of organizing your inputs by completing your copy of Figure 6.4 with Social Security, pension, and lifetime annuity payments. You may note that there are two items that are not in that figure: (1) part-time employment when retired, and (2) annuities with payments for fixed periods that would pay out before death. That's because neither will make payments for life. We will enter values for these two items in Figure 6.6 when we get to that point. But, let's begin work on Figure 6.4 first.

Step 1, enter the current *annual* values of Social Security if you are now receiving payments. If you are under 62, use the estimate you get from the Social Security Administration for age 62 multiplied by 12 even if you would plan to delay taking payments to an older age. If you are over 62 but are still not drawing Social Security, use the annual value you would have received if you were taking Social Security now. These same statements apply to your spouse as well even if he or she is, or will be, taking a nonworking spouse's benefits based on your credits.

There is a substantial amount of information concerning Social Security payments for single and married people in Chapter 5. If you or your spouse are not yet drawing Social Security, we advise you to review that material.

Step 2 is a Social Security adjustment for those who are retiring before age 62. It provides a factor to account for the fact that you are effectively going to

Adjustments to Annual Income from Social Security, Pensions, and Lifetime Annuities

Step	Source	You	Spouse
1	Social Security	13,000	6,000
2	Figure 6.5 factor from Soc. Sec. column	1.0	0.92
3a	Adjusted Soc. Sec. (Step 1 times Step 2)	13,000	5,520
3b	Total for both spouses from Step 3a	18,520	
4	Estimated % of real COLA in above	67%	
5	Escalating Soc. Sec. (Step 3b times Step 4)	12,408	
6	Fixed part of Soc. Sec. (Step 3b minus Step 5)	6,112	
7	Annual pension or annuity payments	15,000 example fixed pension	5,000 example COLA pension
8	1.0 or Figure 6.5 factor if delay till 62	1.0	1.0
9	Adjusted pension (Step 7 times Step 8)	15,000	5,000
10	Estimated % of real COLA in above	0% for a fixed pension	67%
11a	COLA part of pension (Step 9 times Step 10)	0	3,350
11b	Total for both spouses from Step 11a	3,350	
12a	Fixed part of pension (Step 9 minus Step 11a)	15,000	1,650
12b	Total for both spouses from Step 12a	16,650	
13	Total COLA income (Step 5 plus Step 11b)	15,758	
14	Total fixed income (Step 6 plus Step 12b)	22,762	

FIGURE 6.4 Adjusting Social Security and pensions for age and less-than-perfect COLAs.

be borrowing from your other investments until you start taking Social Security in the future. (If you would actually have to borrow money from someone other than yourself, you should not be retired!) Find the factor from Figure 6.5. For example, if you are age 62 or over, the factor is 1.00. If your spouse was age 60, the factor is 0.92. If you are already getting Social Security, enter 1.00. Enter you and your spouse's factors in Figure 6.4.

Step 3a is simply Step 1 values multiplied by Step 2 factors to get an adjusted Social Security value.

Step 3b is the sum of the two spouses' values from Step 3a.

Step 4 requires some judgment. We include it because many people believe that the COLA used to increase Social Security every year will fall short of the actual inflation experienced by retired people. Organizations like the American Association of Retired Persons (AARP) and the Seniors Coalition are vocal about this, particularly since health and drug costs are underweighted in the index for an older person. As a measure of some conservatism in this area, you might do as I do. I know that the cost of the things I buy has increased faster than the government's current market basket used to measure the CPI, so I assume the government will cover only about two-thirds (67%) of inflation. This means that 67% of your Social Security will be inflation adjusted and 33% won't be. If you think Social Security will fully protect you from inflation, enter 100% instead. But remember that in the next few decades we will go from over three workers per retired person to only two workers per retired person. That will put a lot of pressure on the Social Security system. Some of the government's possible solutions are to increase taxes on Social Security or redefine the CPI so that it represents a different basket of goods that includes prices that increase more slowly than the present basket, which is the standard for measuring inflation. That would be a move in the wrong direction for retirees.

Age Factors
(For payments delayed until age 62)

Age	Social Security & COLA Pensions	Fixed Pensions & Annuities
55	0.75	0.54
56	0.79	0.59
57	0.82	0.64
58	0.85	0.69
59	0.89	0.75
60	0.92	0.81
61	0.96	0.88
62 & Over	1.00	1.00

FIGURE 6.5 Factors to account for retiring before Social Security and pensions can begin.

Step 5 calculates the part of Social Security that is inflation adjusted, and then *Step 6* calculates the amount that is not inflation adjusted.

Step 7 records the *annual* amount of any pension or lifetime annuity payments. If you have annuity payments that are very likely to end while you are still living, then do not make an entry here because we'll remind you to do that later in Step 16 in Figure 6.6.

Step 8 requires that you enter either 1.00 if you are already receiving pension payments, or a factor from Figure 6.5 to adjust the pension for a delay in the start of your pension payments until you are age 62. It does not mean that you will be getting less money when you do start getting payments. It's just a way of fooling the computation to account for the delay.

Step 10 gives you an opportunity to show that your COLA pension really doesn't keep up with inflation. It is easy if you have the most common type of a pension, that is, a fixed pension, which gives you the same dollar amount until you die. In this case, just enter zero because there is no COLA part. On the other hand, if you have a COLA pension (as you might if you were a government employee), then you have to estimate the amount of the COLA that you think will be real. If you think retirees have higher inflation rates than reflected in the CPI used to determine COLAs, you won't want to enter 1.00 here, which would mean that your COLA pension would keep up exactly with your costs as a retiree. Therefore, you might consider using 67% value here as with Social Security. You would want to use a value at least this low if your COLA is capped because COLA pensions are often limited to a maximum of 3% inflation a year. If your COLA is capped at 2%, I would use 50% here.

Steps 11a and 11b give the amount of the pension that will be fully adjusted for inflation, while *Steps 12a and 12b* are the amounts that will not escalate with inflation.

Steps 13 and 14 collect all of the COLA income and fixed income inputs, respectively.

Organizing Your Investments

The remaining funds for your retirement must come from your investments. We want to make sure we haven't forgotten anything, so Figure 6.6 provides the reminders. That's important to a retiree, as may be some of the other nonsecurity type items in Step 16 that can be equated to investments and ultimately provide retirement funds.

Step 15 asks you to account for all of your investments. This includes your company savings plans, all IRAs including Roth IRAs, variable annuities, deferred compensation, market value of stock options as if exercised now, stocks, bonds, mutual funds, CDs, savings accounts, and so on. It also includes investment real estate equity, that is, the current market value of your real estate less the current amount of debt on it. You can use Figure 3.7 that you developed to control your allocations to get the data for Step 15, but we've split

Organize Your Investments

Step	Description	Current Balance
15	Investments.	
	Stocks and stock mutual funds.	300,000
	Good investment real estate <u>less</u> related debt.	100,000
	Poor investment real estate <u>less</u> related debt.	
	Fixed income investments excluding money markets.	300,000
	Money markets.	50,000
16	Other sources for retirement funds.	
	Remaining credit from a reverse mortgage, insurance cash value, etc.	
	Investment equivalent to future wages earned in retirement or from annuity or contract with payments for period shorter than life.	50,000
17	Total investments and other sources. (Step 15 items plus Step 16 items.)	800,000
18	Stock, stock funds, and equity in good investment real estate as % of Step 17. In the example above that would be (300,000 + 100,000) divided by 800,000 = 0.50 = 50%.	50%

FIGURE 6.6 Organizing your investments and future contributions to investments from part-time wages and annuities with less-than-lifetime payouts.

investment real estate here into good and poor categories so that your return is not overly optimistic.

You don't have to separate the investments in Step 15 as shown, but it makes it easy to calculate the percent of investments in stock and good investment real estate for Step 18. Good investment real estate is real estate that is appreciating and has positive before-tax cash flow. Poor investment real estate does not meet the criteria for good investment real estate. The latter would include your home if you chose to include part of it, but it's usually not a good idea to include your home equity unless you intend to sell it fairly soon and become a renter. The reason for this is that you need a place to live and at this point it's probably going to be the same home for a long while.

On the other hand, if you plan on renting after selling the house within the next few years, then you can add the current equity (market value less any selling costs, potential capital gains taxes, and your current mortgage principal) to your investments. Or if you know that you are going to sell and buy a less expensive home, you can subtract the forecasted purchase price of the new home from the current market value of your current home less any estimated selling costs and capital gains taxes that would be due on the sale. (There is additional information concerning homes as investments in Chapter 3.)

Step 16 wants you to account for items sometimes forgotten. Don't include automobiles, furniture, or personal effects, and only include investment collectibles at the value you would get from the sale of your collectibles today. If someone owes you money, and you are sure you can collect, include the remaining balance as an investment asset. List life insurance cash value.

If you are considering a reverse mortgage, and you have not included any home equity in Step 15, you can put a fraction such as 40% of the equity in your home as an investment if you're 65, plus another 1.5% for each year over 65 as a very rough guide. When you get within a few years of actually trying to get such a loan, get some quotes from lenders to use in your planning. If you're already using the reverse mortgage as a line of credit for future lump sum draws, ignore the value of your house and any credit already used, but include the remaining line of credit in Step 16. If you're already getting fixed payments for your life, include the payments as a fixed pension in Step 7 of Figure 6.4. If the payments are for a specified number of years, don't count any part of your house as an investment and use the method in Appendix A, Hard-to-Value Investments. Then enter that value in Step 16 of Figure 6.6. Evaluate a reverse mortgage very carefully. The American Association of Retired Persons says to consider reverse mortgages only as a last resort.

There are several items where you can convert annual payments for a certain length of time into an equivalent investment. These include part-time work, annuities with payments that are likely to stop before you die, and payments using a contract payment schedule. Use the method in Appendix A. Unless you have good reason to do otherwise, use the 8% column of the figure in the appendix for anything that will give payments that remain fixed in value each year and the 4% column for anything where the payments will increase with inflation each year.

The most common hard-to-value item is part-time work. First, you have to calculate an adjusted annual wage. This is your current gross annual income (plus employer matching funds, if any) minus taxes for Social Security and Medicare. You should also subtract income taxes to be conservative. Then go to Appendix A and follow the example as illustrated.

Step 17 is your total value of investments and other potential sources of retirement funds.

Step 18 asks for stock and good investment real estate equity as a percentage of your investments in Step 17. This percentage will help you determine a real return in the next gate. That's why we didn't just use the percentage we calculated in the asset allocation analysis. Now that we're in retirement, we want to make sure that we're going to use conservative future returns. Assets like poor investment real estate and cash value of a life insurance policy are likely to bring below average returns. Perhaps you should cash out things like these and find more productive investments.

Organizing Your Debts

We are going to adjust debts so that we account for the fact that high-interest debts are much more punitive than low-interest debts. Make a copy of Figure 6.7 for your own work. You will have to determine the remaining balance of your home mortgage and any other debts. You may already have a schedule showing the remaining principal from your lender. If not, you can call the lender and get a recent value for the remaining amount owed. You might want to use the original home mortgage value if you bought your home less than 10 years ago because there is little reduction in principal early in a long-term mortgage and using a slightly larger debt value is conservative. If any of your debts have interest rates higher than 10%, multiply the remaining debt times the factor from Figure 6.8.

The results of Figure 6.7 will be used to determine a budget for debt payments that will be separate from your other normal living expenses. Because of this, it is prudent to include your home mortgage and personal loans. On the other hand, if you have rental properties as an investment where the loan payments will be made from the rents received, you should not include the debt

Remaining Balance of Mortgages and Debts

(Don't include investment debts covered by their income.)

Description	Value
Home mortgage	142,902
Home equity loan	
Other loans	
Credit card loans if maintain continuing loan balance	1,000
Total	143,902
Note: If any debt has interest higher than 10%, then multiply debt times factor from Figure 6.8 before making entry.	

FIGURE 6.7 Current principal for debts that will be used to determine a budget for debt payments.

Factor for High Interest Rate Debts

Years	Loan Interest Rate								
Left	10%	11%	12%	13%	14%	15%	16%	17%	18%
1	1.03	1.04	1.05	1.06	1.07	1.07	1.08	1.09	1.1
2	1.04	1.06	1.07	1.08	1.1	1.11	1.13	1.14	1.15
3	1.06	1.07	1.09	1.11	1.13	1.15	1.17	1.19	1.21
4	1.07	1.09	1.12	1.14	1.16	1.19	1.21	1.23	1.26
5	1.08	1.11	1.14	1.17	1.19	1.22	1.25	1.28	1.31
6	1.09	1.13	1.16	1.19	1.23	1.26	1.29	1.33	1.36
7	1.11	1.14	1.18	1.22	1.26	1.3	1.33	1.37	1.41
8	1.12	1.16	1.2	1.24	1.29	1.33	1.37	1.42	1.46
9	1.13	1.18	1.22	1.27	1.32	1.37	1.41	1.46	1.51
10	1.14	1.19	1.24	1.29	1.35	1.4	1.45	1.51	1.56
11	1.15	1.21	1.26	1.32	1.38	1.43	1.49	1.55	1.61
12	1.17	1.22	1.28	1.34	1.4	1.47	1.53	1.59	1.66
13	1.18	1.24	1.3	1.37	1.43	1.5	1.56	1.63	1.7
14	1.19	1.25	1.32	1.39	1.46	1.53	1.6	1.67	1.75
15	1.2	1.27	1.34	1.41	1.48	1.56	1.63	1.71	1.79
16	1.21	1.28	1.35	1.43	1.51	1.59	1.67	1.75	1.83
17	1.22	1.29	1.37	1.45	1.53	1.61	1.7	1.78	1.87
18	1.23	1.31	1.39	1.47	1.56	1.64	1.73	1.82	1.91
19	1.24	1.32	1.4	1.49	1.58	1.67	1.76	1.85	1.94
20	1.24	1.33	1.42	1.51	1.6	1.69	1.79	1.88	1.98

FIGURE 6.8 Adjustment factor for high interest rate debts.

here. If you are buying raw land that has no rental income to offset the loan payments, you would include any of its indebtedness here.

You should exclude any debt coming from a reverse mortgage in debts unless you plan to actually repay the debt while you are alive. If you have any remaining balance on a credit line from a reverse mortgage, you should enter that in Step 16 of Figure 6.6.

Organizing Reserves for Large Future Purchases

Reserves are the amount of your investments that you set aside for emergencies, rainy day expenses, or preplanned high-value items. They will not be used for your normal affordable expenses in retirement, so in the planning forms we will subtract the amount of your reserves from the current value of your investments. This means that you will be able to spend whatever is in reserves for whatever you want, but those particular expenses will not be part of your normal budget.

In a copy of Figure 6.9, list the current value of your reserves in terms of their cost today, not some future cost. For example, if you wanted to list the cost of four new automobiles that cost $20,000 today but would be bought at various times in your retirement, you would enter $80,000 even though the price of those automobiles likely would be very much higher when purchased many years from now. In effect, we're going to set aside part of your investments to cover these future costs. Those investments can grow and offset the price escalation. The items on Figure 6.9 are just suggestions for things to consider. You should list whatever items are pertinent to your own future.

It is prudent to increase the size of reserves following years when your investments have grown abnormally fast. This will provide some buffering when the market goes south.

Gate 3. How Much Can You Afford to Spend?

For a retiree, "How much can I afford to spend?" is the most important question this book can answer. If you spend too much early in retirement, you won't have enough for the later part of your life. If you spend too little, you are going to leave more for your heirs and estate taxes and less for you. Of course, you want to be able to increase your spending level each year to compensate for inflation for most of your retirement and ensure that you have enough left for the full life of you and your spouse.

Years ago, when inflation was very low, retirees could often get by with spending all of their after-tax Social Security, pension, dividends, and interest. Things have changed so much that this is no longer practical. It's not just that inflation will destroy your future; ordinary stock dividends, as a percent of investments, are only a fraction of the values in the past. Mergers and acquisitions reduce dividend predictability. And mutual funds declare capital gains dividends in a completely unpredictable fashion. Then you must decide whether you should spend or reinvest capital gains distributions because spending them destroys the future growth of your investments. All of these things indicate that the old-fashioned approach just doesn't work very well in this modern world. You need something better.

Almost all retirees who have deferred tax investments from a 401(k) or IRA can't wait to start drawing as soon as they can avoid tax penalties for early withdrawals. Deferred tax investments make it easy to live off those withdrawals if you withdraw an amount equal to last year's ending balance divided by your current life expectancy, found in IRS Publication 590. Then, in theory, you generally will have some small increase each year early in retirement to help combat inflation until late in life. Also, you will always have some income no matter how long you live. The method, however, gives large year-to-year budget changes. If the market is up 20% this year, you've got 20% more to spend. Unfortunately, the reverse is true. If you have a 20% market decline,

Reserves for Future Large Purchases

Reserve Items	Cost in Today's $
Home appliance replacement, major home repairs or remodeling	10,000
Future autos, RVs, trailers	50,000
Emergency uninsured major medical, dental, and drug costs	20,000
Exceptional vacations, tours, trips	
Assisted care costs above normal living costs	
Additional financial help for children or parents	
Gifts or part of estate for heirs or charity	
Downpayments on vacation home, condo, time-share	
Provisions for other contingencies	20,000
Total (recommend not less than one year's income minus Social Security)	100,000

FIGURE 6.9 List large future expenses that will not be part of your normal annual living expenses.

you've got 20% less to spend. It gets worse as you get older. When your life expectancy is down to 10 years, you are withdrawing funds at 10% a year. That 20% market decline effectively wiped out 2 years of your future life. It's even worse for a surviving spouse using the optional term-certain method (instead of the minimum distribution incidental benefit [MDIB] method) to calculate required minimum distributions. When the last year of the term is over, the surviving spouse has *no* money left. Zip!

Most financial planners use a more esoteric way of determining how much a retiree can spend from investments. Technically, they do an annual calculation each year using financial equations for annual payments from your current investment balance using a real (inflation-adjusted) return and your current life expectancy. The real return is usually based on the long-term average or compound historical returns of securities the same as, or similar to, those you currently hold. More conscientious planners reduce these returns by the costs associated with buying, managing, and selling investments. Do-it-yourselfers, and even some professionals, don't know how to bring fixed pensions into the equations correctly.

Besides the potential mistakes in coping with a fixed pension, most planning methods' forecasts will likely be too optimistic for more than 50% of retirees. This is because of three factors: (1) They usually don't reduce the returns for typical costs and fees of brokers and mutual funds. (2) Long-term real returns correspond to a middle estimate of returns. This means that, 50% of the time, real returns over the lifetime of a retiree are going to be lower than the middle estimate if the future is like the past. (3) Returns for retirees are lower than long-term real returns because of reverse dollar cost averaging.

Retirees cannot afford optimistic forecasts leading to overspending in their early retirement years. Unlike people who are still working, retirees are subject to too many events that can leave them financially helpless the rest of their lives. The security markets can fall; inflation rates can increase; medical and dental costs can soar; they may live much longer; and, inevitably, there are always unforeseen requirements. The roof needs replacing; the furnace falls apart; property taxes or rent increases abruptly; a child has a severe financial problem; insurance no longer covers an expensive drug; reduced physical capacity requires costly assistance; the car must be replaced, and on, and on. I know about these kind of things firsthand because I've helped support three parents, and because I regularly visit and comfort a number of elderly people in our community.

Of course, one almost surefire way of ensuring that the funds will last a lifetime is to keep the initial retirement spending so low that there is plenty of room for market failures and the ability to handle severe economic problems. The major flaw here is that the retiree gets little benefit from hard-earned savings. Instead the heirs and government will get the major share in all likelihood.

The Retirement Autopilot Provides a Better Plan

After working with many retirees and long hours on the computer using simulations with annual historical returns and inflation to test various alternatives, I believe that the following points are the most important elements in a retirement planning method:

- Determine your annual budget using only about half of the real inflation-adjusted return that you might get from historical references, which we'll show you next in Figure 6.10. This offsets reverse dollar cost averaging effects and provides high confidence that your plan will provide adequate funds later in retirement.

- Modify your budget figures using the autopilot feedback calculations that we'll describe when we get to Figure 6.15. This reduces the almost intolerable swings in annual budgets and enhances retirement budgets later in life.

- Set aside significant reserves for contingent large future expenses in years following abnormally high stock market growth. Then scale them back if you must in years when the market really drops. It's a prudent way to achieve some of your future retirement dreams without jeopardizing your normal living expenses.

To use the retirement autopilot planning method we must first complete Figure 6.10. The process is simple and self-explanatory. After the first year of using Figure 6.10, you can use Figure 6.15, which introduces a new technology for retirement planning to absorb the shocks that otherwise occur during the sudden changes of stock market prices. Make a copy of Figure 6.10 and complete the following steps with your own numbers.

Step 1. Enter your age if you are single; otherwise, enter the age of the younger spouse.

Step 2. Get your state and federal income tax from last year's tax return. If you are one of those unlucky people who also have a local income tax, include it as well. But don't include taxes such as property or excise taxes. Only income taxes, please.

Step 3. Gross income is your adjusted gross income from last year's tax return plus any tax-exempt income, plus the untaxed part of Social Security, and any allowable depreciation on investment real estate reported on your income tax.

Step 5. This is your estimate of your future tax rate, expressed as a decimal instead of a percentage (e.g., 0.18 instead of 18%). You might not want to use last year's tax rate from Step 4 if that rate does not reflect the tax rate you think you might have in the future. If not, select a value that you think is better. Remember that this rate effectively establishes a budget for income tax, so it

Affordable Expense Budget in Retirement

Age and Income Tax Information

Step		
1	Current age of younger spouse if married or your age if single.	55
2	Last year's state & federal income tax.	8,000
3	Last year's gross income. (Include tax-exempt income and depreciation.)	50,000
4	Last year's net tax rate. (Step 2 divided by Step 3.)	0.16
5	Enter Step 4 if you think it represents a conservative (slightly high) value for the future, otherwise enter your own estimate considering any special conditions.	0.18
6	1.00 minus Step 5.	0.82

Social Security, Pensions, and Annuities

7	Annual adjusted Social Security and COLA income. (Step 13 from Fig. 6.4.)	15,758
8	Annual fixed pension and/or annuity. (Step 14 from Fig. 6.4.)	22,762
9	Fixed pension factor for inflation and age or life expectancy. (From Fig. 6.11.)	0.475
10	Adjusted fixed pension contribution to budget. (Step 8 times Step 9.)	10,812

Investments, Debts, and Reserves

11	Current market value of investments. (Step 17 from Fig. 6.6.)	800,000
12	Adjusted value of debts. (From Fig. 6.7.)	143,902
13	Adjusted reserves. (Fig. 6.9 results divided by Step 6.)	121,951
14	Step 12 plus Step 13.	265,853
15	Investments for retirement income. (Step 11 minus Step 14.)	534,147
16	Real return from Fig. 4.4 or Fig. 6.13 less costs. Example for 50% stocks in Fig. 6.13 less 1% costs: 4.4% - 1% = 3.4%.	3.4%
17	Step 16 divided by 2 or your own high confidence retirement real return.	1.7%
18	Investment factor. (Fig. 6.12 using Step 1 and column nearest Step 17 result.)	0.040
19	Affordable income from investments. (Step 15 times Step 18.)	21,366

Affordable After-Tax Expenses

20	Affordable before-tax income. (Step 7 plus Step 10 plus Step 19.)	47,936
21	Tax adjustment. (Step 5 times Step 20.)	8,628
22	Affordable expenses. (Step 20 minus Step 21.)	39,308

FIGURE 6.10 Calculate the amount of money you can afford to spend this year for expenses other than income taxes, debt payments, and items specifically listed in reserves.

pays to be a little conservative; that is, use a slightly higher tax rate than you think represents the actual future rate.

Step 9. This factor accounts for the fact that early in retirement you must save a considerable portion of your fixed pension to be used later to offset inflation. Select the column in Figure 6.11 that is nearest your inflation assumption. Then go down that column until you find the factor that corresponds to the age from Step 1. I like to use 5% inflation in my own case. That's because historical studies of inflation for all 30-year periods from 1926 through 1994 show that inflation was higher than 4.8% in 20% of the periods. It is conservative to choose a higher inflation rate than you think may be average in the future.

Figure 6.11 shows the life expectancies we used for fixed pensions as well as for calculating factors in Figure 6.12. Should you want to use a different life expectancy than the one that goes with your age, just use the row with the life expectancy you want. However, remember to use the age that corresponds to that life expectancy when getting a factor for Figure 6.12 as well. We do not recommend using life expectancies to determine the factors unless you come from very long-lived families and feel you are likely to die far later than the average individual. Remember, the life expectancies in Figure 6.11 are already a few years conservative by actuarial standards, and, if you do live beyond your *future* life expectancy, by repeating this analysis every year, you will always have a new life expectancy. You can never outlive your *current* life expectancy, so the method will always provide retirement funds unless your financial institution goes belly-up.

Step 10. This is the before-tax part of your pension you can use as income for this year's expenses. The remaining part of your pension, after paying for taxes, will be reinvested in the mechanization of this program. In future years, you will be able to draw on this investment to counteract the deadly toll inflation exacts on fixed pensions.

Step 16. Over a long period, your real return (approximately the actual return less inflation) is largely dependent on the ratio of stocks and good real estate equity to your total investments. See Figure 6.13. Use your stock and good real estate equity percentage from Step 18 of Figure 6.6 as a reference. The equity in good investment real estate should be included as stock when calculating this percentage, but if real estate equity is more than a third of your investments, it's better to make your own estimate of real return using a calculation as in Figure 4.4. If you use Figure 6.13 for your calculation like we did, don't forget to subtract any fees or costs (as a percentage) from Figure 6.13 numbers. In our example, Figure 6.6 showed 50% in stock and good real estate equities. As long as real estate doesn't dominate your portfolio, you can count good investment real estate as stock. Using 50% stock in Figure 6.13, we got a long-term return of 4.4%. The average mutual fund has costs of between 1 and 2% per year, but your own mutual funds, broker, or agent costs may be more or less than these values. We used 1% in the example, so the net real return was 4.4% minus 1% or 3.4%. If you don't know your investment costs, 1% is a good

Fixed Pension Factors

Age of Younger Spouse	Life Expec- tancy	Fixed Pension Factor for Various Inflation Rates		
		3%	5%	7%
55	**34.4**	**0.627**	**0.475**	**0.370**
56	33.4	0.634	0.484	0.378
57	32.5	0.641	0.492	0.386
58	31.5	0.648	0.501	0.395
59	30.6	0.655	0.509	0.403
60	**29.7**	**0.662**	**0.517**	**0.412**
61	28.7	0.670	0.527	0.422
62	27.8	0.678	0.536	0.431
63	26.9	0.685	0.545	0.441
64	25.9	0.694	0.556	0.452
65	**25.0**	**0.702**	**0.565**	**0.462**
66	24.1	0.710	0.575	0.473
67	23.2	0.718	0.586	0.484
68	22.3	0.726	0.596	0.496
69	21.5	0.733	0.606	0.506
70	**20.6**	**0.742**	**0.617**	**0.518**
71	19.8	0.750	0.627	0.530
72	18.8	0.759	0.640	0.544
73	18.1	0.766	0.649	0.555
74	17.3	0.774	0.660	0.567
75	**16.5**	**0.783**	**0.671**	**0.580**
76	15.7	0.791	0.683	0.593
77	15.0	0.798	0.693	0.605
78	14.2	0.807	0.705	0.619
79	13.5	0.815	0.715	0.632
80	**12.8**	**0.822**	**0.726**	**0.645**
81	12.1	0.830	0.738	0.658
82	11.5	0.837	0.747	0.670
83	10.8	0.845	0.759	0.684
84	10.2	0.852	0.769	0.697
85	**9.6**	**0.859**	**0.780**	**0.710**
86	9.1	0.865	0.788	0.721
87	8.5	0.872	0.799	0.734
88	8.0	0.878	0.808	0.745
89	7.5	0.885	0.818	0.757
90	**7.1**	**0.890**	**0.825**	**0.767**
91	6.7	0.895	0.833	0.776
92	6.3	0.900	0.840	0.786
93+	5.9	0.905	0.848	0.796

FIGURE 6.11 Find your fixed pension factor in the row for your age and the column for your inflation rate selection.

Investment Factors

Age of Younger Spouse	Investment Factors for Various Real Returns								
	-1%	0%	1%	2%	3%	4%	5%	6%	7%
55	**0.024**	**0.029**	**0.034**	**0.040**	**0.046**	**0.053**	**0.060**	**0.067**	**0.075**
56	0.025	0.030	0.035	0.041	0.047	0.054	0.061	0.068	0.076
57	0.026	0.031	0.036	0.042	0.048	0.054	0.061	0.069	0.076
58	0.027	0.032	0.037	0.043	0.049	0.055	0.062	0.069	0.077
59	0.028	0.033	0.038	0.044	0.050	0.056	0.063	0.070	0.077
60	**0.029**	**0.034**	**0.039**	**0.045**	**0.051**	**0.057**	**0.064**	**0.071**	**0.078**
61	0.030	0.035	0.040	0.046	0.052	0.058	0.065	0.072	0.079
62	0.031	0.036	0.041	0.047	0.053	0.059	0.066	0.073	0.080
63	0.032	0.037	0.042	0.048	0.054	0.060	0.067	0.074	0.081
64	0.034	0.039	0.044	0.049	0.055	0.062	0.068	0.075	0.082
65	**0.035**	**0.040**	**0.045**	**0.051**	**0.057**	**0.063**	**0.069**	**0.076**	**0.083**
66	0.037	0.041	0.047	0.052	0.058	0.064	0.071	0.077	0.084
67	0.038	0.043	0.048	0.054	0.060	0.066	0.072	0.079	0.086
68	0.040	0.045	0.050	0.055	0.061	0.067	0.074	0.080	0.087
69	0.042	0.047	0.052	0.057	0.063	0.069	0.075	0.082	0.088
70	**0.044**	**0.049**	**0.054**	**0.059**	**0.065**	**0.071**	**0.077**	**0.083**	**0.090**
71	0.046	0.051	0.056	0.061	0.067	0.073	0.079	0.085	0.092
72	0.048	0.053	0.058	0.064	0.069	0.075	0.081	0.088	0.094
73	0.050	0.055	0.060	0.066	0.071	0.077	0.083	0.089	0.096
74	0.053	0.058	0.063	0.068	0.074	0.080	0.086	0.092	0.098
75	**0.056**	**0.061**	**0.066**	**0.071**	**0.077**	**0.082**	**0.088**	**0.094**	**0.101**
76	0.059	0.064	0.069	0.074	0.080	0.085	0.091	0.097	0.103
77	0.062	0.067	0.072	0.077	0.083	0.088	0.094	0.100	0.106
78	0.066	0.070	0.076	0.081	0.086	0.092	0.098	0.104	0.110
79	0.069	0.074	0.079	0.084	0.090	0.095	0.101	0.107	0.113
80	**0.073**	**0.078**	**0.083**	**0.088**	**0.094**	**0.099**	**0.105**	**0.111**	**0.117**
81	0.078	0.083	0.088	0.093	0.098	0.104	0.109	0.115	0.121
82	0.082	0.087	0.092	0.097	0.103	0.108	0.114	0.119	0.125
83	0.088	0.093	0.098	0.103	0.108	0.114	0.119	0.125	0.131
84	0.093	0.098	0.103	0.108	0.114	0.119	0.124	0.130	0.136
85	**0.099**	**0.104**	**0.109**	**0.114**	**0.120**	**0.125**	**0.131**	**0.136**	**0.142**
86	0.105	0.110	0.115	0.120	0.125	0.131	0.136	0.142	0.147
87	0.113	0.118	0.123	0.128	0.133	0.138	0.144	0.149	0.155
88	0.120	0.125	0.130	0.135	0.140	0.146	0.151	0.156	0.162
89	0.128	0.133	0.138	0.143	0.149	0.154	0.159	0.165	0.170
90	**0.136**	**0.141**	**0.146**	**0.151**	**0.156**	**0.161**	**0.167**	**0.172**	**0.178**
91	0.144	0.149	0.154	0.159	0.165	0.170	0.175	0.180	0.186
92	0.154	0.159	0.164	0.169	0.174	0.179	0.184	0.190	0.195
93+	0.165	0.169	0.175	0.180	0.185	0.190	0.195	0.200	0.206

FIGURE 6.12 Find your investment factor in the row for your age and the column closest to a conservative value of the real return from your investments.

Amount of Stock Largely Determines Real Returns

Stock as % of Investments	Portfolio Description				Long-Term Real Return Excluding Costs
	Large Co. Stock	Growth Co. Stock	Long-Term Corp. Bonds	Trea-sury Bills	
90%	50%	40%	0.0%	10%	**7.0%**
80%	50%	30%	10.0%	10%	**6.4%**
70%	50%	20%	20.0%	10%	**5.7%**
60%	50%	10%	30.0%	10%	**5.1%**
50%	50%	0%	40.0%	10%	**4.4%**
40%	40%		50.0%	10%	**4.0%**
30%	30%		60.0%	10%	**3.5%**
20%	20%		70.0%	10%	**3.1%**
10%	10%		80.0%	10%	**2.7%**
0%	0%		90.0%	10%	**2.3%**

FIGURE 6.13 Use your equity percentage in the first column and find an approximate historical real return in the last column.

number for most situations; you could use 0.5% if you are using all index funds or 2% if you are paying someone to manage your investments.

Step 17. When we divide the real return from step 16 by 2, we account for both reverse dollar cost averaging and achieving roughly an 80% chance of a successful retirement plan if future scenarios are about the same statistically as those in the past. This means that there is still a 20% chance that your investments will not hold up as well as you project, but the retirement autopilot method still will not let you run out of money before you die. You will just have less from investments.

If you are very late in life, or have a life expectancy that is, perhaps, less than 10 years, you may want to use three-fourths of Step 16 instead of one-half. This will increase your affordable expense and your vulnerability to stock market fluctuations, but late in life your stock allocation is likely to be less. Later in this chapter, we'll illustrate in Figure 6.20 what can happen if you take this higher risk too early in your retirement.

Step 18. Find the column in Figure 6.12 that is closest to the Step 17 value. Then go down until you find the factor in the row corresponding to the age from Step 1.

This Year's Cash Requirements

Budget Category	Source	Amount
Affordable expense budget	Step 22 of Figure 6.10 or Step 8 in Figure 6.15	
Major large purchase of item in reserve	Any, part, or all of items listed in Figure 6.9	
Loan principal and interest due plus extra principal if desired	For any items listed in Figure 6.7	
Income taxes	For all items listed in Figures 6.4 and 6.6	
Total	Sum of items above	

FIGURE 6.14 Your plan provides for your budgeted expenses, loan payments, and income tax.

Step 20. Income here is not the kind of income you'd find on your tax return. Rather it's the sum of your affordable expenses and the taxes related to affordable expenses.

Step 21. This is only the tax that relates to the amount of affordable expenses in the last row. Nevertheless, the method accounts for all income taxes even though the Step 21 value may represent only part of the total income tax.

Step 22. This is your affordable expense budget for the year. You now have completed one of the most important parts of a retirement plan. Step up to the platform and get your diploma as the brass band plays and fireworks sound in the distance. Next year you'll be able to improve the results with the autopilot feedback.

Don't forget that you have separately budgeted for income tax, any purchase listed in reserves, and debt payments, so the affordable expense budget excludes those items. You can calculate the amount of cash you'll need for the year using Figure 6.14. The only item you cannot determine specifically at the beginning of the year is income tax, but if your estimate of your net tax rate was slightly conservative, you will be able to afford anything that is within that rate. A good initial tax estimate might be last year's tax plus 3% or so for inflation.

Gate 4. The Retiree's Autopilot

We have already shown part of the retirement autopilot's features when we used one-half of the real return in the calculations of Figure 6.10 to survive about

80% of the scenarios from past history. We'll show how another part of the autopilot works here: how it provides a practical transition from one year to the next to avoid getting budgets that change dramatically each year. We need to explain the mechanics initially, then show some demonstrations.

As you can see in Figure 6.15, you must have the calculations from last year to complete the analysis. That's because we're using feedback from last year's results to modify this year's results.

Step 1. This is last year's affordable expense budget.

Step 2. Here we calculate the annual growth factor either from last year's inflation rate, which you can get from your public library, or, if you were getting Social Security last year, you can divide this year's Social Security by last year's Social Security. That's because Social Security is supposed to be adjusted upward every year by the amount of last year's inflation.

Step 5. This provides the smoothing or shock absorber action. In effect, it brings a bias toward maintaining last year's results modified for inflation.

Step 6. This slowly introduces this year's results because we're going to use only 25% of this year's results. Therefore, the result in Step 7 is not so sensitive to abrupt changes in budgets brought on by severe security market changes.

Step 8. This step restrains the growth of affordable expenses. Use this budget for this year's normal expenses. Remember that this budget does not include income taxes, items that were budgeted in reserves, or debt payments.

As a pilot of your retirement plan, you must decide whether to use these calculations. As long as there have been no major changes in your plan, historical simulations show that the autopilot results are a benefit. However, if you change your plan abruptly by, say, adding much larger reserves this year that were not part of last year's calculation or a major change in investment return assumptions, you should probably stick to this year's Step 22 result from Figure 6.10.

The Retirement Autopilot's Benefits

We've seen that the mechanical part of the retirement autopilot is easy to apply. We're going to look at its benefits now by establishing some standard conditions in order to compare various planning possibilities using *The Retirement Autopilot* program from www.analyzenow.com that uses Figure 6.15 in simulations. So we'll consider a 55-year-old whose savings and a recent inheritance totals $1 million. We chose to start with a 55-year-old so that we can show what would happen over a long retirement period of 40 years. We picked $1 million as an initial investment balance because we wanted to get retirement expense levels of roughly $30,000 a year, which together with Social Security would be a goal many people would seek. We used a 15% net tax rate in anticipation of higher future tax rates, but since the tax rates are the same for all cases, it does not affect the comparison. We did not include any Social Security because those payments are inflation adjusted and would just add a constant amount each year.

Autopilot Feedback Calculations Are Simple

(Must have information from last year)

Step		Example	
1	Step 8 from last year's Figure 6.15, or, Step 22 from last year's Figure 6.10 if you did not use autopilot feedback last year.	32,000	
2	1.000 + last year's inflation, e.g., 1.000 + 4% = 1.040. Or, you can divide this year's Social Security by last year's to get the same result.	1.040	
3	Step 1 times Step 2.	33,280	
4	Step 22 from this year's Figure 6.10.	39,308	
5	Step 3 times 0.75.	24,960	
6	Step 4 times 0.25.	9,827	
7	Step 5 plus Step 6.	34,787	
8	Affordable expense budget for this year. (Use the smaller of Step 3 or Step 7.)	33,280	

FIGURE 6.15 Use this figure to adjust your affordable expense budget on an annual basis.

We assumed the same allocation of investments for all alternatives. This based the amount of stock as a percentage equal to 110 minus the retiree's age. Stocks are represented by the S&P 500 index less 1.5% for investment costs. Ten percent of investments is always in money markets represented by short-term Treasury bills less 0.3% costs. The remainder of investments is in long-term corporate bond funds with costs of 1.0%. This means that the initial allocation at age 55 is 55% stocks, 10% money markets, and 35% long-term corporate bonds. At age 90, the allocation has changed to 20% stocks, 10% money markets, and 70% long-term corporate bonds.

Let's first see how the retirement autopilot compares with some other planning methods by reviewing some alternatives in Figure 6.16, which uses a 40-year scenario that starts in 1955 and ends in 1994. The shortcut represents results a person could get using any one of the many methods on web sites or magazines that do not account for the costs of buying, owning, and selling securities. Unlike most shortcut methods, we assume that the person using the method makes a new calculation each year considering the particular allocation of that year. The shortcut uses a real return that is about one-third higher than what a conscientious planner would use. The planner case represents the results you might get from a professional and many of the more comprehensive software programs.

Obviously, the shortcut provides some short-term advantages for a retiree because it provides a larger initial budget. Spending at this higher budget level rapidly depletes investments so that future budgets must be much smaller. It doesn't take long for the planner to provide a better budget for expenses than the shortcut. Still, both of these planning methods would begin to show signifi-

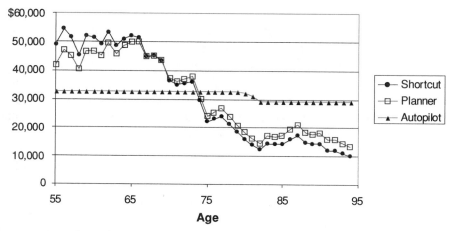

Only the Autopilot Provides for Late Retirement Expenses

FIGURE 6.16 Scenarios starting in 1955 for annual expense budgets using three different methods: shortcut, planner, and autopilot.

cant stress at age 70. It's even worse by age 80 when the budgets would be only about one-third of the amounts planned on at age 55. The autopilot provides an almost constant inflation-adjusted budget throughout the period. Of course, by comparison with the other two methods, it offers significantly less budget early in retirement but equally significantly more later in retirement.

You can derive about the same results as in the planner by just making Step 17 equal to Step 16 in Figure 6.10. Or you can get halfway in between the planner and the autopilot by making Step 17 three-fourths of Step 16. The problem with making these adjustments to Figure 6.10 is that you may so severely restrict spending late in life that you will not be able to cope with the financial stress that most often accompanies old age. I have friends in their 80s spending significantly more (real) money than in their 60s largely because of a whole new set of costs relating to health and the need for assistance. I also have friends in their 80s who are engaged in far more recreation and entertainment than they were in their 60s. I don't think a person should plan on dying early and spending wildly early in retirement at the expense of late retirement financial penalties and stress.

There will be those who criticize the autopilot approach because the annual budget doesn't go up in good times (even though they know that will hurt when bad times follow). However, you must keep in mind that these figures are showing only the affordable expense budget, not the budget for large future purchases that would be included in reserves. In fact, if you take our suggestion for increasing those reserves following prolonged periods of substantial investment growth, retirees can buy some of those extra things added to reserves if subsequent market declines don't force the retiree to reduce reserves before actually using them.

There are a number of financial analysts recommending that people use a very simple rule for their retirement planning. That is to withdraw a fixed percentage of their investments each year. In Chapter 1 we saw the disaster from a 6% draw each year. More responsible analysts recommend 4%, so let's take a look at that in Figure 6.17, which starts in 1955 just as in previous examples. The 4% withdrawal method provides a higher budget than the retirement autopilot for the first 10 years, but in the second half of retirement, the budget is only about half of that in the first 10 years. That too is pretty painful. Using smaller percentage draws starts to level the spending but the budgets are almost always lower than the autopilot's. Not only that, but they change significantly from year to year. And I've never heard any of the advocates of the constant-percentage draw ever mention how retirees would get money for large purchases that occur infrequently. Apparently they should buy such items on time, a decidedly poor thing for most retirees.

The previous examples were all for scenarios starting in 1955 and ending in 1994. Figure 6.18 shows what would have happened to a person retiring a decade earlier in 1945, and Figure 6.19 shows what would have happened in

Annual Expenses in Today's Dollars Starting in 1955

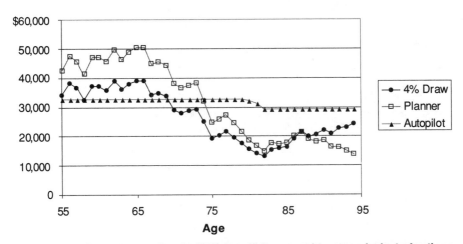

FIGURE 6.17 Scenarios starting in 1955 comparing annual expense budgets for three methods: 4% draws each year, the planner, and the autopilot.

scenarios starting in 1935. The scenarios starting in 1945 provide the best showing for the 4% withdrawal method and planner. If people could foresee that they would die before age 75 or 80, and if they could choose a year like 1945 to retire, and if a large part of their retirement budget was for discretionary items that could come and go with the ever changing budget each year, then the planner would be a great way to go. Of course, this is completely unrealistic.

Annual Expenses in Today's Dollars Starting in 1945

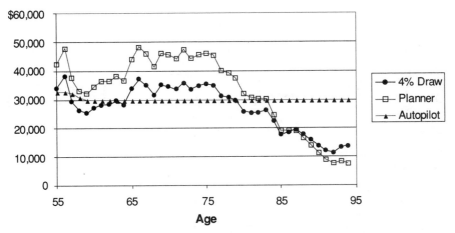

FIGURE 6.18 Scenarios starting in 1945 comparing annual expense budgets for three methods: 4% draws each year, the planner, and the autopilot.

Annual Expenses in Today's Dollars Starting in 1935

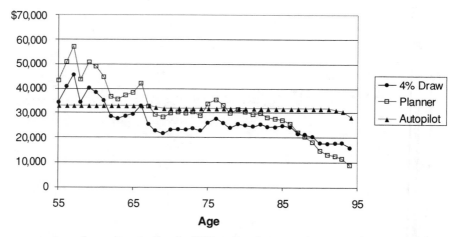

FIGURE 6.19 Scenarios starting in 1935 comparing annual expense budgets for three methods: 4% draws each year, the planner, and the autopilot.

Overall, we conclude that the retirement autopilot does the best job of providing a stable budget that provides funds for a long life.

If you have confidence that you will die earlier than the average person, you might consider using the full retirement autopilot features in Figure 6.15 but use three-fourths of step 16 as your input for Step 17 in Figure 6.10. Then you may enjoy a higher, but stable budget for a shorter period of time. We demonstrate this in Figure 6.20 in a scenario starting in 1955 with a modified auto-

Modify the Autopilot If Expect Short Life

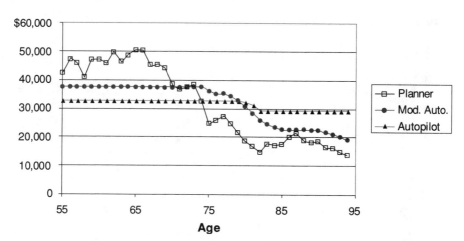

FIGURE 6.20 Scenarios starting in 1955 comparing annual expense budgets for three methods: planner, autopilot, and a modified autopilot.

pilot. However, if there's a prolonged bear market ahead, and you live longer than you thought, you'll be worse off because you spent too much too early.

Gate 5. Staying on Track

You now have a plan for your retirement consistent with an allocation of investments that is appropriate for you; you know the vehicles for the best tax leverage; you've selected investments that you can manage; and you have budgets for normal living expenses as well as reserves for future large purchases. You also have de facto budgets for income taxes and debt payments because income tax rates and debt balances were inputs into the planning process. Next we'll discuss how you need to execute that plan, not only this year, but in the years that follow.

There are at least four things that you should do to make sure your money is sufficient for your lifetime.

1. Analyze your investment status at least once a year for allocations and returns.
2. Calculate how much you can spend annually.
3. Make some kind of a budget breakdown.
4. Institute a top-down cash control policy.
5. Try to say no!

Analyze Your Investment Status at Least Once a Year

I originally used a commercial software program to keep the status of my investments, but I now feel that it takes more effort to input the data than the value I receive at this stage in my life. I know other people who love to enter everything they do on the computer, but I'd rather do other things. The main advantage the software program had was for detailed record keeping. I even kept backup copies in my safe deposit box so that I could reconstruct my files in case of fire or theft. I've given up on that now. Instead I use a ledger for recording any action I take with my securities and I use one of the free Internet services to keep track of most of my investments. I also have a file drawer with a file of information for each investment that we own as well as the last few years' of tax returns. In addition, I have a file where I stuff information that will be needed when I do my taxes next year. I use a computer to keep track of my allocations, returns, and retirement autopilot calculations, but you could do those by hand and put them in a file as well.

You may choose to control your allocations with greater detail than I do. There is nothing wrong with this, and, in fact, there may be some gain if you have the energy. I think that my best risk control tool is Figure 3.7 for the calculation of the percentage of investments I have in equities—that is, stocks, stock funds, and investment real estate. It tells me whether I'm running too high or too low relative to my percentage target for equities, which is between 100 minus my age on the low side and 110 minus my age on the high side. I try to look at my security information quarterly (or if there is a huge change in the market), and I adjust my portfolio after that. As a practical matter, I seldom get out of my equity target percentage more than once a year, and often it's two years before I have to make an adjustment. If you are in the highest tax bracket, you may want to use an after-tax version of Figure 3.7 because deferred tax investments are worth relatively less than taxable investments after considering taxes.

The other thing I recommend for analyzing investments is the use of Figure 4.2 to determine the total return of all of your investments during the past year. If your actual returns are below the assumptions you used in Step 16 of Figure 6.10, you should ask yourself whether it was your particular choice of investments or whether the market as a whole was also down. To help answer this question you will want to look at your stock equities alone, again using Figure 4.2, and then compare your own results with last year's returns of the S&P 500 index, which you can find in almost any library or on the Internet. If your actual returns are not much less that 1% below the S&P 500 index, you don't have to worry too much, but if your stock returns are lower than this, particularly for a couple of years in a row, you may need some (different) professional help. If you have given control of your stock to a money manager, you will want to do this last calculation every year for a while to see if you are getting substandard performance.

Calculate How Much You Can Spend

Once you've gone through the process in this book using Figures 6.10 and 6.15, it takes only a short time to do it again the following year. I consider this more important than how my money is invested. I have an 80-year-old neighbor who has had a great life. He says, "The most important thing about your investments is how much you don't spend. It's more important than earning a big return." I think that he's right.

Make Some Kind of a Budget Breakdown

Divide your annual budget into categories that you can measure. There are many ways to measure your spending, but Figure 6.21 has a useful set of categories for many retired people. If you're going to control by a budget, you may have to break it down so that if fits whatever is the appropriate time period, that is, annually, monthly, or weekly. Of course, everything should have an annual value as in the first blank column of Figure 6.21. The total should not exceed the results you get from Figures 6.10 or 6.15. Those items that you pay monthly should have monthly values, which you can get from the annual values by dividing by 12. And sometimes you'll have to seasonally adjust even these.

Budget Control for Affordable Expenses

Date: ___ / ___/ ____	Annually	Monthly If Applicable	Weekly If Applicable
Rent if applicable (but not mortgage)			
Utilities and maintenance			
Property taxes			
Auto and transportation			
Insurance			
Uninsured medical and dental			
Groceries			
Restaurants			
Other essentials			
Support of others			
Clothing			
Vacation and travel			
Entertainment and hobbies			
Gifts and charities			
Subscriptions and education			
Other discretionary items			
Total			

FIGURE 6.21 Divide your annual budget into categories you can measure.

Items involving weekly expenditures such as items paid from cash should have a weekly budget determined by dividing the annual budget by 52.

There are a number of commercial software programs that can be used to sort amounts on your checks into categories that are meaningful to you. Ask at your local computer store if this interests you. Another alternative is to manually sort last month's checks into categories. Then add the check values in each category to see where your money actually went. It's a good alternative, and after you do it a couple of times to establish a baseline, you only need to do it again when you overrun your budget. It will help locate problems.

The budget in Figure 6.21 excludes any payments on debts listed in Figure 6.7 or large item purchases listed in Figure 6.9 provided that the results from Figures 6.7 and 6.9 were used to calculate the affordable expense budget in Figure 6.10. The same is true of income taxes, provided that the net tax rate used in Step 5 of Figure 6.10 represents your true tax position. The only other control you need for cash outflows excluded from Figure 6.21 is the discipline to make sure you do not step beyond the budgets for reserve items in Figure 6.9.

Of course, if part of your investments are businesses you control, those need their own budgets to succeed. If you are saddled with an enterprise that is a continual drain on your personal cash, then you should include a budget item for that in Figure 6.21. Needless to say, few retirees need that kind of business.

Institute a Top-Down Cash Control Policy

Our family finds that the most effective way to control expenses is to pay for all of the items on Figure 6.21 from a checking account and everything else from a money market. The money market is our source of funds for the checking account and also for income taxes that may be over our withholding and items that were large purchases budgeted in Figure 6.9. We only put the amount that we will spend monthly into the checking account. If we end up spending too much in a month, we know it right away because our checking account has reached its minimum balance. In fact, I hear about it as fast as the speed of sound because my wife keeps the checkbook, and I maintain the money market. Sometimes it's a very loud sound.

Try to Say No!

It's one thing to create a budget, and it's another thing to follow it. I've learned that following a budget is similar to following a diet. It's very hard. But the same advice holds, "Just say no!" Just as you would say no for dessert, say no when tempted by extra expenses.

Actually, it can be a heart-wrenching experience in many circumstances to say no. I think that the toughest cry for help I've heard is the cry of a parent who would like some financial assistance. I've seen retired people who hardly had enough funds for their own existence part with money to help a parent. This is a very noble thing to do, and I'm sure that sometime in the hereafter the retirees will be blessed for the sacrifice. However, often there are other sources of help or alternative lifestyles that may not be as ideal, but still may be suitable for the parent considering the circumstances. Do some research to identify these possibilities. Call in other family members to participate. Look at downsizing, public assistance, support from other family members, and so on.

Another situation that's tough for the *no* answer is a pleading adult son or daughter. Most often, I've found that the adult child could have acted differently and avoided the financial crisis. The question then becomes, "Should a retired parent bail out an adult child?" Keep in mind that doing so may just enable the adult child to repeat a similar performance. Tough love may be the better approach.

But there are times when the adult child got into financial difficulty through an unfortunate set of circumstances without any self-contributing factors. (Or at least that is what you may rationalize.) Parents always like to help their children, but if there is any chance that recovery is possible without parental help, and if your help will most certainly lead to your own financial disaster, you really have no choice but to say no. Again, explore as many alternatives as you can think of.

Modern living and the lifestyle of the neighboring Joneses have a lot to do with what you consider necessities. A one-room log cabin with a wood-burning stove just won't do. Maybe you won't have to go that far, but consider whether you really need a cell phone, a pager, a computer(s), a high-speed Internet service, two telephone lines, cable and/or satellite TV, a second (or any) car, season tickets, the choice of your own doctors, vitamins, a gym or club membership, a traditional vacation, restaurant dining, holiday gifts for all of the family, and so forth.

I see people hang on to suburban life because that's where their friends are as well as all of the necessities. Nevertheless, sometimes they are living far beyond their means. They could do much better living in a small city apartment near a bus line. But they won't even consider that. Perhaps they think they will not live through another year, or worse yet, be embarrassed by their peers! Big mistake!

Another way to say no is to make it difficult to say yes. Credit cards are the biggest enablers of all. To minimize spending, destroy all your cards, or those of your pleading parents or adult children. A credit card not only makes it too easy to purchase something, it also lets you borrow money when you don't have any. For the same reason that you buy something on credit, it is even more difficult to repay. The reason, of course, is that you don't have the money now. In the case of retirees, if they don't have the money now, they surely aren't likely to have it later.

Over the years, I've worked with a number of people in the 70-plus age bracket with precious few financial resources who have learned how to live within their budget. Those I admire the most have taken on a part-time job to make money to pay for something special. How sweet it is when they finally reach their objective.

If you follow these five steps, you'll keep your retirement finances in control and on track.

Gate 6. Always Look Ahead

A winning retirement plan requires that you always look to the future. Be aware that success often depends on knowing about alternatives before they happen so that you understand your choices and the potential impact. Then make your plans accordingly. Let's look at some of the key things here. Perhaps, you've already passed some of these points in time.

Age 59½

You can now take money out of deferred tax investments without the 10% tax penalty even if you are working. Actually, if you follow rigorous methods prescribed by the IRS, you can start withdrawals even earlier, but I always ask people if they are retiring too early if they need early withdrawals.

This is a good time to look into long-term health care insurance. As you get older the rates increase. You may not need such insurance if you have either very small savings or if your savings exceed a million dollars or so and your plans make some provision for some period of nursing care costs. There are many insurance alternatives. Check them out and compare.

Age 62

This is the earliest you can start taking Social Security. It also may be the earliest you can start using your employer's pension plan. If there is any reasonable chance that you may live longer than the average person, consider waiting until you are at least 65 or what the Social Security Administration calls the full retirement age. There is more information on this in Chapter 5.

If you or your spouse are still getting a paycheck, and your pay exceeds certain thresholds, your Social Security check will be smaller. Call and find out details from the Social Security Administration.

At this age, or sometimes younger, you often can get "senior" rates for things like entertainment, recreation, or airplane tickets.

Age 65

A few months before your 65th birthday, register for Medicare even if you do not plan on starting Social Security. This is a good time to review your choices for Medigap health insurance.

Some other things are keyed to age 65. After 65, the standard deduction for income tax increases and you can now work without fear of losing some Social Security benefits.

Age 70

It's time to review your estate plan (again) and learn about the method you'll use for required minimum distributions (RMDs) from any IRAs, 401(k)s, and so forth. By age 70½, or in some circumstances a little later, you must start withdrawals from such deferred tax investments using IRS Publication 590 instructions. Otherwise, you'll be penalized 50% of the amount you should have withdrawn.

Age 80

Now you can ski free at most resorts. We have a number of friends who are still nimble enough to benefit from this perk.

Age 85

If you have a variable annuity, you must now either withdraw the entire amount or annuitize your contract. See your policy, because the age for annuitizing may be earlier.

Age 100

Notify the White House. You'll get a birthday card signed by the President. And you might want to start thinking about making some plans for your funeral including selecting a burial plot.

IRA and 401(k) Withdrawal Rules

You must learn something about your alternatives when you want to withdraw money from an IRA or a 401(k). We'll just give you enough information here so that you know something about the subject and can see some of the language, but be aware that the government often changes requirements in areas like this. The firm that administers your IRA will be able to give you current detailed information and assistance.

Under Age 59½

I've always felt that if you had to start withdrawals under age 59½ to support retirement, you probably should not be retired. However, I know that there are many practical exceptions to this. The general rule is that withdrawals before age 59½ incur not only income tax but a 10% penalty as well. Withdrawal rules for 401(k)s are generally similar to IRA rules. Most people elect to roll their 401(k)s into IRAs so that they have more investment flexibility and heirs often have better withdrawal alternatives.

The government does provide some freedom for hardship cases. Penalties may be excused if you withdraw for medical insurance premiums if you have been unemployed more than 12 weeks, a first-time home purchase (up to $10,000), higher education expenses for your children, and medical costs for permanent disabilities or if medical expenses exceed 7.5% of your gross income.

Another alternative is to start withdrawals using an annuity formula based on your life expectancy. These withdrawals must last at least five years or until you are 59½, whichever is later. Confirm the annual amount with your IRA provider and/or an accountant.

If you still have a 401(k) or equivalent and have not yet converted to an IRA, you may be able to borrow up to 50% or your current balance or $50,000, whichever is smaller, but you have to pay off the loan within five years. You cannot borrow money from an IRA. Borrowing from a 401(k) is a decidedly bad idea if you are not sure you will be employed until the loan is paid. As soon as you leave employment, the loan and accrued interest are due. If you can't come up with the cash, you'll receive a bill for both income tax and a 10% penalty.

Between Ages 59½ and 70½

If you are between the ages of 59½ and 70½, you are free to let your investment grow without any required distributions, or you can make any size withdrawal you want (unless you have a converted Roth IRA that's not five years old). As a practical matter, most people will want to start some regular withdrawals after retirement. There is no perfect answer for the pattern you choose. The important thing is to keep your overall spending within the budgets determined with the retirement autopilot.

The best strategy for most people is to minimize IRA or 401(k) withdrawals during this period if you have other funds that can provide cash for your affordable retirement expenses. The reason for delaying withdrawals is that your investments continue to grow on a tax-deferred basis. Doing this will help delay the onset of lower retirement budgets late in life as reflected in Figure 2.8.

However, people with substantial wealth wanting to leave money to heirs might want to start accelerated withdrawals because of the potentially high taxes on an inheritance by someone other than a spouse.

Over Age 70½

The general rule is that once you have passed April 1 of the year after you reach age 70½, you must start taking a specified minimum distribution. Failure to do so will incur a 50% penalty on the difference between the specified minimum and your actual withdrawals, if any. (A Roth IRA not only incurs no income taxes but also has no required minimum distributions, so there is no penalty for not withdrawing adequate Roth funds each year.)

Mercifully, the IRS changed the rules for IRA required minimum distributions in 2001. The intent of the new regulations is to simplify the calculations. The previous system was terribly complex. Even experts had difficulty understanding all of the implications. The major item that remains unchanged is the need to start RMDs after age 70½.

Even with the simplifications, there are a lot of complex issues and small print, so before you reach 70½, review your decision with a professional planner or accountant. Ask about estate ramifications and the best way to designate beneficiaries. At this point in your life, this review is worth much more than an annual physical or dental checkup and may not cost as much.

The new RMDs are based on the life expectancy in IRS Publication 590 for an IRA owner with a beneficiary who is 10 years younger, even though the owner may be single and have no beneficiary. (There is an exception when a spouse is more than 10 years younger.) This is called the minimum distribution incidental benefit (MDIB).

The revised method requires that you divide the total balance of your IRAs at the end of the previous year by the period from the MDIB table, which is the same as the last column of Figure 2.1. If you were age 71, you would divide the balance of your IRA accounts at the end of last year by 25.3 to get the minimum amount you must withdraw this first year. The next year, you would be 72, so you would divide the end of the previous year's balance by 24.4. Each year you divide by a smaller number from the figure, so the amount of the minimum withdrawal increases each year until you are withdrawing more than your investments earn.

The surviving beneficiary generally must make a different kind of calculation and use a single person's life expectancy instead of the the MDIB period. The beneficiary starts the withdrawals the year after the owner died. (The owner, or the owner's estate, must take out the MDIB amount in the year of the death.) To illustrate, suppose the beneficiary was a spouse who was age 69 the year following the death. A 69-year-old has a life expectancy of 16.8 years according to the "Single" column in Figure 2.1. You begin the same way by dividing the previous year-end IRA balance by a life expectancy, but now you divide last year's ending balance by the single person's value, 16.8 in this case. Another difference is that in the next year you subtract 1 from your previous life expectancy, that is, 15.8 becomes the divisor. You never go back to the life expectancy table again. Each year thereafter, you keep subtracting one year. This means that the surviving spouse will run out of money in the 17th year, or age 86 in this case.

However, spouses, unlike other beneficiaries, have another alternative in many cases. They can roll the deceased spouse's IRA into their own IRA. Then they can use the same type of calculation as the deceased spouse starting after age 70½ with MDIB periods. If you want to stretch your IRA to its limits, this is the best thing to do. The surviving spouse can name children or grandchildren as beneficiaries to really stretch the funds. A year after the death of the surviving spouse, the beneficiaries start collecting using their own single age life expectancy in the first year as the divisor. In subsequent years, they subtract one from the previous year's life expectancy.

Give careful consideration to naming beneficiaries. The owner may want to name a spouse as primary beneficiary and children as contingent beneficiaries in case the spouse dies before the owner. A person who inherits an IRA may want to name children or grandchildren as beneficiaries to stretch funds as long as possible. People who inherit IRAs may outlive their IRA funds. However, if they use the autopilot method and don't spend more than the calculated affordable expense, they should not outlive their resources. If the IRA required minimum distribution is bigger than you need, just reinvest the excess in an account other than an IRA.

IRA Withdrawals' Effect on Your Plan

We have shown some simple examples to help you understand the basics of the new IRA rules. Contrary to what you may hear elsewhere, required minimum distribution alternatives have little impact on affordable expenses in retirement, but failing to observe the IRS regulations may have severe penalties otherwise. Unless you have tax penalties, the main difference between your required minimum distribution alternatives concerns estate planning. That's because these alternatives determine the proportion of your investments at death in deferred tax accounts. While it may not matter much to your lifestyle, it may make a significant difference to your heirs.

Estate Planning

Gifting

The purpose of this book is not to give a tutorial on estate planning, but rather to show how to calculate how much you can afford to spend. Believe it or not, there are many people who feel that they don't need to spend all they can. This is a great opportunity to take the surplus and give it to your children or some other worthy cause. Gifting before you die will reduce your estate taxes, and, if your children or a charitable fund invests the money, they will get more in the long run. You and your spouse can each give $10,000 to each child each year for a total of $20,000 to each child. With a number of children and a number of years of giving and compounding, the sums for heirs can grow substantially.

But you aren't limited to the annual $10,000 from each person to another person. Over your lifetime, you can give an additional amount up to $1 million by 2006 (see Figure 6.22) from you and another $1 million from your spouse without having to pay any gift tax, but you do have to file a gift tax return for the record. However, the amount that passes tax free through your estate is later reduced by whatever amount over the $10,000 per person per year you gifted before you died. These amounts can change at the whim of Congress, so check by calling the IRS or your accountant before committing to gifts much in excess of $10,000 per person per year.

Increasing
Estate Tax Exemption

2000 and 2001	$675,000
2002 and 2003	$700,000
2004	$850,000
2005	$950,000
2006 and on	$1,000,000

FIGURE 6.22 Limits on tax-free gifts excluding $10,000 per person gifts.

Mutual Funds Can Amplify Your Gifts and Return Income

If you can do more than gift to your children or grandchildren, consider the charitable gift funds from some of the major mutual fund companies. Donate appreciated stock or part of an appreciated mutual fund and never pay the capital gains tax that would otherwise be due if you sold the securities first. You'll receive a tax deduction on the full amount. Then, whenever you want to make a contribution, just direct the charitable fund to send the amount you want to the charity of your choice. Until you deplete the fund, the money will grow in whatever mutual fund you choose within the charitable fund's portfolios. All of this growth will be outside of your estate and so will escape estate taxes as well as income taxes.

These charitable gift funds also offer the option of providing some income for yourself from the contribution. Of course, your tax deduction will then be less. If you have some really large sums, you can set up your own charitable remainder trust and draw some income as well, or set up a charitable lead trust and get back part of the principal.

A Special Deal for Grandparents

Grandparents should consider using 529 plans to accumulate money for their grandchildren's college education. These are plans created by individual states as provided by the 1997 Taxpayer Relief Act. Plans differ in each state, and because you are not obliged to use the plan from your home state, you may want to shop around. You can use the money for college expenses at any accredited U.S. college. These expenses are not limited to tuition and can include room, board, and books.

The 529 plans defer taxes on the investments so that you can ultimately gift more to grandchildren. You still are limited to $10,000 per year per person, but a provision allows you to gift up to $50,000 in one year that can count as a contribution over five years. Your spouse can do the same thing and effectively double the gift. Residences of some states also get a state income tax deduction. Lower-income people can transfer their savings bonds to the fund without having to pay tax on the savings bonds' income. (File form 8815 with your income tax return.) Because the money is now out of your estate, the gift reduces your ultimate estate taxes. The student must pay income taxes that are likely to be at the lowest rates possible considering a student's low income. The distributions may reduce elegibility for other student assistance however.

You must invest in one of the alternatives created by the state you choose. Your funds will go into a pool with everyone else's funds in that state. You name a relative such as a grandchild as the beneficiary of the fund. You can change the beneficiary to another family member at any time. Further, your participation in the fund is revocable, so you can pull out if you need the money. Expect to pay both income tax and a 10% penalty on the earnings you withdraw. More information is available on the Internet from such sites as Kiplinger.com or Savingforcollege.com.

Some IRA Estate Considerations

Under current tax law, it is theoretically possible for a person with a very large IRA to get into a situation where his or her heirs would get only about one-fourth of the pretax value of an IRA after federal taxes and even less after state taxes. There are several ways to mitigate this, but in general, the government and/or an insurance company is going to get a substantial part of your hard-earned savings in IRAs and annuities after you and your spouse die. If you can gift the money before you die or arrange to gift it in your will after you die, you can reduce the taxes on your IRA after your death.

If estate preservation for your heirs is important, you may want to start drawing down your IRA at any time after age 59½ and investing the money in stocks or stock mutual funds because the tax basis of your securities not in deferred tax accounts generally gets marked up to the market value on the day the first spouse dies and marked up again on the death of the second spouse. This means that the heir escapes capital gains taxes.

If you have substantial sums, you should consult an accountant or knowledgeable financial planner about naming IRA beneficiaries and/or using part of your IRA withdrawals to make insurance premium payments to a trust to maximize your heirs' returns on your death. If your spouse inherits your IRA and transfers it to her/his own IRA, she or he can name new, younger beneficiaries such as a son, daughter, or grandchild to stretch out the tax deferral time. This won't eliminate the estate taxes when the surviving spouse dies, so heirs will need cash for that. Still, most people can get better results by giving the money away before they die—even if they have to pay gift taxes.

If the non-IRA part of your estate is not significant and liquid, your heirs may have trouble coming up with the estate taxes. This is a good situation to consider an insurance policy, which would not be part of your estate, or a family partnership. Consult an expert before embarking on this step.

Something for Everyone

Finally, have you wondered whether you need a complex will or trust? Do you need some way to get around the confiscatory death taxes? In spite of what you may read or hear, the chances are that you don't. Most people die with pitifully little. Still, you need at least a simple will and some documents your lawyer can prepare to make it easier on people who will administer your care if you become incapacitated, or your estate when you die. Wills, trusts, powers of attorney, and so forth, are not do-it-yourself projects in this modern world saturated with complexities and legalities. Use a professional.

That's It Folks!

Well, there you are. You've done the things required in Chapter 3 about investments and passed through all six gates here. You've allocated your assets, selected good vehicles for reducing taxes, picked investments you feel you can manage, considered your Social Security and pension alternatives, looked ahead to find potential large future expenses, established a budget for normal living expenses, set up a control system to keep you on track, settled your insurance and IRA distribution questions, and worked out plans for distributing your estate before and after you die. You now have a winning retirement plan. Go out and take some well-earned time to relax! That is until this same time next year when you review your asset allocation and calculate a new annual budget. In the meantime, I wish you a happy and bountiful retirement.

POSTSCRIPT

> As life is action and
> passion, it is
> required of a man
> that he should share
> the passion and
> action of his time, at
> peril of being judged
> not to have lived.*

May your future retirement be long and healthy! I hope that the material in this book contributes to your prosperity and outlook for those many years ahead.

There may be a few of you who understand the pros and cons of every point, but, statistically, you are probably a neophyte in many aspects of this book. If you still feel intimidated, make sure you seek professional help instead. Use the subject matter of the book to help form your questions to ask the expert.

But don't just sit there and do nothing. The penalty may be far worse than anything you can currently imagine. I see far too many cases of people who didn't save and/or spent their resources too early. Their hardships are likely to be exacerbated by the increasing part of our population that is dependent on the decreasing part of our population that is working. Reduced benefits for retirement are almost certainly going to be part of your future.

By applying even part of the material in this book to your life, you will distinguish yourself from the average person. By going a step further and helping others understand the benefits, you will gain much satisfaction by improving other lives as I hope I have in doing this work.

Henry K. Hebeler

---

*Oliver Wendell Holmes, Jr., Memorial Day Address, 1884.

Hard-to-Value Investments

You may have trouble valuing a number of different types of investments. Keep in mind that you do not always need a perfect answer because, if you have the diversity you should, an imperfect answer will not change your final result by a large amount.

Annuities

People generally have more questions about what to do about annuities than anything else. Here is some guidance.

If you have already annuitized, that is, are already receiving payments and those payments are for life, include the amount of the annual payments under Step 7 in Figure 6.4 and enter 0% in Step 10. Do not enter anything in this case under investments in Figure 6.6.

If you have not yet started getting payments, include the current balance of your contract as an investment in Step 16 as a fixed income investment in Figure 6.6 even though your annuity investments may be mostly in stocks, unless you don't plan to annuitize for more than, say, five years. Ignore any estimate of future payments for Figure 6.4.

If you are already getting payments but those payments are for a term-certain that is less than your life expectancy, use the method under contracts that follows. Enter the resulting equivalent investment in Step 16 of Figure 6.6. Although those payments may seem like fixed income, they must be payments for life to use in Figure 6.4.

Contracts, Notes Owed to You, and Term-Certain Annuities

In the case of contracts, notes owed to you, and term-certain annuities, you will get a series of regular payments for a certain period of time. We are going to estimate the size of an equivalent investment that would return the same future payments. Figure A.1 provides a factor to multiply by the first year's worth of payments to get the size of the investment. As you can see, the result depends on the return. You should use actual, not real, returns if you want to represent equal annual payments. Real returns would represent an investment that would give payments that increased every year with inflation.

Unless you are using a table like Figure A.1 to negotiate the sale of some income property where you would like to get a high price, you would normally want to use a lower value for retirement planning to be conservative. The higher the return, the lower the equivalent investment value. The bottom line for our planning purposes is that good rough estimates would be a return of about 8% to represent something that will give fixed annual payments and 4% for something that will give escalating payments. If you really want to fine-tune your results you can use the real return for escalating payments from Step 16 of Figure 6.10. For fixed payments, add your estimate of inflation to the real return from Step 16. Note that we are looking for a real return that is about the same as you have assumed for your investments. That's because we're going to add this equivalent investment to your other investments, so we want both returns to be the same.

Suppose you had part-time work that would last five years with an annual income of $5,000, and you thought your pay would increase by the amount of inflation every year. You would go to the 4% column, for example, in Figure A.1 and look in the five-year row where you would find the factor 4.54. Multiply that times the $5,000 first-year income and get an equivalent investment of $22,700.

Or let's suppose that you thought your wages would stay the same for five years. Then, using 8% actual return, in the five-year row of Figure A.1, you find the factor 4.15. Therefore, the equivalent investment there would be $5,000 times 4.15 or $20,750.

Trusts

If a trust is one where the earnings are distributed to you and you can draw down the principal if necessary (as with a marital trust or bypass trust), then put the current balance of the principal under Step 15 of Figure 6.6 as a fixed investment. Do not enter the earnings distributions anywhere.

If the trust is one where you receive only the income and have no access to the principal (as with a charitable remainder trust), put the current value of annual income in Step 7 of Figure 6.4. If the amount is relatively constant year to year, enter 0% in Step 10 of Figure 6.4. If the amount is increasing every year

Factors for Equivalent Investments

Years	Return on Investment								
	2%	3%	4%	5%	6%	7%	8%	9%	10%
1	0.99	0.99	0.98	0.98	0.97	0.97	0.96	0.96	0.95
2	1.96	1.94	1.92	1.91	1.89	1.87	1.85	1.84	1.82
3	2.91	2.87	2.83	2.79	2.75	2.72	2.68	2.65	2.61
4	3.85	3.77	3.70	3.63	3.57	3.51	3.44	3.39	3.33
5	4.76	4.65	4.54	4.44	4.34	4.24	4.15	4.06	3.98
6	5.66	5.50	5.35	5.20	5.06	4.93	4.81	4.69	4.57
7	6.54	6.32	6.12	5.93	5.75	5.58	5.41	5.26	5.11
8	7.40	7.12	6.87	6.62	6.40	6.18	5.98	5.78	5.60
9	8.24	7.90	7.58	7.29	7.01	6.74	6.50	6.27	6.05
10	9.07	8.66	8.27	7.91	7.58	7.27	6.98	6.71	6.45
11	9.88	9.39	8.94	8.51	8.12	7.76	7.42	7.11	6.82
12	10.68	10.10	9.57	9.08	8.64	8.22	7.84	7.48	7.15
13	11.46	10.79	10.19	9.63	9.12	8.65	8.22	7.82	7.46
14	12.23	11.47	10.77	10.15	9.57	9.05	8.57	8.14	7.74
15	12.98	12.12	11.34	10.64	10.00	9.43	8.90	8.42	7.99
16	13.71	12.75	11.89	11.11	10.41	9.78	9.21	8.69	8.21
17	14.43	13.36	12.41	11.56	10.79	10.10	9.49	8.93	8.42
18	15.14	13.96	12.91	11.98	11.15	10.41	9.75	9.15	8.61
19	15.84	14.54	13.40	12.39	11.49	10.70	9.99	9.35	8.78
20	16.51	15.10	13.86	12.77	11.81	10.96	10.21	9.54	8.94
21	17.18	15.65	14.31	13.14	12.12	11.21	10.42	9.71	9.08
22	17.83	16.18	14.74	13.49	12.40	11.45	10.61	9.87	9.21
23	18.48	16.69	15.15	13.83	12.67	11.67	10.79	10.01	9.33
24	19.10	17.19	15.55	14.14	12.93	11.87	10.95	10.14	9.43
25	19.72	17.67	15.93	14.45	13.17	12.06	11.10	10.26	9.53
26	20.32	18.14	16.30	14.73	13.39	12.24	11.24	10.38	9.62
27	20.91	18.60	16.66	15.01	13.61	12.41	11.37	10.48	9.70
28	21.49	19.05	17.00	15.27	13.81	12.56	11.49	10.57	9.77
29	22.06	19.48	17.32	15.52	14.00	12.71	11.60	10.66	9.84
30	22.62	19.89	17.64	15.76	14.18	12.84	11.71	10.74	9.90
31	23.17	20.30	17.94	15.98	14.35	12.97	11.80	10.81	9.95
32	23.70	20.69	18.23	16.20	14.51	13.09	11.89	10.87	10.00
33	24.23	21.08	18.51	16.40	14.66	13.20	11.97	10.94	10.05
34	24.74	21.45	18.78	16.60	14.80	13.30	12.05	10.99	10.09
35	25.25	21.81	19.04	16.78	14.93	13.40	12.12	11.04	10.13

FIGURE A.1 Multiply your annual payments by one of these factors to get an equivalent investment. Note: Use Figure 2.6 for a single future payment.

about as fast as inflation, enter 100% in Step 10. If it's someplace in between, use 50% in Step 10 or some value you can rationalize.

Insurance

If you have a life insurance policy that has cash value or the features of a variable annuity, put the amount of the cash value in Step 16 of Figure 6.6. Don't enter the death value. The only time that you should ever consider using the death value of a life insurance policy is if you are within weeks of dying and you're estimating what the affordable expenses will be for your widow(er). Then include the death value as an investment if your widow(er) is the beneficiary.

Depreciating Assets

You may own something that you would consider selling in the future if you really need the money, but you fear that its real value is declining each year. Estimate its current value and go to Figure 2.6 to adjust it for whatever depreciation rate you feel is appropriate. (This is not the bookkeeping kind of depreciation rate that you would use for income tax calculations. It is the reduction in market value every year.) For example, if you had something that you thought was going down in value every year by 10%, use the 10% column and the row for the number of years in the future that you might sell it. For example, if you had something in this category worth $10,000, and you thought you might sell it in 10 years, multiply $10,000 by 0.386 from Figure 2.6 and get $3,860. If this is something like a racehorse that might die within 10 years or a stud that is losing his amorous intentions faster than a 10% rate, reduce the value much more.

But wait, you're still not ready to enter the value in investments. You first have to multiply the result by another fraction from Figure 2.6 depending on your real return. Continuing with the previous example, if that's 4%, then find the factor 0.676 in the 10-year row of Figure 2.6. Multiply that times its value in the future of $3,860 and get an investment value of $2,548 to add to the fixed income part of Step 15 in Figure 6.6.

Technical Notes

Preretirement Investment Growth

All of our preretirement planning is done on a before-tax basis so that it will be easy for the user to compare forecasted postretirement income with current income from wages. Most people relate to this concept better than the details of a postretirement plan. Of course, this forecasted postretirement income is not the kind of income that would be on an income tax statement. It's simply the sum of the affordable expenses in retirement plus the taxes associated with that income.

The basic preretirement planning investment model is based on tax-deferred accounts. Some critics would argue that the part of savings that goes into taxable accounts grows at a slower after-tax rate. However, for most people that's not true in practice. Most people pay all of their income tax from their wages, not by withdrawing money quarterly from investments to pay the associated taxes. In effect, people are actually saving more than the amounts deducted from their paychecks. Or said another way, their savings are growing at a before-tax rate of return if you don't count investment taxes paid from wages as savings.

For those few people who actually withdraw money from investments to pay taxes, our method is set up so that they reduce their annual savings contribution by the amount of these taxes. That means that the returns are still growing at a before-tax rate of return, but the annual savings input is smaller.

Postretirement Investment Analysis

On close inspection, a student of various retirement planning methods would see that the theory for the mechanization that we use for postretirement planning is based on investments in deferred tax accounts. However, there is very little difference when investments are in taxable accounts except with extremely high income tax rates as we'll show here.

To demonstrate the difference between our projections using a deferred tax method with a more accurate model that separates deferred and taxable accounts, let's look at some comparisons. Figure B.1 shows results for a 65-year-old couple starting retirement with $1 million. In all cases, the couple spent only the affordable expense budget each year. However, withdrawals from deferred tax accounts were always the greater of affordable expenses plus taxes or the last year's investment balance divided by the current life expectancy. Any surplus withdrawal was deposited to a taxable account.

Whether the investments are tax deferred makes only a small difference when net tax rates are around 10% as can be seen in Figure B.1. Most retirees have even lower net tax rates. However, when net tax rates are up to 30%, there is a difference. It takes a very large income to reach 30% using our definition for net tax rate. In fact, you must be in the 40% marginal tax rate bracket and not have much in the way of capital gains or tax-exempt income.

Figure B.1 shows that even in this 30% net tax rate case, our method provides good results for any mix of deferred and taxable accounts. Through the 10th year, there is less than 4% difference between the largest and smallest result. The very high tax rate, of course, takes the highest toll when investments are all in a deferred tax account. Since we want our method to err on the conservative

Autopilot Works with Taxable Accounts Too!

With 10% net tax rate:	Affordable Expenses (Today's $)		
	1st Year	10th Year	20th Year
100% investments in IRA	51,685	49,892	41,258
50% in IRA plus 50% in taxable	51,685	49,468	41,300
100% taxable investments	51,685	49,045	41,343

With 30% net tax rate:	Affordable Expenses (Today's $)		
	1st Year	10th Year	20th Year
100% investments in IRA	40,200	37,991	30,999
50% in IRA plus 50% in taxable	40,200	39,452	34,531
100% taxable investments	40,200	38,456	34,586

FIGURE B.1 Affordable expenses for different mixes of deferred and taxable accounts for a 65-year-old couple with $1 million investments with a 6% return and 3% inflation.

side, we chose to use that as our basis. In the case of 100% taxable investments, in the 20th year our method would budget spending at 12% less than a more accurate method that separated taxable and deferred accounts. The chances are that someone with a 30% net tax rate wouldn't mind being 12% conservative after 20 years. In the meantime, the vast majority of retirees benefit from the simplicity of our approach.

Fixed Pension Factors

The fixed pension factors in Figure 6.11 are calculated using financial equations. The factor equals the following ratio:

$$\frac{\text{Payment (Real Return, Life Expectancy, Present Value} = 1)}{\text{Payment (Actual Return, Life Expectancy, Present Value} = 1)}$$

This equation assumes that the part of the fixed pension that is not spent is invested. These investments build up over time and ultimately provide the income that offsets the ever diminishing real value of the pension itself. The most forceful element in the equation is the amount of inflation, which you can select yourself in Figure 6.11. The other assumptions are 15% tax rate and 1.0% real return. This may appear to be a low return, but remember we're looking for a high confidence factor, and the investment return is most important late in retirement at a time when the allocations will favor fixed income investments and their lower returns. Tax rates and real returns may be lower or higher than some would like, but changes in these values are much less critical than the inflation assumption. I often tell people they can approximate this factor just by dividing their age by 100. Or said another way, a 65-year-old retiree should not spend more than about 65% of her or his after-tax pension receipts.

Reverse Dollar Cost Averaging

Our example of reverse dollar cost averaging was highly idealized. Here we'll look at more realistic cases. For example, consider a portfolio that is continually rebalanced so that it always has 50% large company stocks (like the S&P 500), 40% bonds (like long-term corporate bonds), and 10% money markets (like short-term Treasury bills). We'll use data going back to 1926 for these securities, using returns from Global Financial Data on www.globalfindata.com. All dividends and interest are reinvested. Investment costs are 1.5% for the stocks, 0.5% for the bonds, and 0.3% for the Treasury bills. We'll compute real returns from rolling 20-year periods using 1927 as the beginning point of the first 20-year period, and then we'll look at 50 such 20-year periods so the last period will begin in 1976 and end in 1995. For each period we're going to calculate three real returns:

1. A real return based on compound growth of $1 deposited at the beginning of the first year. This is the basis used by mutual fund companies to report performance on actual returns.

2. A real return based on depositing $1 in the middle of each year, but that $1 will be adjusted for inflation each year so that we always deposit $1 of real value. This is the assumption that is used in most savings calculations for retirement planning.

3. A real return based on withdrawing $1 in the middle of each year, but that $1 also will be adjusted for inflation each year so that we always withdraw $1 of real value. This is the basic assumption used in almost all retirement planning programs.

Figure B.2 shows the results of those calculations. The first column is the year in which each 20-year period begins. The next three columns show the returns for each of our three cases. But wait, look at the first result. The return for deposits is less than the long-term return, and the return for withdrawals is more. Isn't this exactly the opposite of what was supposed to happen? The answer is yes, but that's not what happens in the average case. In fact, the majority of the cases show that dollar cost averaging helps and reverse dollar cost averaging hurts. The average of all of those 50 periods shows real returns of 2.9% for long-term, 3.2% for deposits, and 2.6% for withdrawals. This substantiates the principle of reverse dollar cost averaging.

Eighty Percent Chance of Success

The final perspective we'd like to illustrate is in Figure B.3. There we sort the return columns from Figure B.2 so that the lowest return is at the top. The median or 50th percentile returns for the three cases are 3.3, 4.1, and 2.4% respectively. That shows that in half of the past 20-year periods retirees fared a lot worse than savers. Retirees need more than a 50% chance that their money will last, so let's look at the 80th percentile for a possible value to use in planning for a retiree. There we find 0.3% for the retiree making regular withdrawals. That's virtually no return and much less than one-half of the long-term return used in the retirement autopilot calculations.

We decided to use the factor of one-half of the long-term real return from Figure 4.5 after looking at perhaps a thousand simulations. We tried to find a factor that would allow retirees to spend a relatively large part of their investments over their lives and not suffer impractical penalties late in life. Figures B.2 and B.3 assume that we will exhaust the investments at the end of the 20 years, whereas in retirement planning we use a conservative value for life expectancy and update it every year. Thus, theoretically, we never outlive our life expectancy or our investments. So we still say that we have roughly an 80% chance of success, even though in the vast majority of cases the retiree will

Real Returns for 20-Year Rolling Periods

Year	Growth	Deposits	Draws
1927	3.7%	1.8%	6.3%
1928	2.3%	0.8%	4.2%
1929	1.2%	0.6%	1.9%
1930	2.0%	1.5%	2.4%
1931	2.6%	2.1%	3.3%
1932	3.7%	2.2%	5.8%
1933	3.6%	2.6%	4.9%
1934	2.3%	2.2%	2.4%
1935	3.6%	4.2%	2.8%
1936	3.3%	5.3%	1.0%
1937	2.5%	5.0%	-0.3%
1938	3.3%	4.1%	2.3%
1939	3.2%	5.4%	0.6%
1940	3.4%	5.6%	0.8%
1941	3.7%	5.4%	1.7%
1942	5.2%	6.2%	3.9%
1943	4.9%	5.4%	4.3%
1944	5.0%	5.9%	3.8%
1945	5.0%	6.2%	3.4%
1946	4.4%	6.2%	2.2%
1947	5.0%	5.0%	5.2%
1948	5.8%	5.2%	6.8%
1949	5.9%	4.8%	7.6%
1950	4.7%	3.1%	6.9%
1951	4.3%	2.7%	6.5%
1952	4.4%	2.9%	6.5%
1953	4.4%	3.2%	6.1%
1954	3.6%	1.2%	6.9%
1955	1.1%	-1.7%	4.1%
1956	1.0%	-0.4%	2.6%
1957	1.6%	0.6%	2.9%
1958	1.6%	-0.5%	4.0%
1959	0.4%	-1.1%	2.1%
1960	0.0%	-1.6%	1.7%
1961	0.1%	-1.4%	1.6%
1962	-0.9%	-2.1%	0.3%
1963	0.2%	-0.2%	0.6%
1964	0.2%	0.8%	-0.3%
1965	0.1%	1.3%	-1.1%
1966	0.9%	3.2%	-1.4%
1967	2.1%	4.5%	-0.4%
1968	1.6%	4.1%	-1.0%
1969	1.9%	4.7%	-1.1%
1970	3.3%	5.9%	0.3%
1971	3.1%	5.3%	0.5%
1972	3.6%	6.5%	0.0%
1973	3.4%	6.7%	- 0.5%
1974	4.5%	7.1%	1.3%
1975	5.7%	6.4%	4.8%
1976	5.2%	6.3%	3.7%
Average	2.9%	3.2%	2.6%

FIGURE B.2 Real returns are significantly different depending on whether using scenarios of simple growth, regular deposits (as in dollar cost averaging), or regular withdrawals (as in reverse dollar cost averaging).

Real Returns in Ascending Order

Percentile	Growth	Deposits	Draws
100	-0.9%	-2.1%	-1.4%
98	0.0%	-1.7%	-1.1%
96	0.1%	-1.6%	-1.1%
94	0.1%	-1.4%	-1.0%
92	0.2%	-1.1%	-0.5%
90	0.2%	-0.5%	-0.4%
88	0.4%	-0.4%	-0.3%
86	0.9%	-0.2%	-0.3%
84	1.0%	0.6%	0.0%
82	1.1%	0.6%	0.3%
80	**1.2%**	**0.8%**	**0.3%**
78	1.6%	0.8%	0.5%
76	1.6%	1.2%	0.6%
74	1.6%	1.3%	0.6%
72	1.9%	1.5%	0.8%
70	2.0%	1.8%	1.0%
68	2.1%	2.1%	1.3%
66	2.3%	2.2%	1.6%
64	2.3%	2.2%	1.7%
62	2.5%	2.6%	1.7%
60	2.6%	2.7%	1.9%
58	3.1%	2.9%	2.1%
56	3.2%	3.1%	2.2%
54	3.3%	3.2%	2.3%
52	3.3%	3.2%	2.4%
50	**3.3%**	**4.1%**	**2.4%**
48	3.4%	4.1%	2.6%
46	3.4%	4.2%	2.8%
44	3.6%	4.5%	2.9%
42	3.6%	4.7%	2.9%
40	3.6%	4.8%	3.3%
38	3.6%	5.0%	3.4%
36	3.7%	5.0%	3.7%
34	3.7%	5.2%	3.8%
32	3.7%	5.3%	3.9%
30	4.3%	5.3%	4.0%
28	4.4%	5.4%	4.1%
26	4.4%	5.4%	4.2%
24	4.4%	5.4%	4.3%
22	4.5%	5.6%	4.8%
20	4.7%	5.9%	4.9%
18	4.8%	5.9%	5.2%
16	4.9%	6.2%	5.8%
14	5.0%	6.2%	6.1%
12	5.0%	6.2%	6.3%
10	5.0%	6.2%	6.5%
8	5.2%	6.3%	6.5%
6	5.2%	6.4%	6.8%
4	5.7%	6.5%	6.9%
2	5.8%	6.7%	6.9%

FIGURE B.3 Sorting the numbers from Figure B.2 reveals that you must use very low returns if you want to get high confidence results, especially in withdrawal scenarios.

have a smaller budget later in life. There is no way to get an exact value in such a highly judgmental situation. The 80% number is meaningful only in the sense that perhaps 80% provides significantly more comfort than a 50% number conveys. After all, 50% means that you have a 50% chance of failure, while the retirement autopilot provides much better results because it uses somewhat conservative values for both returns and life expectancy.

Poor Man's Monte Carlo

Jersey Gilbert, financial editor of *Smart Money* magazine, humorously called my method a poor man's Monte Carlo analysis. (Most Monte Carlo programs are very pricey and require time-consuming inputs from an expert. My program simply adds an Excel spinner button that costs nothing but still lets you see different historical results with each click of the button.) For those who don't know anything about statistical analysis, a Monte Carlo analysis is one where you assign a statistical distribution to a variable and experiment by running hundreds or thousands of simulations to find out what will happen. One of the earliest popular sites was financialengines.com where you could watch what would happen to a combination of mutual funds over some 500 trials. It helped you to understand that the outcome of your savings for retirement was far from certain.

A number of sophisticated financial planners acquired Monte Carlo programs such as Crystal Ball from Decisioneering, Inc. I think that Monte Carlo analysis is a step up in planning technology because it gives people a quantitative feel for the wide range of possible future outcomes. However, the common practice of ignoring transaction costs and poor modeling of the combination of returns and inflation can give misleading results.

The retirement autopilot is a poor man's analysis, but it does not lack quality. It has certain benefits that are not in most financial planning statistical simulations. The major benefit is that the analysis for this book uses real returns in their actual historical sequence as opposed to a statistical representation of actual returns.

Statistical models should be based on real returns, not actual returns. The value of an investment at the end of a year depends on inflation of that particular year, not some statistical value of inflation for a large group of years. Using actual returns in a statistical analysis and later bringing the result to a present value with some average inflation really bothers me.

I also believe that the actual historical sequence of returns has some meaning. Statisticians say that there is very little serial correlation for investment returns, but I think that actual events of history affect both returns and inflation. The problem is that historical events are not numbers and therefore don't fit well into the rich man's Monte Carlo analysis.

Finally, it's important to remember that the future will not be exactly like the past, even statistically. Any competent planner must recognize this and provide for contingencies. In the aerospace business, we used to call these *unk-unks,* short for unknown-unknowns—in other words, things that you are not even smart enough to know to list as possibilities much less how big they will be. I think it's a benefit to have a reserve of one or two years' expenses (not otherwise covered by Social Security and a pension) as potential cover, so the retirment autopilot encourages you to set some amount aside just in case our theoretical predictions for the future aren't exactly right—as is most certain.

Forms for Your Own Calculations

The forms that follow are copies of key figures used in the text of this book, but the example values are deleted so that you can make copies and fill them in with your own numbers each year. We advise that you do the work with the book open to the example and the relevant instructions. Each figure number here is the same as that in the text except that it is followed by a *C*.

Current Balances and Allocations

Vehicles and Real Estate	Current Vehicle Balances	Allocation Classes			
		Equities		Fixed Income	Cash
		Real Est.	Stock		
Roth IRA					
401(k)/deductible IRA					
Nondeductible IRA					
Taxable or tax-exempt					
Variable annuity					
Total allocation					

FIGURE 3.10c Begin by listing balances for current vehicles and desired allocations.

Calculate Your Own Return

Row	Item	Value
1	Year-end balance.	
2	Starting balance.	
3	Ending balance divided by starting balance. (Row 1 divided by Row 2.)	
4	Deposits.	
5	Withdrawals.	
6	Net deposits. (Row 4 minus Row 5.)	
7	Net deposits divided by starting balance. (Row 6 divided by Row 2.)	
8	Return from Figure 4.3 using inputs from Row 3 and Row 7. See how this compares with a comparable market index for last year.	
9	Last year's inflation.	
10	Subtract Row 9 from Row 8 and compare this approximate real return with the assumptions used in your planning analysis.	

FIGURE 4.2C Find out if your own return for last year met your expectations.

Calculate the Real Return for Your Plan

1 Security	2 Investment Value	3 % of your Investments	4 Representative Real Returns	5 Real Return Col. 3 x Col. 4
Stocks			6.7%	
Growth stocks			9.0%	
Other equities				
Bonds			2.4%	
Other fixed income investments				
Money markets, T-bills, short-term CDs, etc.			0.8%	
Totals		100%		
		Estimated costs (for funds, brokers, etc.)		
		Net real return (total real return minus estimated costs)		

FIGURE 4.4C Use this table to calculate a net real return on your investments.

Use Quick and Dirty to
Estimate Your Retirement Income

Step	Item	
1	Retirement investments.	
2	Current annual wages.	
3	Investments divided by wages. (Step 1 divided by Step 2.)	
4	<u>Annual</u> savings. (Don't include returns from investments.)	
5	Annual savings as % of annual wages. (100 times Step 4 divided by Step 2.)	
6	Years until retire.	
7	Aggressive, moderate, or conservative investor.	
8	Value from following figures closest to inputs above, e.g., use Fig. 5.4 for 9 years. Under Moderate, get 0.52 using Steps 3 & 5 inputs above. (See text.)	
9	Step 2 times Step 8.	
10	Annual Social Security & COLA pension.	
11	Annual fixed pension times current age as %.	
12	Estimated retirement income. (Step 9 plus Step 10 plus Step 11.)	

FIGURE 5.1C Follow these quick and dirty steps to estimate your before-tax income in retirement.

Preretirement Worksheet

Step	Description	
1	Annual Social Security and COLA pension for you and spouse. See Step 1 instructions in text.	
2	Annual fixed pension or annuity. Today's $ value equals employer's estimate times Fig. 2.6 factor. See Step 2 instructions.	
3	Calendar year you will retire _____. Enter your age (or younger spouse if couple) in that year.	
4	Factor from Fig. 5.16 using Step 3 and your chosen inflation estimate.	
5	Step 2 times Step 4.	
6	Current annual before-tax cash flow from investment real estate.	
7	Estimated annual retirement expenses (including income tax & debt payments) in today's $.	
8	Step 1 plus Step 5 plus Step 6.	
9	Step 7 minus Step 8.	
10	Real return before retire. See Fig. 4.4 or Fig. 4.5. Example: 70% stock and 1% costs.	
11	$1/2$ x real return after retire. See Fig. 4.4 or Fig. 4.5. Example: $1/2$ x (4.0% at 40% stock less 1% cost).	
12	Factor from Fig. 5.17 using values closest to Steps 3 & 11.	
13	Step 9 times Step 12.	
14	Major purchases during retirement, e.g., condo. See text for tax adjustment.	
15	Step 13 plus Step 14.	
16	Current balance of all investments less equity used to produce cash flow in Step 6.	
17	Large expenses before retirement, e.g., kid's college expenses. See text for tax adjustment.	
18	Step 16 minus Step 17. If negative, show minus sign.	

(Figure 5.15C continued on next page.)

19	Number of years until you retire.	
20	Factor from Fig. 5.18 for values closest to Step 10 and Step 19.	
21	Step 18 times Step 20. (Show a minus sign if Step 18 is negative.)	
22	Step 15 minus Step 21. (If negative, congratulations!)	
23	Factor from Figure 5.19 using values closest to Step 10 and Step 19.	
24	Step 22 divided by Step 23. (Enter 0 if negative.)	
25	The amount of Step 6 that you are reinvesting.	
26	Savings from wages this year equals Step 24 minus Step 25.	
27	Current gross annual wages excluding employer matching contributions to savings.	
28	Estimated savings as percentage of wages: 100 times (Step 26 divided by Step 27). If the non tax-deferred part of Step 16 is less than Step 17, then most of Step 28 should go to non tax-deferred accounts.	

FIGURE 5.15C Use this preretirement worksheet to determine how much you need to save in order to support your future retirement expenses along with any preretirement purchases you will fund with investments.

Autopilot Adjustments

Step

29	Results from Step 28 of this year's analysis.	
30	Results from Step 28 of last year's analysis.	
31	If Step 29 is less than Step 30, enter 75% of Step 30; otherwise, enter 0.	
32	If Step 29 is less than Step 30, enter 25% of Step 29; otherwise, enter 0.	
33	Add Step 32 to Step 31.	
34	If Step 29 is less than Step 30, enter Step 33 here; otherwise, enter Step 29.	

FIGURE 5.20C Apply the retirement autopilot to determine what percentage of your wages should be going into savings each year.

Retirement Income If Retire at Different Ages

Step		Retire at Age:		
		e.g., 58	e.g., 62	e.g., 66
1	Your retirement age.			
2	Years till retire.			
3	Your Social Security * & COLA pension.			
4	Spouse's Social Security * & COLA pension.			
5	Fixed pension. (See Step 5 instructions.)			
6	Fixed pension factor: Figure 5.16 using Step 1.			
7	Step 5 times Step 6.			
8	% stock in investments before retirement and real return, e.g., Figure 4.5 less 1%.			
9	Factor from Figure 5.18 using values closest to Step 2 and real return in Step 8.			
10	Current retirement investment balance times Step 9.(Example: current balance = $200,000.)			
11	Factor from Figure 5.19 using values closest to Steps 2 and 8.			

12	Annual new savings from wages.			
13	Step 11 times Step 12.			
14	Balance at beginning of retirement. (Step 10 plus Step 13.)			
15	Major purchases during retirement, e.g., auto purchases. See text for tax adjustment.			
16	Remaining balance for other expenses. (Step 14 minus Step 15.)			
17	% Stock in investments after retirement and ½ real return, e.g., ½ times (Figure 4.5 less 1%).			
18	Factor from Figure 5.17 using values closest to Step 1 and real return in Step 17.			
19	Retirement income from investments (Step 16 divided by Step 18.)			
20	Total retirement income in today's dollars (Sum of Steps 3, 4, 7, and 19.)			

* If retiring before age 62, reduce age 62 Social Security by 3.6% for each year retirement will be under 62 (e.g., at 58, 4 x 3.6% = 14.4% reduction).

FIGURE 5.26C Use this analysis to determine your retirement benefits at different retirement ages.

Evaluating an Early Retirement Offer

Step	Description	Cases		
		Accept offer and retire now	Reject offer but stay with same firm	Accept offer and work elsewhere
1	Your retirement age.			
2	Years till retire.			
3	Your Social Security * and COLA pension.			
4	Spouse's Social Security * and COLA pension.			
5	Fixed pension.			
6	Fixed pension factor from Figure 5.16.			
7	Step 5 times Step 6.			
8	% stock in investments before retirement and real return, e.g., Figure 4.5 less 1% costs.			
9	Factor from Figure 5.18 using Steps 2 & 8.			
10	Add any lump sum offer to your current retirement investment balance. Then multiply that result times Step 9.			

11	Factor from Figure 5.19 using Steps 2 & 8.							
12	Annual new savings from wages.							
13	Step 11 times Step 12.							
14	Balance at beginning of retirement. (Step 10 plus Step 13.)							
15	Major purchases during retirement, e.g., auto purchases. See text for tax adjustment.							
16	Remaining balance for other expenses. (Step 14 minus Step 15.)							
17	% stock in investments after retirement and $\frac{1}{2}$ real return, e.g., $\frac{1}{2}$ times (Figure 4.5 minus 1%).							
18	Factor from Figure 5.17 using Steps 1 & 17.							
19	Retirement income from investments (Step 16 divided by Step 18.)							
20	Total retirement income in today's dollars. (Sum of Steps 3, 4, 7, and 19.)							

* If retiring before age 62, reduce age 62 Social Security by 3.6% for each year retirement will be under 62 (e.g., at 58, 4 x 3.6% = 14.4% reduction).

FIGURE 5.27C Compare your alternatives when faced with an early retirement offer.

Adjustments to Annual Income from Social Security, Pensions, and Lifetime Annuities

Step	Source	You	Spouse
1	Social Security		
2	Figure 6.5 factor from Soc. Sec. column		
3a	Adjusted Soc. Sec. (Step 1 times Step 2)		
3b	Total for both spouses from Step 3a		
4	Estimated % of real COLA in above		
5	Escalating Soc. Sec. (Step 3b times Step 4)		
6	Fixed part of Soc. Sec. (Step 3b minus Step 5)		
7	Annual pension or annuity payments		
8	1.0 or Figure 6.5 factor if delay till 62		
9	Adjusted pension (Step 7 times Step 8)		
10	Estimated % of real COLA in above		
11a	COLA part of pension (Step 9 times Step 10)		
11b	Total for both spouses from Step 11a		
12a	Fixed part of pension (Step 9 minus Step 11a)		
12b	Total for both spouses from Step 12a		
13	Total COLA income (Step 5 plus Step 11b)		
14	Total fixed income (Step 6 plus Step 12b)		

FIGURE 6.4C Adjusting Social Security and pensions for age and less-than-perfect COLAs.

Organize Your Investments

Step	Description	Current Balance
15	Investments	
	Stocks and stock mutual funds.	
	Good investment real estate <u>less</u> related debt.	
	Poor investment real estate <u>less</u> related debt.	
	Fixed income investments excluding money markets.	
	Money markets.	
16	Other sources for retirement funds.	
	Remaining credit from a reverse mortgage, insurance cash value, etc.	
	Investment equivalent to future wages earned in retirement or from annuity or contract with payments for period shorter than life.	
17	Total investments and other sources. (Step 15 items plus Step 16 items.)	
18	Stock, stock funds, and equity in good investment real estate as % of Step 17. In the example above that would be (300,000 + 100,000) divided by 800,000 = 0.50 = 50%.	

FIGURE 6.6C Organizing your investments and future contributions to investments from part-time wages and annuities with less-than-perfect payouts.

Remaining Balance of Mortgages and Debts

(Don't include investment debts covered by their income.)

Description	Value
Home mortgage	
Home equity loan	
Other loans	
Credit card loans if maintain continuing loan balance	
Total	
Note: If any debt has interest higher than 10%, then multiply debt times factor from Figure 6.8 before making entry.	

FIGURE 6.7C Current principal for debts that will be used to determine a budget for debt payments.

Reserves for Future Large Purchases

Reserve Items	Cost in Today's $
Home appliance replacement, major home repairs or remodeling	
Future autos, RVs, trailers	
Emergency uninsured major medical, dental, and drug costs	
Exceptional vacations, tours, trips	
Assisted care costs above normal living costs	
Additional financial help for children or parents	
Gifts or part of estate for heirs or charity	
Down payments on vacation home, condo, time-share	
Provisions for other contingencies	
Total (recommend not less than one year's income minus Social Security)	

FIGURE 6.9C List large future expenses that will not be part of your normal annual living expenses.

Affordable Expense Budget in Retirement

Age and Income Tax Information

Step		
1	Current age of younger spouse if married or your age if single.	
2	Last year's state & federal income tax.	
3	Last year's gross income. (Include tax-exempt income and depreciation.)	
4	Last year's net tax rate. (Step 2 divided by Step 3.)	
5	Enter Step 4 if you think it represents a conservative (slightly high) value for the future, otherwise enter your own estimate considering any special conditions.	
6	1.00 minus Step 5.	

Social Security, Pensions, and Annuities

7	Annual adjusted Social Security and COLA income. (Step 13 from Fig. 6.4.)		
8	Annual fixed pension and/or annuity. (Step 14 from Fig. 6.4.)		
9	Fixed pension factor for inflation and age or life expectancy. (From Fig. 6.11.)		
10	Adjusted fixed pension contribution to budget. (Step 8 times Step 9.)		

Investments, Debts, and Reserves

11	Current market value of investments. (Step 17 from Fig. 6.6.)				
12	Adjusted value of debts. (From Fig. 6.7.)				
13	Adjusted reserves. (Fig. 6.9 results divided by Step 6.)				
14	Step 12 plus Step 13.				
15	Investments for retirement income. (Step 11 minus Step 14.)				
16	Real return from Fig. 4.4 or Fig. 6.13 less costs. Example for 50% stocks in Fig. 6.13 less 1% costs: 4.4% - 1% = 3.4%.				
17	Step 16 divided by 2 or your own high confidence retirement real return.				
18	Investment factor. (Fig. 6.12 using Step 1 and column nearest Step 17 result.)				
19	Affordable income from investments. (Step 15 times Step 18.)				

Affordable After-Tax Expenses

20	Affordable before-tax income. (Step 7 plus Step 10 plus Step 19.)			
21	Tax adjustment. (Step 5 times Step 20.)			
22	Affordable expenses. (Step 20 minus Step 21.)			

FIGURE 6.10c Calculate the amount of money you can afford to spend this year for expenses other than income taxes, debt payments, and items specifically listed in reserves.

This Year's Cash Requirements

Budget Category	Source	Amount
Affordable expense budget	Step 22 of Figure 6.10 or Step 8 in Figure 6.15	
Major large purchase of item in reserve.	Any, part, or all of items listed in Figure 6.9	
Loan principal and interest due plus extra principal if desired	For any items listed in Figure 6.7	
Income taxes	For all items listed in Figures 6.4 and 6.6	
Total	Sum of items above	

FIGURE 6.14C Your plan provides for your budgeted expenses, loan payments, and income tax.

Autopilot Feedback Calculations Are Simple

(Must have information from last year)

Step		
1	Step 8 from last year's Figure 6.15, or, Step 22 from last year's Figure 6.10 if you did not use autopilot feedback last year.	
2	1.000 + last year's inflation, e.g., 1.000 + 4% = 1.040. Or, you can divide this year's Social Security by last year's to get the same result.	
3	Step 1 times Step 2.	
4	Step 22 from this year's Figure 6.10.	
5	Step 3 times 0.75.	
6	Step 4 times 0.25.	
7	Step 5 plus Step 6.	
8	Affordable expense budget for this year. (Use the smaller of Step 3 or Step 7.)	

FIGURE 6.15C Use this figure to adjust your affordable expense budget on an annual basis.

Budget Control for Affordable Expenses

Date: ___ / ___ / ___	Annually	Monthly If Applicable	Weekly If Applicable
Rent if applicable (but not mortgage)			
Utilities and maintenance			
Property taxes			
Auto and transportation			
Insurance			
Uninsured medical and dental			
Groceries			
Restaurants			
Other essentials			
Support of others			
Clothing			
Vacation and travel			
Entertainment and hobbies			
Gifts and charities			
Subscriptions and education			
Other discretionary items			
Total			

FIGURE 6.21C Divide your annual budget into categories you can measure.

Glossary

Affordable Expenses. Annual budget in today's values at level to provide life-time support with inflation adjustment. In Chapter 5 on preretirement planning this includes all expenses such as annual normal living expenses, expenses for large infrequent costs, income taxes, and debt payments. In Chapter 6 for postretirement planning, affordable expenses are a separate budget item that covers only annual normal living expenses. The rest of the items have their own budgets.

After-Tax. The value of income after income tax deduction or the value of a return on investment after deducting income taxes.

Aggressive Investments. High-yield investments. Usually high risk in comparison with moderate or conservative investments.

Annuitize. Convert a variable annuity into a contract for monthly or annual payments starting in the year of the annuitization.

Annuity. An insurance contract that ultimately provides regular payments for life or a set period.

Balanced Fund. A fund with a mixture of stocks and bonds.

Before-Tax. The value of income or a return before income tax deduction.

Bond. Security for a debt paying fixed interest. Before maturity, market value may change with economic conditions or changing interest rates.

Capital Gain. The net amount received after sale of a security minus the original cost.

Certificate of Deposit (CD). A security that pays fixed interest like a bond.

Charitable Lead Trusts. Trusts designed to give the income to a charity and the principal to heirs.

Charitable Remainder Trusts. Trusts designed to give a charity the principal and the investor the income from it.

COLA. Cost of living adjustment to compensate for inflation.

Compound Return. The annual percentage gain needed to correspond to the growth of an investment over several years.

Conservative. Not optimistic. Not risky. Also used in this text as a technical definition for a group of investments that have less return than moderate or aggressive investments.

Conservative Investment. Mostly fixed income investments like savings accounts, money markets, certificates of deposits, and bonds.

Debt. An amount owed to someone else.

Deferred Taxes. Taxes not due on an investment until redeemed.

Dividends. The earnings paid to an investor.

EE Bonds. The modern equivalent of savings bonds that can be purchased at a bank.

Equity. Stock, stock mutual fund, or, if real estate, current market value less current debt.

ETF. Exchange traded funds such as Spiders (S&P Depository Receipts representing the S&P 500 index) or Qubes (QQQs representing the NASDAQ 100 index). The advantage over mutual funds is that there is no undistributed capital gain, and they trade throughout the day, not just at market closing prices.

Excise Tax. An additional tax.

Feedback. The process of periodically feeding data back into a system to better control system response.

Fees. Brokers or funds charges for service.

FICA. Federal Insurance Contribution Act. The total of your taxes for Social Security.

529 Plans. State-administered plans that will fund a child's higher education on a tax-deferred basis.

Fixed Pension. A pension that has a constant dollar value each year.

401(k) and 403(b). Employer's deferred tax savings plans.

Fraction. A factor usually expressed as a decimal equivalent (e.g., 0.40 is equivalent to 40% or $\frac{4}{10}$).

Future Dollars. Less-valuable dollars degraded by inflation.

Future Value. The value of something in the future in its then-year values. Inflation makes the present value or real value of it smaller.

GNMA. Government National Mortgage Association securities (with government backing) similar to bonds. Usually sold by mutual funds.

Gross Income. As used herein, total of all income sources including ones that are not taxable.

Guaranteed Income Contract. A fund that pays fixed interest that is usually adjusted annually, but the principal is guaranteed.

I Bond. Inflation-adjusted bond. A government bond that is periodically adjusted for inflation and can be purchased at banks just like savings bonds.

Income. Wages from job or earnings from investment.

Inflation. Percentage of annual increase in prices.

Interest. Earnings from a loan, bond, or savings account.

Investment. A single security or group of securities like stocks, bonds, and so on.

IRA. Individual Retirement Arrangement for investments with deferred taxes and penalties for early, late, or other situations.

IRS. Internal Revenue Service for federal tax collection.

Keogh. Approved savings plan with deferred taxes.

Leverage. Borrowing money to make an investment.

Life Expectancy. Years to live based on 50% probability.

Limiting Equations. A logic equation such as, if A is less than B, then the equation equals X; otherwise it equals Y.

Loads. Part of a mutual fund's charges for service.

MDIB. Minimum distribution incidental benefit. A method prescribed for IRA owners' withdrawals.

Moderate Investments. Lower-risk stocks or a mixture of conservative and aggressive investments.

Muni. Municipal bond with interest free from federal income tax and, in some states, free of state tax.

Mutual Fund. A group of investments managed by a fund manager in an investment firm. A mutual fund provides diversification within the asset class the fund represents.

Net Tax Rate. Total of state and federal income tax divided by gross income.

New Savings. The annual amount you are able to save from wages.

Pension. Retirement payments for life from a former employer.

Present Value. Future value adjusted to today's value.

Rate. A percentage. Either inflation or the annual growth of an investment expressed as a percentage.

Real Return. The actual return adjusted for inflation: (actual return − inflation) / (1.00 + inflation).

Real Value. Future value adjusted to today's value by taking out inflationary effects.

REIT. Real Estate Investment Trusts are traded like a stock.

Reserve. An amount that is set aside for something other than a source for your normal retirement expenses.

Risk. Volatility, or subject to considerable value variations.

RMD. Required minimum distributions established by the IRS so that an IRA owner is forced to take out some money each year after age 70½.

Roth IRA. An IRA made with nondeductible savings but with no income taxes due on withdrawals. Of course, future tax law changes may affect this definition.

S&P 500. Standard and Poor's index measuring value of stock of 500 largest firms on U.S. stock market.

SEP. Simplified Employee Pension plan with deferred taxes.

Social Security. Federal government payments during retirement.

Spend-All. A theory of retirement planning that says you can spend all of your after-tax income from Social Security, pension, and investments.

Stocks. A security representing ownership in a company.

Tax-Deferred Investments. Investments with tax deferrals on income and (sometimes) principal, for example, IRA, 401(k), Keogh, deferred compensation, variable annuity, I and EE bonds.

Then-Year Dollars. Less-valuable future dollars degraded by inflation.

Today's Values or Dollars. Dollars with current purchasing power.

Variable Annuity. Insured investment with deferred taxes and early withdrawal penalties. Can either take voluntary withdrawals or establish fixed monthly or annual payments, that is, annuitize.

Index